"*Affluenza* is an engagingly conversational, thought-provoking look at where we have perverted the American dream. Though the nature of books like these is to preach to the converted, *Affluenza* offers enough support to the arguments and enough depth to the solutions to have a good chance of reaching the unconvinced."

—DETROIT FREE PRESS

"You'll laugh . . . You'll cry . . . You'll cheer . . . You'll growl. But you'll be challenged and moved by this book. *Affluenza* looks at our epidemic of over-consumption and shows how we can live simpler, more meaningful lives. It's a fantastic book, very funny yet deeply serious."

—PETER BARNES, COFOUNDER, WORKING ASSETS

"If you sometimes suspect that American life has become a nightmare, but you dare not admit the truth to yourself or talk about it to others, take a peek inside *Affluenza*. The way to end a nightmare is to wake up, and this book is an alarm clock. We have created a world that dishonors all that is honorable, good, and meaningful. There is another possibility."

—PAUL HAWKEN, AUTHOR
Ecology of Commerce AND *Natural Capitalism*

"*Affluenza* brings society's consuming malaise into sharp focus. But rather than dwell only on the illness, it provides suggestions for healing on an international, national, local and individual level. I've recommended that our community read and discuss its concepts as a first step toward living more carefully and consciously. As we find each other in conversation, good things are happening."

—AMY LEVEK, MAYOR, TELLURIDE, COLORADO

" . . . one of the wittiest, most dynamic treatments of the linked problems of our frenetic lives and the destruction of the planet. If you want to feel exhilarated, like jumping up and down and cheering humanity on as we find ways to save the Earth and ourselves, read this book!"

—CECILE ANDREWS, AUTHOR
The Circle of Simplicity

"Using humor, facts, and compelling stories, [Affluenza] exposes the disease of over-consuming that threatens our health, families, budgets, friendships, communities, and the environment. But it doesn't stop there; it offers concrete ideas that can contribute to healthier, happier lives and a more livable planet. You should read it. You'll laugh, you'll cry, and you might even change your life—or extend it!"

—DAVID R. BROWER, CHAIRMAN, EARTH ISLAND INSTITUTE, AND FOUNDER, FRIENDS OF THE EARTH

"The material basis for the American way of life is not sustainable here and is not replicable elsewhere. Our feverish mindset is burning up the natural systems that support us. Affluenza provides a witty, informed roadmap out of this unfulfilling dead end, and describes sustainable alternatives that are stimulating, healthy, diverse, and fun."

—DENIS HAYES, CHAIR, EARTH DAY NETWORK

"Affluenza lays out the symptoms, the causes, and (gratefully) the cure. With wit, intelligence and pizzazz, this trio of authors has brought together a complete guide to the disease that most ails America. Proof of having read the book should be a requirement for opening a charge account, applying for a boat loan, or running a large corporation."

—Yes!
A JOURNAL OF POSITIVE FUTURES

AFFLUENZA

AFFLUENZA

The All-Consuming Epidemic

SECOND EDITION

John de Graaf
David Wann
Thomas H. Naylor
In association with Redefining Progress
With new research by Pamela Rands

Illustrations by David Horsey
New foreword by Vicki Robin

BK

BERRETT-KOEHLER PUBLISHERS, INC.
San Francisco
a BK Currents book

Berrett-Koehler Publishers, Inc.
235 Montgomery Street, Suite 650
San Francisco, CA 94104-2916
Tel: (415) 288-0260   Fax: (415) 362-2512   www.bkconnection.com

Ordering Information

Quantity sales. Special discounts are available on quantity purchases by corporations, associations, and others. For details, contact the "Special Sales Department" at the Berrett-Koehler address above.

Individual sales. Berrett-Koehler publications are available through most bookstores. They can also be ordered directly from Berrett-Koehler: Tel: (800) 929-2929; Fax: (802) 864-7626; www.bkconnection.com.

Orders for college textbook/course adoption use. Please contact Berrett-Koehler: Tel: (800) 929-2929; Fax: (802) 864-7626.

Orders by U.S. trade bookstores and wholesalers. Please contact Ingram Publisher Services, Tel: (800) 509-4887; Fax: (800) 838-1149; E-mail: customer.service@ingrampublisherservices.com; or visit www.ingrampublisherservices.com/Ordering for details about electronic ordering.

Berrett-Koehler and the BK logo are registered trademarks of Berrett-Koehler Publishers, Inc.
Printed in the United States of America

Berrett-Koehler books are printed on long-lasting acid-free paper. When it is available, we choose paper that has been manufactured by environmentally responsible processes. These may include using trees grown in sustainable forests, incorporating recycled paper, minimizing chlorine in bleaching, or recycling the energy produced at the paper mill.

Library of Congress Cataloging-in-Publication Data
De Graaf, John.
Affluenza: the all consuming epidemic / by John De Graaf, David Wann, and Thomas H. Naylor; in association with Redefining Progress; with new research by Pamela Rands; illustrations by David Horsey; foreword by Vicki Robin.—2nd ed.
    p. cm.
"Based in part on the PBS television programs Affluenza and Escape from Affluenza.
Includes bibliographical references and index.
ISBN-10: 1-57675-357-3; ISBN-13: 978-1-57675-357-6
1. Quality of life—United States. 2. Wealth—United States. 3. Consumption (Economics)—United States. 4. United States—Social conditions—1980- 5. United States—Economic conditions—1981- 6. United States—Civilization—1970- I. Wann, David. II. Naylor, Thomas H., 1936-. III. Redefining Progress (Organization). IV. Affluenza (Television program: 1997). V. Escape from Affluenza (Television program: 1998). VI. Title.

HN60 .D396 2005
306'.0973–dc22   2005045324

First Edition
12 11 10 09 08 07   14 13 12 11 10 9 8 7 6

Interior design and composition: Seventeenth Street Studios.
Copyeditor: Karen Seraguchi. Indexer: Medea Minnich.
Photo credits: The Surrender of the Joneses, Francine Strickwerda; Skeen Family, Pearland Texas ©1994D Peter Ginter, Peter Menzel/Material World; Yadev Family, Ahraura, India © 1994D Peter Ginter/Material World.

In memory of
DAVID ROSS BROWER
(1912-2000)

a giant of twentieth-century thought and action on behalf
of the earth. He hoped that one day

We may see that progress is not
The accelerating speed with which we multiply
And subdue the Earth, nor the growing number
Of things we possess and cling to.
It is a way along which to search for truth,
To find serenity and love and reverence for life,
To be part of an enduring harmony…

And in memory of
DONELLA MEADOWS
(1941-2001)
Scientist and sheep farmer, she pointed us all
toward a more sustainable society.

CONTENTS

The Skeen family with their possessions, Pearland, Texas

The Yadev family with their possessions, Ahraura, India

FOREWORD TO THE FIRST EDITION

When I was first approached to host the television program *Affluenza*, the idea sounded just about as appealing as a lukewarm cup of boiled root tea. I imagined a stern sort of brew that would make me cringe with every breath and sip, while earnestly pious activists in earth sandals and dun-colored parkas spun from discarded soda pop bottles hectored innocent bystanders strolling into coffee bars and shopping malls: "Materialist stooge! Self-gratifying spendthrift! Polluting pirate!" I opened their proposal determined to quickly fill my schedule with conflicting activities.

But I had worked with this production group before, had liked and respected them. More: I enjoyed spending time with them. And then, I read. And I was impressed. The program they proposed had wit, feeling, and style. It was pointed without being overbearing. It had character. And it held my interest.

I enlisted. I didn't imagine that *Affluenza* would become wildly popular. At most, I thought it might present a few significant scenes and ideas to an interested audience. It would impart a warm feeling and then, like most broadcasting, evaporate, leaving only a small, wet spot in its place.

What I hadn't figured on was timing, timing. *Affluenza* was aired in the late 1990s, a time when more Americans were feeling fatter bank accounts—and more hollowness inside. Shopping and stock market speculation were becoming the genuine national pastimes. But at the same time, greater numbers of Americans were seeking to cash themselves out of what was becoming to them a daily rough-and-tumble struggle for mere things. So, against all expectation (or at least mine), *Affluenza* generated a small but fierce enthusiasm. Discussion groups were convened. Tapes and transcripts were passed around, read, and replayed. Viewers who were drawn in by unexpected flashes of wit in the program stayed around to find that their consciences could be tickled, too.

This book is the cheerful result of accumulated curiosities from people who would like to run some of *Affluenza*'s thinking through their minds and hearts. It is not a how-to book, so much as a what-if book. While it contains some staggeringly practical suggestions for small and large proposals that could reform our cities, reorder our tax code, and build new kinds of communities that emphasize sharing over competition, it is not a book that shakes a finger in our faces and reprimands hard-working Americans for wanting a little more comfort, elegance, and enjoyment in our lives. On the contrary. *Affluenza* respects those perfectly human desires and seeks to create ways that make comfort, elegance, and enjoyment more genuine and durable than purchasable, perishable commodities. More than most start-ups or dot-coms, it creates something of real value—a new way of accounting for true happiness in our lives.

Scott Simon
Weekend Edition Saturday Host
National Public Radio

Washington, D.C.
February 2001

Feel like a failure: splurge. Economy slows down: splurge. . . collectively. The late and sorely missed Donella Meadows saw affluenza as the tendency to fill nonmaterial needs materially.

If shopping is a response to joy *and* sorrow, good fortune *and* bad, despair *and* hope, I think that's substance abuse. If so, might we learn from the 12-step programs? **Step one: We admit that we are powerless over our personal and collective shopping habit and that our lives have become unmanageable.** Y'know what? That sounds true to me. Our personal lives are unmanageable—overextension, stress, loss of relationships, and debt combine to put us into a downward spiral. Our collective lives are unmanageable: we overharvest, overmine, overbuild, overheat the atmosphere, and suffer from a rise in asthma, cancers, and autoimmune diseases. All of this and more depletes our capacity to sustain life and give the next generation a planet as healthy as the one our forebears gave us. One hope of this book is to show—gently and with humor—that we've already hit bottom.

Affluenza—*the book*—then, could be seen as an intervention. With kindness and firmness it asks us to face our consumption-generated problems. It doesn't ridicule us, but it doesn't pull punches. And, like an intervention for other substance-abuse problems, it offers the experience, hope, and strength of those who've kicked the habit and regained their self-respect, integrity, and belonging through "the program." In this case, though, the programs offered at the end of the book work on many levels, from making personal choices to changing the rules of the game to reward all actions moving us toward a thriving, just, and sustainable future. So enjoy! This is a great book about a tough-to-face set of problems…but a spoonful of humor really helps this medicine go down.

Vicki Robin
Coauthor of *Your Money or Your Life*

Whidbey Island, Washington
March 1, 2005

PREFACE

As I write these words, a news story sits on my desk. It's about a Czech supermodel named Petra Nemcova, who once graced the cover of *Sports Illustrated*'s swimsuit issue. Not long ago, she lived the high life that beauty bought her—jet-setting everywhere, wearing the finest clothes. But then, she happened to be vacationing in Phuket, Thailand, when the great Southeast Asian tsunami struck. Her boyfriend was swept away and killed. Badly injured, she survived by clinging to a palm tree for eight hours till she was rescued.

After leaving the hospital she announced that the tragedy had transformed her. She no longer wanted to model; she wanted to work on relief projects for the United Nations. She told reporters she no longer cared about her old life of fashion, fame, and fortune. "Believe me, it isn't really important," she said. "There are so many more important things in the world, like health and love and peace in your soul."

In the Age of Affluenza, it's a lesson we all need to learn. I've also got an "invitation" on my desk, offering me free tickets to the Millionaire Conference with Reed West. The invitation says I'll learn how to cut my tax bill by 31 percent and reduce all my capital gains taxes to zero. Sounds good . . . until I consider what would happen if we all did that. No taxes would mean no schools, parks, public amenities. It would mean even more reckless consumption. And every study I know of shows that getting rich won't make me happy. Sharing with those in need, building for the common good, living rich in friendships, family, and community—that's what will. I don't wish a tsunami on Reed West, whoever he is. But he, and all the rest of us, need to understand what tragedy taught Petra Nemcova.

So welcome to the second edition of *Affluenza: The All-Consuming Epidemic.* Most movies start with a book, but this book started with a movie. In 1996, together with Vivia Boe, a fellow public-television producer, I set out to craft a documentary about the subject of overconsumption and its many not-so-benign consequences for American society. Our research told us the subject was a huge one, touching our lives as Americans in more ways than any other social or environmental issue. But how to make sense of it? How to present the issue so that viewers could see that multiple problems were caused by our consuming passion and that they were connected to each other?

After videotaping more than two-thirds of the program, we were still wondering how to weave together the wide range of material we had collected. Then, on a flight from Seattle to Washington, D.C., to do still more videotaping, I happened to see the word *affluenza* used in passing in an article I was reading. For me, it was like that moment in cartoons when the light bulb goes on over someone's head. This was it: *affluenza*. A single word that not only would make a catchy (pun intended) TV title, but that also suggested a disease resulting from overconsumption.

Vivia and I agreed that here was a way to make the impacts of overconsuming more clearly understandable—as symptoms of a virus that, in the United States at least, had reached epidemic proportions. We could then look at the history of this disease, trying to understand how and why it spread, what its carriers and hot zones were, and finally, how it could be treated.

From that point on, we began to use the term, asking interviewees if the idea made sense to them. And indeed, real doctors told us they could see symptoms of affluenza in many of their patients, symptoms often manifesting themselves physically. A psychologist offered his observation that many of his clients "suffer from affluenza, but very few know that that's what they're suffering from."

To be certain that *Affluenza* would be carried by as many PBS affiliate stations as possible, Vivia and I borrowed a page from the marketers and promoted it shamelessly. At a Chicago meeting of PBS programmers, we wore lab coats and stethoscopes, with name pins labeling us Dr. John and Dr. Vivia, Affluenza Epidemiologists. We passed out medicine vials labeled Affluenza Vaccine (containing candy). We wanted the programmers to know that our show would be entertaining as well as informative. With a teaspoon of sugar to make the medicine go down.

Our documentary, *Affluenza*, premiered on PBS on September 15, 1997, and was greeted with an outpouring of audience calls and letters from every part of the United States, making it clear to us that we had touched a deep nerve of concern. Viewers as old as ninety-three wrote to express their fears for their grandchildren, while twenty-year-olds recounted sad tales from the lower depths of credit card debt. A cover story in the *Washington Post* Sunday magazine about people trying to simplify their lives introduced them as they were watching the program. A teacher in rural North Carolina showed it to her class of sixth graders and said they wanted to talk about it for the next two weeks. On average, the kids thought they had three times as much "stuff" as they needed. One girl said she could no longer close her closet door. "I've just got too many things, clothes I never wear," she explained. "I can't get rid of them."

CROSSING POLITICAL LINES

Though past criticisms of consumerism have come mostly from the liberal side of the American political spectrum, we were pleased to find that *Affluenza* spoke to

© 2001 by Joel Pett

the concerns of Americans of all political persuasions. The head of one statewide conservative family organization wrote to congratulate us, saying, "This issue is so important for families." Ratings and audience response were as high in conservative cities like Salt Lake and Houston as they were in liberal San Francisco or Minneapolis. In colleges, the program has been more popular at Brigham Young than at Berkeley. At Appalachian State University in Boone, North Carolina, students and faculty showed it to audiences in both poor mountain communities and upscale churches, recording audience comments and producing a video of their own called *Escaping Affluenza in the Mountains.*

THE WHOLE WORLD IS WATCHING

In 1998, we followed *Affluenza* with a closer look at treating the disease, called *Escape from Affluenza.* Since that time, both television programs have been widely shown throughout the United States and abroad. The *Affluenza* videos have become best-sellers for their distributor, Bullfrog Films, and have now been released as DVDs, with extra interviews, Adbusters' "uncommercials" (see chapter 27), teachers' and viewers' guides, and connections to Web resources. They continue to be popular.

We've become convinced that this issue troubles people throughout the world. The "Great Malls of China" are now the largest on earth. We've heard from countries where we couldn't imagine anyone would be concerned about affluenza—Thailand, Estonia, Russia, and Nigeria, for example—but where, indeed, citizens hoped to adopt what was good about the American lifestyle and avoid what was harmful.

An Islamic business magazine in Sri Lanka asked us for a short article about the disease. Activists in rural northern Burma wanted to translate the TV program into a local dialect called Kachin. A sixteen-year-old Israeli girl sought permission to project it onto the wall of a Tel Aviv shopping center. Seeing overconsumption as a disease, they said, helped them understand it better and explain it to others.

A SOCIAL DISEASE

Often, writers speak of "affluenza" with different emphases. Some have used the term primarily with reference to the spoiled children of the super-rich. Others, to what they call "sudden-wealth syndrome." Defined as such, it loses the sociopolitical message we put forward and becomes a matter of purely personal behavior. In our view, the virus is not confined to the upper classes but has found its way throughout our society. Its symptoms affect the poor as well as the rich, and our two-tiered system (with the rich getting richer and the poor, poorer) punishes the poor twice. They are conditioned to want the good life but are given very little possibility of attaining it. Affluenza infects all of us, though in different ways.

AFFLUENZA: THE BOOK

After the TV broadcasts, calls from three individuals convinced me of the need to write a book on the subject. Thomas Naylor, an economist, and David Wann, an environmental scientist, both suggested a collaboration, while Todd Keithley, a New York literary agent, added his opinion that such a book would find an eager readership. I was immensely gratified by the reaction to the *Affluenza* television specials. But television, even at its most informative, is still a superficial medium; you simply can't put that much material into an hour. And that's the reason for this book: to explain "affluenza" in more depth, with more examples, more symptoms, more evidence, more-thorough exposition. If you've seen the video, you'll recognize a few of the characters and stories. But the first edition of the book represented three more years of research, updated data, and additional stories. In the jargon of consumer culture, it was "new and improved!"

The first edition arrived on the market just before the tragedy of September 11, 2001. Like the impact of the tsunami on Petra Nemcova, the World Trade Center attacks caused many Americans to reevaluate their priorities. Families and friends suddenly seemed more important than things and work. But then, the consumption propaganda machine kicked into high gear again. If you want to be patriotic, President Bush told Americans, go to the malls and shop. Buy to fight terror.

From Democrats, the message was the same. Former San Francisco mayor Willie Brown had a million shopping bags printed, with big flags on them and the bold words "AMERICA: OPEN FOR BUSINESS." Washington senator Patty Murray proposed "Let's go shopping" legislation that would have removed sales taxes on products during the 2001 holiday shopping season. Almost no one dared to mention that anger and envy over the profligate spending of Americans might encourage sympathy for terrorists in developing countries.

Since the first edition of *Affluenza: The All-Consuming Epidemic* was published, it's been used widely by book groups and in university classes. We've been thrilled by the response from readers, and at least six foreign translations of the book are now in print, showing that concern about the issue is worldwide. In Australia, another book called *Affluenza*, with similar content, has just been published

We had hoped *affluenza* would become a household word. That actually seems to be happening. An Internet search before our PBS broadcast turned up about 200 cases of the word on the Web—all of them in Italian, where *affluenza* simply means affluence. Today, I checked the word on Google and found 232 *thousand* references to it(!), referring, in the vast majority of cases, to overconsumption. London's *Independent* newspaper picked it as one of its most popular new words for the year 2003, and dictionaries are considering including it in the next few years.

Moreover, use of the term continues to grow: a popular play called "Affluenza" is now touring the country. Recently, a National Hockey League official pointed out that only in 1918 (when the Spanish flu killed 20 million people) and in 2005 had the NHL season been canceled. The first time, he said, the season was canceled because of influenza, and the second time because of affluenza (presumably referring to players' salary demands).

THE SECOND EDITION

Now, four years have passed since the first edition of *Affluenza* hit the bookstores. In some ways, the United States is a different place—the supercharged economy of the late '90s has cooled appreciably, and many of the facts in the first edition of the book are outdated. So here is a new edition, fully updated, thanks to the research work of Pamela Rands. Again, it's "new and improved." With more pages! It also contains a little of the new thinking that David, Thomas, and I have been doing since the first edition came out, particularly where simplicity-friendly public policies are concerned. And we've prepared a Study Guide for high school and college curricula, available for downloading at www.bkconnection.com/affluenza.

A COUPLE OF QUICK CAVEATS

With apologies to other citizens of North, Central, and South America, we frequently use the terms *America* and *Americans* to refer to the United States and its citizens. We mean no disrespect to other Americans, but simply recognize the colloquial usage that the term has throughout the rest of the world. Further, we do not mean to imply in this book any generalized condemnation of wealthy Americans or of money itself. Used properly for the common good, money can contribute to the health of our society instead of encouraging affluenza. Indeed, this book would not have been written without the financial support of generous individuals.

Happy reading!

John de Graaf
Seattle, Washington
February 23, 2005

ACKNOWLEDGMENTS

The authors wish to extend their heartfelt thanks to the following people:

To Vicki Robin, for all of her inspiration and support, for her tremendous work for simplicity, and for the foreword to this edition of *Affluenza: The All-Consuming Epidemic.*

To Vivia Boe, John's fellow producer on both the *Affluenza* and *Escape from Affluenza* television programs. Her insights and ideas strengthened those works immeasurably. To Scott Simon for his terrific work as the host of *Affluenza,* and for the foreword to the original edition of this book. To Chris De Boer, Francine Strickwerda, and Hope Marston, for their research and production interviews during the making of those programs. And to all the other people who worked on the programs, including all of John's longtime colleagues at KCTS Television.

To Susan Sechler, the Pew Charitable Trusts, the Merck Family Fund, the Summit Foundation, KCTS Television, Oregon Public Broadcasting, the New Road Map Foundation, and ITVS, whose support helped make those programs possible. To John Hoskyns-Abrahall and Winnie Scherrer at Bullfrog Films, and Anne Robinson at PBS. To Peter Barnes, Leyna Bernstein, and Pam Carr, for their support at the Mesa Refuge writers' retreat, and to Mesa Refuge co-writers Jonathan Rowe, Terry Tempest Williams, and Carl Anthony, who helped think some of this through.

To all those people whose stories, words, and ideas are included in this book. To Arnie Anfinson, Monique Tilford, Wanda Urbanska (the host of *Escape from Affluenza*), Frank Levering, Cecile Andrews, and other friends in the voluntary simplicity movement. To those who read this manuscript and offered helpful input: Dawn Griffin, Trish Padian, Joseph Webb, Stuart Lanier, Scott Gassman, and Jennifer Liss. And to Robert Meier for research assistance.

To Paula Wissel, David de Graaf, and Oliver and Vivian de Graaf for their love, support, and patience. To the memory of David Wann Sr., whose convictions drove his actions; to Marjorie Wann, a very wise and resourceful woman; and to Colin and Libby, who inspire Dave to keep working. To all of Dave's friends at Harmony Village, who supported this project in many ways, but especially to Macon and Ginny Cowles, Matt and Linda Worswick, Wendy Hanophy, Claire Lanier, Bob Paulson, and Edee Gail. To our agent Todd Keithley.

Special thanks to the Merck Family Fund, the True North Foundation, the Threshold Foundation, the Weeden Foundation, and the Fred Gellert Foundation, who supported the writing of this book.

To Joanne Kliejunas and everyone at Redefining Progress, who helped and trusted in us, and to Steven Piersanti and all of our friends at Berrett-Koehler Publishers, who believed in this book. And to our friends in the Simplicity Forum and the Center for a New American Dream, and all the other wonderful people out there who are working to build a simpler, slower, and happier world.

We owe a special debt of gratitude to Pamela Rands, who cheerfully and tirelessly re-researched all the time-sensitive facts (and a few others) contained in the first edition of this book and updated them for the second edition, meeting a tough deadline.

Another such debt is owed to David Horsey, of the *Seattle Post-Intelligencer,* who provided his marvelous cartoons to both editions at a price far more reasonable than we should have expected. We are tremendously honored to have the gifts of so talented an artist (and two-time Pulitzer Prize winner) included in the book. His pictures are worth much more than a thousand of our words.

Finally, for all those whose help we have failed to remember, we thank you and ask your forgiveness. It took a village to write this book, but all errors and omissions should be blamed only on the authors.

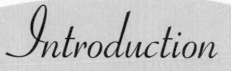

Introduction

*I*n his office, a doctor offers his diagnosis to an attractive, expensively dressed
*female patient. "There's nothing physically wrong with you," he says. His
patient is incredulous. "Then why do I feel so awful?" she asks. "So bloated
and sluggish. I've got a big new house, a brand-new car, a new wardrobe. And I just got a
big raise at work. Why am I so miserable, doctor? Isn't there some pill you can give me?"
The doctor shakes his head. "I'm afraid not," he replies. "There's no pill for what's wrong
with you." "What is it, doctor?" she asks, alarmed. "Affluenza," he answers gravely. "It's the
new epidemic. It's extremely contagious. It can be cured, but not easily."*

Of course, the scene is an imaginary one, but the epidemic is real. A powerful
virus has infected American society, threatening our wallets, our friendships, our
families, our communities, and our environment. We call the virus *affluenza*. And

because the United States has become the economic model for most of the world, the virus is now loose on every continent.

Affluenza's costs and consequences are immense, though often concealed. Untreated, the disease can cause permanent discontent. Were you to find it in the *Oxford English Dictionary,* the definition might be something like the following:

> **affluenza,** *n.* a painful, contagious, socially transmitted condition of over-load, debt, anxiety, and waste resulting from the dogged pursuit of more.

EARTH IN THE BALANCE

Quietly, like some sort of unseen mind-snatcher, the virus has consumed the American political dialogue. Consider Al Gore. In 1992, while still a senator, he wrote a popular book called *Earth in the Balance.* America, Gore noted then,

> is holding ever more tightly to its habit of consuming larger and larger quantities every year of coal, oil, fresh air and water, trees, topsoil, and the thousand other substances we rip from the crust of the earth, trans-forming them into not just the sustenance and shelter we need but much more that we don't need. . . . The accumulation of material goods is at an all-time high, but so is the number of people who feel an empti-ness in their lives.[1]

Americans, Gore suggested, had become addicted to stuff. Our civilization, he wrote, promises happiness through "the consumption of an endless stream of shiny new products. . . . But the promise is always false." A year later, Al Gore was inaugu-rated as vice president of the United States. During the ceremony, a soprano sang the beautiful old Shaker hymn, "Simple Gifts" (*'Tis the gift to be simple, 'tis the gift to be free . . .*). During the song, Gore nodded in agreement. Then, in the next cou-ple of years, something happened. The mind-snatcher came and took Al Gore.

In the 1996 vice presidential debate, Gore's opponent, Jack Kemp, vowed to "dou-ble the size of the U.S. economy in the next fifteen years." Gore never questioned whether it would be a good thing for Americans to consume twice as much. By the 2000 election, the transformation of Al Gore into an agent of affluenza was complete. In a presidential debate, he vowed to increase the size of the U.S. economy by 30 per-cent in ten years. And what happened to Al Gore seems to be happening to all of us.

"Who wants to be a millionaire?" asks the ABC show. Apparently, nearly everyone.

Of course, there's a downside to this obsession, and in our hearts most of us know it. Pollster Richard Harwood found that out back in 1995, when he conducted a sur-vey for the Merck Family Fund about American attitudes concerning consumption.

"People are saying that we spend and buy far more than we need. That our children are becoming very materialistic and that we're spending for what we want today at the expense of future generations and our own future," Harwood explains. "It crosses religious lines, age lines, race, income, and education. There is a universal feeling in this nation that we've become too materialistic, too greedy, too self-absorbed, too selfish, and that we need to bring back into balance the enduring values that have guided this country over generations: values of faith, family, responsibility, generosity, friendship."[2]

NEEDING MORE PLANETS

In our view, the affluenza epidemic is rooted in the obsessive, almost religious quest for economic expansion that has become the core principle of what is called the American dream. It's rooted in the fact that the supreme measure of national progress is that quarterly ring of the cash register called the gross domestic product. It's rooted in the idea that every generation will be materially wealthier than its predecessor and that, somehow, each of us can pursue that single-minded end without damaging the countless other things we hold dear.

It doesn't work that way. The contention of this book is that if we don't begin to reject our culture's incessant demands to "buy now," we will "pay later" in ways we can scarcely imagine. The bill is already coming due. At its most extreme, affluenza threatens to exhaust the earth itself. "We human beings have been producing and consuming at a rate that far exceeds the ability of the planet to absorb our pollution or replenish the stock," says corporate critic Jeremy Rifkin. Scientists say we'd need several more planets if everyone on earth were to suddenly adopt the American standard of living.

CONNECTIONS

Consider the following scenario, as reported in a 1998 article in *Parade* magazine:

> The US economy defied experts' predictions and stayed healthy despite a global financial crisis and the threat of presidential impeachment, thanks to the resilience and stamina of the American consumer. . . . There was plenty of bad news. . . . Much of the nation's weather was awful. Torrential rains in California, a devastating flood on the Ohio River, weeks of triple-digit heat in Texas, lethal ice storms in Virginia and the worst Atlantic hurricane season in 200 years. The 1997 poverty rate was still higher than in the early '70s. And although the federal deficit is gone, Americans are deeper in debt than ever. . . . But nothing distracted us

from the good news: high employment, low inflation, real wage increases and the best mortgage rates and gasoline prices in decades. . . . Consumer spending remained strong throughout the year, guaranteeing continued economic growth.

The best gasoline prices, awful weather; continued economic growth, persistent poverty; consumer confidence, spiraling debt. Are they all somehow connected? We think so.

In each of the past eight years more Americans have declared personal bankruptcy than graduated from college. Our annual production of solid waste would fill a convoy of garbage trucks stretching halfway to the moon. We have twice as many shopping centers as high schools. We now work more hours each year than do the citizens of any other industrial country, including Japan. Though we constitute only 4.7 percent of the earth's people, we account for 25 percent of its global-warming greenhouse gas emissions. Ninety-five percent of our workers say they wish they could spend more time with their families. Forty percent of our lakes and streams are too polluted for swimming or fishing. A CEO now earns 475 times as much as the average worker, a tenfold increase since 1980. Since 1950, we Americans have used up more resources than everyone who ever lived on earth before then.

However unrelated they may seem, all of these facts—the diverse symptoms of affluenza—are also connected. Much of this book focuses on the United States because its citizens are the world's most profligate consumers. But what is happening in the United States is clearly beginning to happen elsewhere as the American lifestyle becomes the model for nearly all of the rest of the world. But other countries may have more choice than the United States does. Those in countries where affluenza is not so full-blown an epidemic can keep themselves from greater infection and preserve more balanced lifestyles. We believe there are lessons for every country and every person, rich and poor, to be found in America's mistakes. The global economy means that all of us are in this together and need to understand and control this disease.

SYMPTOMS

We have divided the book into three sections. The first explores many of the symptoms of affluenza, each—only half whimsically—compared to a real flu symptom. Think of how you feel when you've got a bug. You're likely to be running a temperature. You're congested. Your body is achy. You may have chills. Your stomach is upset. You're weak. You might have swollen glands, even a rash.

In the Age of Affluenza, America as a society shows all of these symptoms, metaphorically at least. We present each as a chapter. We start with individual symptoms, then move to the social conditions, and finally turn to the environmental impacts of affluenza.

Some chapters may greet you with the shock of self-recognition—"Honey, that's me!" You might have noticed the conditions discussed in other chapters taking hold of your friends. You might find some symptoms more troubling than others, because you worry more about your children than about your Mother Earth. You might be well off materially but feel continually stressed out or as though your life lacks purpose or meaning. Or you might be poor, and angry at your inability to give your children what marketers say they "gotta have" to fit in. You might have just felt the sting of insults from another driver, red-faced with road rage. Or watched bulldozers destroy the only open space left around your community—to make room for row upon row of identical tract homes with three-car garages. If you're elderly, you may have noticed your children's inability to balance their checkbooks, and you may worry for their children. If you're young, you may be anxious about your own future.

Wherever you're coming from, we believe you'll clearly recognize that at least some of the symptoms of affluenza affect you. Then, as you read on, you'll begin to see how they're connected to others less obvious from your vantage point.

GENESIS OF THE DISEASE

In part 2 of this book, we look beneath the symptoms to search for causes. Is affluenza simply human nature, as some would suggest? What was the genesis of this powerful virus? How has it mutated through history and when did it begin to reach epidemic proportions? What choices did we make as a society (between free time and "stuff," for example) that deepened our infection? We look carefully at warnings from across time and cultures, and at early efforts to eradicate the disease with controls and quarantines.

Then we discover how the spread of the disease has become not only socially acceptable, but encouraged by all the powerful electronic carriers our technological civilization keeps perfecting. We suggest that affluenza promises to meet our needs in inefficient and destructive ways. And we contend that an entire industry of pseudo-physicians, handsomely rewarded by those with a huge stake in the perpetuation of affluenza, conspires to keep the diagnosis of the disease and the extent of its symptoms from reaching the general public.

CURING AFFLUENZA

But far be it from our intent to leave you permanently depressed. Affluenza can be treated, and millions of ordinary Americans are already taking steps in that direction. A 2004 poll by the Center for a New American Dream (www.newdream.org) found that 48 percent of Americans claim to have cut back on their spending.

The same poll also revealed that 85 percent of Americans think our priorities as a society are out of whack. Of the respondents, 93 percent feel Americans are too focused on working and making money, 91 percent believe we buy and consume far more than we need, 81 percent think we'll need to make major changes in the way we live to protect the environment, more than half say they have too much debt, and 87 percent feel our current consumer culture makes it hard to instill positive values in our children. The poll conducted by Widmeyer Communications, a national polling firm, surveyed nearly 1,300 American adults and had a margin of error of 3 percent.

Our increasingly harried lifestyles continue to produce rat-race refugees. Enough to make corporate marketers salivate over millions of potential new customers. Hence, companies urge us to "simplify" our lives by buying their products, and new publications, like Time Warner's *Real Simple* (it would be more aptly called *Real Cynical*, as most of it is devoted to ads for expensive products), build an audience of 400,000 subscribers before printing their first issue.

What that says to us is that a lot of people are looking for answers to affluenza. Part 3 of this book is devoted to offering some answers we've found.

As with symptoms, we look at treatments starting with the personal and advancing to the social and political. Our treatments, too, employ the medical metaphor. We start as you do when you've got the flu, with bed rest, aspirin, and chicken soup—individual prescriptions popularized by the "new frugality" and "voluntary simplicity" movements.

We encourage a restored interest in the natural world outdoors, with its remarkable healing powers. We agree with futurist Gerald Celente, the author of *Trends, 2000.* "There's this commercial out," he says, "and it shows this middle-aged man walking through the woods pumping his arms, and all of a sudden in the next cut, there he is on the back porch, woods in the background, walking on this treadmill that must have cost a fortune. It doesn't make sense. It was so much nicer walking through the woods and it cost nothing at all." [3]

We suggest strategies for rebuilding families and communities and for respecting and restoring the earth and its biological rules. We offer "political prescriptions," with the belief that some well-considered legislation—like that suggested by the

Take Back Your Time campaign (www.timeday.org) to allow us to choose time instead of more money—can help create a less affluenza-friendly social environment and make it easier for individuals to get well and stay that way.

We also present preventive approaches, including vaccines and vitamins, to strengthen our personal and social immune systems. And we suggest an annual checkup. Ours comes in three phases:

1. You can test how you're doing personally in staying well.

2. You can help your community assess its own true health, using indices of sustainability developed by several American cities.

3. And finally, as a people, Americans can find a truly useful substitute for the current outmoded measure of national health, the gross domestic product (GDP).

We recommend an index called the genuine progress indicator (GPI), being fine-tuned by Redefining Progress, an Oakland, California, think tank. Using multiple indices to discover how Americans are doing, the GPI paints a different picture of our real success as a society. While GDP has risen steadily throughout history, the GPI has been falling since 1973.

Then, for fun, we've added a new measure in this edition of the book—a fever thermometer that measures whether the collective illness is getting worse or better.

LET'S BEGIN A DIALOGUE

Little in this book is truly new information, yet the issue in this "information age" isn't more information. It's how to make sense of what we already know. We offer a way of understanding seemingly disconnected personal, social, and environmental problems that makes sense to us—as symptoms of a perilous epidemic that threatens your future and that of generations to come. We don't expect you to agree with everything in these chapters, nor do we even expect to immediately convince you that affluenza is a real disease. Our intention is to encourage a national dialogue about the American consumer dream so that whatever choices you make about consumption are made with a clearer understanding of their possible consequences.

The message of this book isn't to stop buying; it's to buy carefully and consciously with full attention to the real benefits and costs of your purchases, remembering, always, that the best things in life aren't things.

Symptoms

Shopping fever

Gotta listen to me honey/Gotta get all your money/Gotta know just where I stand/ If you want to be my date/Well you better get it straight/I'm a big time shopping man. . . . / Baby come on, there's a whole lotta shoppin' going on. . . ./Get that money out of your ' savings account/There's a whole lotta shoppin' going on. . . .

—FOLKSINGER ALAN ATKISSON

It's Thanksgiving Day, and eight-year-old Jason Jones has just finished stuffing himself with turkey, cranberry sauce, and pumpkin pie à la mode. He sits at his PC, frantically typing a list of presents he hopes to receive from Santa Claus at Christmas. He plans to deliver the list to Santa the next day, the opening day of the Christmas shopping season and, incidentally, of affluenza season. Jason's list contains ten items, including a trip to Disney World, a mountain bike, a cell phone, a DVD player, and several compact discs.

Jason is no dummy; he doesn't really believe in Santa Claus, but he knows his parents usually give him what he asks Santa for, so he gets up bright and early on Friday to play the game. Jason and his mother, Janet, set out in their Lincoln Navigator and, half an hour later, arrive at the All-Star Bazaar, where thousands of people are already fighting for the remaining parking spots nearest the entrance.

The mall is jam-packed with frantic holiday shoppers, unwitting and at risk in an affluenza hot zone, armed only with credit cards and checkbooks. In one store, a crowd gathers to watch two parents duke it out over the last remaining Dino-Man, the latest hot kids' toy, a doll with the body of a weightlifter and the head of a tyrannosaur (and selling faster than Beanie Babies did). In a corner, a mother sobs, knowing she got there too late to get a Dino-Man for her son. "I knew I should have camped out here last night," she wails. Other customers, already exhausted, sit on benches near an escalator, beside mountains of merchandise, looking both tense and bored.

It takes Jason nearly an hour to get through the line to Santa's lap and deliver his list. His mom leaves him in the video arcade with a roll of quarters while she makes the rounds of the dozens of shops in the mall. Hours later, on the way home, they stop at Blockbuster's to rent a couple of movies so Jason won't complain of boredom that night. Though the day is sunny and warm, unusually so for late fall, even the park in Jason's upper-middle-class subdivision is devoid of kids. There are plenty of children in this neighborhood of young professionals. But if they're not shopping, they're indoors communing with Xbox or the Cartoon Network. It's a tough choice for Jason, but he's tired of the games he has, so he turns on the TV.

Jason is, admittedly, an imaginary, composite kid. But his experience at the mall is far from atypical. In 1999, according to the National Retail Foundation, Americans spent nearly $200 billion on holiday gifts, more than $850 per consumer. Affluenza season, the month between Thanksgiving and Christmas, generated 25 percent of all retail profits.

Seventy percent of Americans tell pollsters they want less emphasis on holiday spending and gift giving. A third cannot even remember what they gave their significant other the previous year and, on average, do not pay off their Christmas debts until the following summer, if then. Yet the urge to splurge continues to surge. It's as if we Americans, despite our intentions, suffer from some kind of Willpower Deficiency Syndrome, a breakdown in affluenza immunity.

MALL MANIA

Since World War II, Americans have been engaged in a spending binge unprecedented in history. We now spend nearly two-thirds of our $11 trillion economy on consumer goods. For example, we spend more on shoes, jewelry, and watches ($100 billion) than on higher education ($99 billion). We spend as much on auto maintenance as on religious and welfare activities. Nearly 30 percent of Americans buy Christmas presents for their pets; 11 percent buy them for their neighbors.[1]

In 1986, America still had more high schools than shopping centers. Less than twenty years later, we have more than twice as many shopping centers (46,438) as high schools (22,180). In the Age of Affluenza (as we believe the current period will eventually be called), shopping centers have supplanted churches as a symbol of cultural values. In fact, 70 percent of us visit malls each week, more than attend houses of worship.[2]

Our equivalent of Gothic cathedrals are the megamalls, which continually replace smaller shopping centers, drawing customers from ever-greater distances. Typically, they cover areas of formerly fertile farmland that produced bumper crops instead of traffic jams. Indeed, 137 acres of prime American farmland are lost to "development" every hour.[3] When a new megamall opens, the pomp and ceremony rival anything Notre Dame or Chartres might have witnessed in medieval times.

The Super Mall in Auburn, Washington, opened in October 1995 to a stampede of a hundred thousand shoppers. The crowd gathered under a model of Washington's 14,410-foot Mount Rainier. Rising above the Super Mall's front entrance, the imitation mountain provided one show that the real thing could not: a display of fireworks, set off as soon as the ribbon-cutting ceremony was over.

In a spirit of boosterism that would have impressed Sinclair Lewis's Babbitt, speaker after speaker extolled the wonders of the new shopping center, the biggest in the state. "The number of shoppers expected to visit here over the next year exceeds 1.2 million," bubbled Auburn's mayor, who added that "committed shoppers can shop till they drop in 1.2 million square feet of shopping space." Along with a new racetrack and casino in the area, the mall was expected to become a "destination attraction" for vacationers from the entire western United States and Canada. It would, they said, create four thousand jobs and "improve the quality of life throughout the region." Thirty percent of the expected business would come from tourists who would each spend about five hours and more than $200 at the mall.[4]

FUN FOR THE WHOLE FAMILY

The thousands of eager shoppers on hand for the opening wore bored and impatient expressions during the speeches but pushed eagerly through the open doors when the rhetoric stopped. One woman said she was "really excited about the mall because this is something we haven't had in this part of Washington. We were waiting for something like this."

"We said, 'If we build it, they will come,' and they did," said a happy shopkeeper. Another explained that the hardwood floors "add a little sense of excitement to the mall. They're much easier than walking on tile or granite and make the Super Mall really special." She hoped children would enjoy it, "because shopping has become such a family experience that's really important."

Really. And it's a good thing, too, since we Americans now spend six hours a week shopping and only forty minutes playing with our kids.[5] "Shopping malls have really become the centers of many communities," says Michael Jacobson, founder of the Center for the Study of Commercialism, in Washington, D.C. "Children as well as adults see a shopping center as just the natural destination to fill a bored life."[6]

WHAT ELSE MATTERS?

"If you've seen one mall, you've seen them all," sneer critics, but "committed shoppers" (some psychologists say they *should* be committed) disagree. They're willing to jet across the country for new shopping experiences. So much so that some airlines now offer package flights to shopping meccas like Potomac Mills, a giant "discount" mall divided into sections that are euphemistically labeled "neighborhoods." Potomac Mills bills itself as the "number-one tourist attraction in Virginia," with more visitors each year than Shenandoah National Park, the most visited site in the National Park System.

The host of *Affluenza*, Scott Simon, visited Potomac Mills while filming the television program. Shoppers were eager to answer his questions about where they came from and what they thought of the mall. None of the people Simon talked to were sweating profusely. But all seemed infected by shopping fever, often the first symptom of affluenza.

Two women from Dallas, Texas, said they'd been at the mall for three days straight, while their husbands golfed nearby. "We're always looking for a bargain. You've got to know the brands and we have experience, we're proud to say," they proclaimed. "I didn't need anything. I just went to shop," said a man with a cart full of merchandise. "Whatever I like I buy." "I bought a lot more than I planned to," another woman admitted. "You just see so much."

Yes, you do, and that's the idea. It's why big malls sell much more per square foot than do their smaller counterparts. Seeing so much leads to impulse buying, the key to mall profitability and to the success of big-box stores like Wal-Mart. Impulse: a devilish little snake that cajoles first, then bites later when the credit card bill comes due. Only a quarter of mall shoppers come with a specific product in mind. The rest come just to shop. "What else matters?" asked one of the ladies from Dallas, only half in jest.

"I came here with one overriding interest, to spend money," said a proud teenage girl, who was getting rid of the hundred dollars her mother had given her for this particular spree. "I like to shop," she explained. She's not alone. One poll found that 93 percent of teenage American girls rate shopping as their favorite activity.[7]

An older couple passed by with a shopping cart piled to the brim. "This is only half of what we've purchased," the man said cheerfully. "We brought a long list of things to buy," his wife added, "and then we bought a lot of stuff that wasn't on the list." They were examining the fold-out map Potomac Mills provides to shoppers, saying, "We'd be lost without it."

But Potomac Mills is a mere mini-mall compared to the Mall of America in Bloomington, Minnesota, America's number one visitor attraction. With 4.2 million square feet of shopping space (one hundred acres), our biggest mall ("Where It's Always 72 Degrees!") spreads over an area the size of seven Yankee Stadiums. It employs ten thousand people and attracts forty-two million visits a year. The Mall of America is more than metaphorically a cathedral; some people even get married there. It is also a world-class affluenza hot zone.

In the Age of Affluenza, nothing succeeds like excess. "Good malls are usually the most profitable kind of real estate there is," says one Los Angeles real estate consultant. "Good malls are money machines."[8] *Good*, he points out, means bigger. Because of that, the frenzy to attract megamalls pits city against city, each offering sweetheart deals in hopes of capturing tax revenue later on. To win such deals, mall developers compete for the most-profitable stores. According to the *Sacramento Bee*, the Seattle-based Nordstrom Company received $30 million in direct subsidies and incentives to put a store in Roseville, California's, Galleria Mall. Why? "Nordstrom does the highest sales per square foot in the industry," says mall developer Michael Levin. Most people, says Levin, will drive only about half an hour to a mall, "but with Nordstrom, they will drive much farther."[9]

HOME SHOPPING

Of course, these days you don't have to drive at all (or fly either) to shop, though most people still do. But while malls, and vast discount megastores like Wal-Mart and Costco, still boast growing sales (and still drive smaller, locally owned stores out of business), Americans are doing a whole lotta shopping right from their couches. Eighteen *billion* mail-order catalogs flooded our homes last year, about seventy for every one of us,[10] selling everything from soup to nuts (to refrigerators to underwear). "Buy Now, Pay Later!" they shout. While some of us resent their arrival, most Americans eagerly await them and order with abandon. In some cases, we even pay for the catalogs (such as Sears's) so that we can pay for what's in them. In 2005, mail-order catalog sales are expected to total $143 billion.

Then there are the home shopping channels. Critics mock them as presenting a continuous succession of baubles on bimbos, but for a sizable percentage of Americans, they're the highlight of our cable TV systems, and they're highly profitable. And to think someone once called TV "a vast wasteland." That was before the shopping channels, of course.

Mail-order catalogs and shopping channels carry a lot more than products. They are highly effective carriers of affluenza. Next time a catalog comes, check it with a high-powered microscope.

CYBERSHOPPING

In the past several years, a new affluenza carrier has come online. And it threatens to someday outdraw malls, catalogs, and shopping channels combined. The intense frenzy with which the ubiquitous Internet has been embraced as a shopping center can only be compared to that which followed the discovery of gold in California and Alaska, or oil in Texas. Americans now spend an average of eleven hours a week online, and much of that time is spent shopping—nearly half of Internet sites are now selling something.

During the 2003 affluenza season, consumers spent $17 billion online, nearly double what they spent four years earlier. Now that's growth! E-spending for the Thanksgiving weekend 2004 was up a third from 2003.[11] For the year, e-sales topped $50 billion.[12] That's still only a tiny fraction of total retail sales ($3.4 trillion), but soon Internet shopping should eclipse catalog sales. Everything imaginable (and some things unimaginable) can now be bought online.

Much of it can be bought from eBay, the biggest winner in the online shopping sweepstakes. The company has been in existence for only eight years, but it did $23 billion in business in 2003. It offers such fanciful purchases as kangaroo scrotums ($10) and Paul McCartney's germs from a used tissue. Every second, $729 worth of goods is sold on eBay.[13]

SHOPPING AS THERAPY

When Scott Simon visited Potomac Mills, the mall was running one of the cleverest ad campaigns we've ever seen, featuring an alluring actress named Beckett Royce, whose persona combined bubble-headed ditziness with a winking "joke's on you" sophistication. "Shopping is therapy," she intoned, lying on a couch. "Listen to that little voice in your head: SHOP, SHOP, SHOP."

Royce's monologues mocked the shopping channels and catalog shopping, but definitely not shopping at Potomac Mills. She pranced between its aisles, grabbing item after item, then added up what she'd bought and chirruped, "I *spaved* a hundred dollars!" *Spaving* means spending and saving at the same time, she explained, suggesting that at Potomac Mills everyone could become a "spaver."

"The more you buy, the more you save," proclaimed an ad for Bon-Macy's, a Seattle department store. As our next chapter demonstrates, large numbers of Americans apparently believe this mathematical impossibility. Beckett Royce is no fool; she gets paid plenty to persuade the credulous that "spaving" works. Simple mathematics says otherwise. But then, math scores have been falling.

And, as we discover in our next chapter, the road to bankruptcy is *spaved* with good intentions.

CHAPTER 2

A rash of bankruptcies

Uh oh, we're in the red, dear
On our credit card it shows
Christmas is almost over
But the debit line still grows.

—"ALTERNATIVE" CAROL
from the Center for a New American Dream
(to the tune of "Rudolph,
the Red-Nosed Reindeer")

On the Monday after Thanksgiving, Janet Jones, Jason's mom, drops him off at school, winds her way through heavy traffic back to the mall—a fairly new one, built in 10 BHP (Before Harry Potter)—and enters, eyes wide for sales. She carries the wish list Jason wrote for Santa Claus. Making sure Mom knew what he wanted, Jason printed a copy of the list for her and left it, as if by accident, on his bed.

The first purchases go fine, and by her reckoning Janet has soon saved a hundred dollars, but when she tries to buy the mountain bike, there's a hitch. "I'm sorry," says the smiling clerk, "but you're over your limit on this card. Do you have another?" Momentarily embarrassed, Janet reaches in her purse. "No problem," she says. "I've got several." She remembers the slogan "Some things are priceless, but for everything else there's MasterCard," and hands hers to the clerk, who runs it through a scanner. "Sorry," the young woman says with a sympathetic look. "Same results. Insufficient credit remaining." Janet looks quickly *around, hoping no one has seen her in this predicament, and muttering, "There must be some mistake," walks out of the bicycle shop.*

On the way home from the mall, she passes the offices of Consumer Credit Counseling Service and wonders if it might be time.

If she'd gone inside, she would have found things humming. These days, Consumer Credit Counseling Service (CCCS), a network with 1,100 offices in several countries, gets plenty of referrals—people who have gotten themselves deep in debt and do not see any way out.

PLASTIC NATION

According to Marielle Oetjen, a former member of the CCCS staff in Colorado Springs, Colorado, "One of the first things we do when people come here is cut up their credit cards. . . . The whole availability and ease of credit makes it hard for people to remember that they're dealing with real money."[1]

Oetjen removed a large box from a shelf and poured the contents on the floor— hundreds, perhaps thousands, of cut-up credit cards. The average American possesses 6.5 credit cards, for a nationwide total of 1.2 billion.[2] One in three high school seniors and 83 percent of college undergraduates have cards. The more you have, the more you're likely to be offered. The son of coauthor Thomas Naylor was sent an offer for a card when he was only twelve! A steady stream of such offers fills American mailboxes, each offer with its own incentives: frequent-flier miles, introductory low interest rates, lower minimum payments. According to the *Guinness Book of World Records*, one American now has a whopping 1,497 credit cards, a dubious honor.[3]

"There's a lot of marketing ploys from the credit card companies to not only encourage customers but have those customers carry as much debt as possible," Oetjen says. That's how the companies, the banks, make their money. Say you spend $2,000 on a typical credit card (at 18 percent interest), and make minimum payments to pay it off. It will take you eleven years, and you will end up paying double the original price. And that's if you never buy anything else with the card.

"The credit card companies push instant gratification," Oetjen points out. "Buy it now. Don't worry about it. Pay it off in little monthly installments. You can take as long as you want. You can handle it. That's the ethic that's being pushed. That's what most of the folks that come in here get caught up in."

In fact, fewer than a third of Americans avoid interest by paying off their credit card balances each month (though 55 percent usually do).[4] The average American

household carried about $9,000 in credit card debt during the year 2002, for a total
of $764 billion. Even college students average $2,500. Total American credit card
indebtedness tripled in the 1990s.[5]

The news was even worse for Cindy and Keaton Adams, an attractive young couple with two children who were in many ways typical Consumer Credit Counseling
Service clients. They turned to CCCS in 1995 when they found themselves $20,000
in debt and unable to make credit card payments. "We started out thinking we could
finance the world," Keaton says. "And we tried, but it didn't work."[6]

It almost never does.

It all started when Keaton got a Mervyn's credit card at the age of eighteen.
"With that," he says, "I managed to get a Visa card, and Cindy managed to get a Visa
card, and we ended up with lots of Visa cards." They began buying plenty of things,
all on credit. Besides credit card purchases, they found a way to get financing for
new cars. "But it wasn't just 'Let's get a nice $8,000 car,'" Cindy confesses. "It was
'Let's try and finance the nicest car we can get.'"

But what they got was deeper and deeper into debt, until finally a debt collector
just asked, "Why can't you pay your bills?" Keaton says it made him stop and think.
When the debt collector suggested Consumer Credit Counseling, he took her
advice. It was hard to watch their credit cards being cut up, Keaton and Cindy say
now, but they're glad someone did it.

IS AMERICA BECOMING A DEBTORS' PRISON?

The situation that faced the Adams family is not all that unusual these days.
According to the *Los Angeles Times*, Americans are "straining under record debt
loads amassed in a spending binge powered by the booming economy."[7] Current
bankruptcy rates exceed those experienced during the Great Depression.

Rising debt, says one economist, is the "soft underbelly" of the U.S. economy.
A soft underbelly covered with little red dots, as shopping fever leads to another
affluenza symptom, a rash of bankruptcies. Six million Americans are as close to
bankruptcy as the Adamses were. Each year, in fact, more than a million and a half
people—up from 313,000 in 1980, and including one of every seventy Americans—
file for personal bankruptcy, more than graduate from college. That's been the case
since 1996. Every fifteen seconds, an American goes bankrupt.[8] On average, the
debt load for such filers equals twenty-two months of income.[9] Ninety-two percent
of bankruptcies are filed by middle-class Americans. About half of them are the
result of reckless spending; the rest come from sudden medical bills (40 million
Americans still lack health insurance) or a job loss. In response to the situation,
lending institutions have successfully lobbied Congress to make it harder to declare

bankruptcy, while at the same time they continue to push their customers toward financial ruin.

In 1980, U.S. household debt stood at 65 percent of disposable income. Today, debt is 125 percent of income. "Families are overextending themselves as never before as indicated recently when total household debts surpassed total after-tax incomes for the first time in history," writes *Los Angeles Times* reporter Leslie Earnest.[10]

A PENNY SAVED—BARELY

There is a strange irony at work in contemporary America: The more incomes rise across the board, the less we save. It should be the other way around. Fatter paychecks ought to leave more dollars for savings accounts. Not so. When the film *Affluenza* was produced, Americans were saving just under 4 percent of their incomes, half the German rate and only a quarter that of Japan. That seemed, at the time, very bad news, since the savings rate had been about 10 percent as recently as 1980. But today our national savings rate hovers near *zero* and in some months falls below that line.[11] Steve Lohr of the *New York Times* reports that Americans now save only 0.2 percent of their personal income—about $1.50 a week on a salary of $40,000.[12] Meanwhile, residents of the European Union save 12 percent, and impoverished Chinese, Indian, and Pakistani workers save a quarter of their incomes.

Advertisements often use exaggeration to touch popular social chords. Consider, for instance, the back cover of one *USA Weekend* magazine. An attractive woman, identified as "Veronica Lynn, Beverly Hills, FL, Doral Smoker," smiles from one half of the page while she is quoted on the other half as saying, "It lasts longer than my paycheck."[13] *It,* in this case, is a Doral cigarette, the product the ad is selling. The underlying message is none too subtle: paychecks don't last long in contemporary America.

The United States of America. Land of history's biggest five-minute paychecks. But why worry? Light up. If you've already got affluenza, what's a little cancer?

WILL BOOMERS GO BUST?

Boston College sociologist Juliet Schor points out that most Americans live without an adequate financial cushion. "Sixtypercent of families," Schor writes, "have so little in the way of financial reserves that they can only sustain their lifestyles for about a month if they lose their jobs. The next richest can only hold out for about three and a half months."[14]

Some economists suggest there's no cause for alarm. Half of all Americans now own stocks (though in most cases, not many), they point out, and could sell them if need be. In a time of surging stock prices, many higher-income, stock-owning baby boomers see no need to be thrifty. They are relying on selling their stocks at a hefty profit to take care of their retirement needs a few years from now. It's a risky gamble, argues Thornton Parker, an economic consultant and the author of *What If Boomers Can't Retire?* Rising stock prices depend on the ability of boomers to sell their stocks to the next generation of workers, who, they expect, will pay top dollar.

But there are problems with that scenario, Parker suggests. In the future, there will be fewer workers to buy the stocks, and retirees will have to sell more cheaply to unload them. Moreover, as the Crash of '29 made only too clear, stock prices can plummet as well as climb, and many of them are already overvalued and not backed up by real corporate earnings.

Even former millionaires have joined the bankruptcy ranks. Some used their stocks—whose value had continued to rise—as collateral for loans to finance expensive vacations or homes. "I could call up Solomon Smith Barney anytime to ask for $10,000," said one. But when the value of her stock began to fall, Solomon Smith Barney called her up—to demand repayment. By then, her debts were greater than the amount she could cash her stock in for.

So why are we spending so much more now? Stay tuned. . . .

CHAPTER 3

Swollen expectations

*Greed has infected our society.
It is the worst infection.*

—DR. PATCH ADAMS

*I was sad because I had no onboard fax until
I saw a man who had no mobile phone.*

—1993 *New Yorker* cartoon
BY WARREN MILLER

ake a walk down memory lane. Way down. If you're as old as we are,
your memories carry you back to the 1950s, at least. The Second
World War and the Great Depression were over, and America was on
the move. Suburban houses going up everywhere. New cars rolling from the assembly lines and onto new pavement. Ground breaking for the National System of
Interstate and Defense Highways, soon to stretch from sea to shining sea. A TV dinner (introduced in 1953) in every oven.

"It's a great life, eh, Bob?" a man in a '50s commercial intones as a young couple
and their tow-headed son sit on a couch watching the tube. "And tomorrow will be
even better, for you and for all the people." Of course, the great life wasn't great for
the millions who were poor or discriminated against. And even for middle-class
America, it wasn't worry free. On the same day in 1957 (October 4) that *Leave It to
Beaver* premiered on American television, those pesky Russians shot Sputnik into

space. Nikita Khrushchev promised to bury us "in the peaceful field of economic competition." We know how that came out.

But 1957 was important for another, less-heralded reason. It was the year the percentage of Americans describing themselves as "very happy" reached a plateau never exceeded and seldom matched since then.[1] The following year, a year when Americans bought millions of hula hoops, economist John Kenneth Galbraith published an influential book calling the United States "the affluent society."

We *felt* richer then than we do now. Most Americans today don't really think of themselves as affluent, says psychologist Paul Wachtel, "even though in terms of gross national product we have more than twice as much as we did then. Everybody's house has twice as much stuff in it. But the feeling of affluence, the experience of well-being, is no higher and perhaps even lower."[2]

Liberal economists argue that since about 1973 the real wages earned by middle-class Americans haven't risen much and, for many workers, have actually declined. Young couples talk of not being able to afford what their parents had. By contrast, conservative economists contend that the rate of inflation as calculated by the federal government has been overstated and, therefore, that real wages have risen considerably. But one thing is incontestable: *We have a lot more stuff and much higher material expectations than previous generations did.*

STARTER CASTLES

Take housing, for example. The average size of new homes is now more than double what it was in the 1950s, while families are smaller. LaNita Wacker, who owns Dream House Realty in Seattle, has been selling homes for more than a quarter of a century. She takes us on a drive through the neighborhoods near her office to explain what's happened.

She shows us houses built during every decade since World War II and describes how they've gotten bigger and bigger. Right after World War II, Wacker points out, 750 square feet was the norm (in Levittown, for example). "Then in the '50s," she says, "they added 200 square feet, so 950 was the norm. By the '60s, 1,100 square feet was typical, and by the '70s, 1,350. Now it's 2,300." Beginning with the recession in 2000, the average new house size stabilized at 2,320 feet, but larger sizes can be expected when the next round of prosperity arrives.

Wacker started selling homes in 1972, "right about the time we moved from a single bath to the demand for a double bath."[3] Two-car garages came in then, too, and by the late '80s many homes were being built with three-car garages. That's 600 to 900 square feet of garage space alone, "as much square footage as an entire family used in the early '50s," Wacker says. "It would house an entire family. But we have acquired a lot of stuff to store."

To drive the point home, Wacker takes us by a huge home with a four-car garage. Expensive cars and a boat are parked outside. The owner comes out wondering why she is so interested in his place. "I own Dream House Realty," she says. "And yours is a dream house." "It was built to the specifications of my charming wife," the man replies with a laugh. "So why four garages?" asks Wacker. "It's probably because of storage," the man replies, explaining that the garage is filled with family possessions. "You never have enough storage, so you can never have enough garages," he adds cheerfully. Wacker asks if he has children. "They're gone now," he replies. "It's just me and the wife."

The four-car garage is an exception, no doubt. But everyone expects larger homes now. "A master bedroom in the '50s would be about 130 square feet," explains Wacker. "Now, even in moderately priced homes, you're talking about maybe 300 square feet devoted to the master bedroom."

More than ever, homes have become a symbol of conspicuous consumption, as beneficiaries of the '90s stock market boom began in many communities to buy real estate, bulldoze existing (and perfectly functional) homes, and replace them with megahouses of 10,000 square feet and more. "Starter castles," some have named them. Others call them monster homes.

On America's Streets of Dreams, the competition is fierce. McMansions . . . Double McMansions . . . Deluxe McMansions . . . Deluxe McMansions with Cheese . . . Full Garage Deals . . . each one a little bigger and glitzier, popping up like mushrooms in a frenzy of home wars. In places like the spectacular mountain towns of the West, many such megahomes are actually second homes, mere vacation destinations for the newly rich.

BETTER THAN TAIL FINS

A similar story presents itself with automobiles. In 1957, when Ford had a better idea called the Edsel, cars were big and chromey, but they were far from the sophisticated machines we drive today. A 1960 Ford commercial shows crowds of people admiring the new Fairlane, Thunderbird, and Falcon, surrounded by twinkling stars as if touched by Tinkerbell. It is, the ad proclaims, "the Wonderful New World of Ford." But in that wonderful new world, much of what we now take for granted as standard automobile features wasn't available even in luxury models.

In 1960, for example, fewer than 5 percent of new cars had air conditioning. Now more than 90 percent do. Mike Sillivan, a veteran Toyota salesman in Seattle, says

...AND THEY JUST GET BIGGER AND BIGGER AND BIGGER AND...

that "today, people's expectations are much higher. They want amenities—power steering, power brakes as standard, premium sound systems."[4] The car of today is a different animal from that of a generation ago. It's filled with computer technology. And, after a hiatus following the "energy crisis" of the mid-1970s, big is back.

Until recently, gasoline costs for Americans were at an all-time low in real dollar terms. Worries about fuel efficiency were forgotten as we bought gas-guzzling four-wheel-drive wagons called sport-utility vehicles (some call these suburban assault vehicles; others use the term "axles of evil"). In the late '90s half of all new cars sold were SUVs and light trucks, exempted from federal fuel-efficiency standards. Roomy, comfy, and costly, SUVs just keep getting bigger.

CAR WARS

Until 2000, the eighteen-foot-long Chevy Suburban set the standard for gigantism. Then, not to be outdone, Ford introduced the Excursion, a 7,000-pound titan that is a foot longer than the Suburban. Ford Motors chairman William Ford even apologized for making so many SUVs, calling his Excursion "the Ford Valdez" for its propensity to consume fuel. He condemned SUVs as wasteful and polluting, but said Ford would continue to manufacture them anyway because they were extremely profitable.

"For a lot of people an SUV is a status symbol," says car salesman Sillivan. "So they're willing to pay the thirty- to forty-odd thousand dollars to drive one of these vehicles."

Never one to give up without a fight, General Motors has come charging back at Ford, acquiring ownership of the Hummer, a more luxurious version of the military transport vehicle used during the Gulf War. GM is "placing a big bet that the decade-long trend toward ever larger and more aggressive-looking sport utility vehicles would continue," according to the *New York Times*.[5] "It's like a tank with fashion," says one teenager quoted by the *Times*. The kid says he loves the Hummer because "I like something where I can look down into another car and give that knowing smile that says 'I'm bigger than you.' It makes me feel powerful." More than a foot wider than the Excursion, the Hummer retails for more than $100,000. GM predicts these behemoths will be especially popular in (we are not making this up) Manhattan, which is probably a good thing because you need to be on the viewing platform of the Empire State Building to see over them.

A Hummer dealer Web site (www.lynchhummer.com), features a link to "Stupid Hummer Tricks." The link offers photos of, among other things, a Hummer in a standoff against a buffalo, another proudly knocking aside trees as it plows up an incline in a forest, and a third nearly submerged in a pretty mountain stream. Now what will Ford counter with, an even bigger SUV called the Extinction?

WEIGHTLESS TOURISM

Hummers on the streets of Manhattan. You might call them Saddam's revenge. Or Ho-Hummers, if you compare them with yet another way to drop big bucks.

In 2001, American Dennis Tito became the world's first space tourist, for only $20 million. The next year, South African Mark Shuttleworth followed, for the same price.[6] In June 2004 SpaceShipOne took off on its first flight, rising sixty-two miles above Earth and entering officially into space.[7] Soon, seats will be available for as little as $100,000.

If that sounds like a deal, you might want to stick a thermometer in your mouth right away. Ten . . . nine . . . eight . . . .

LET'S DO LUNCH

We've talked about houses and cars. Now consider food. The '50s did give us TV dinners. Turkey, peas, and mashed potatoes in a throwaway tray for sixty-nine cents: thank you, Swanson's. As kids, we considered them delectable. Our standard diets were pretty bland. *Exotic* meant soggy egg rolls, chow mein, and chop suey. *Mexican* was tacos and tamales. (How did we cope without chimichangas and chalupas?) *Thai* wasn't even part of our vocabulary. Now, city streets and even suburban malls sport a United Nations of restaurants. We remember waiting for certain fruits and vegetables to be in season. Now, there is no season; everything is always available. When it's winter here, it's summer in New Zealand, after all. Yet we often feel deprived. Strawberries lose their flavor when you can have them all the time. More food choices certainly aren't a bad thing, but they come at a cost. The exotic quickly becomes commonplace and boring, requiring ever newer and more expensive menus.

Take coffee. Until recently, we took it as watery brown stuff made bearable by gobs of sugar. Now, specialty coffees are everywhere. NPR radio host Scott Simon was surprised some years ago when he stopped at a service station in rural Washington state. In the station's mini-mart was an espresso stand with so many types of coffee drinks that Simon wanted an Italian dictionary to identify them. No need. The kid behind the counter with his baseball cap on backward knew them all.

Eating out used to be a special occasion. Now we spend more money on restaurant food than on the food we cook ourselves. Swelling expectations. Swelling stomachs too, but that's another symptom.

INVENTION IS THE MOTHER OF NECESSITY

Consider, also, the kinds of goods that were deemed luxuries as recently as 1970 but are now found in well over half of U.S. homes and thought of by a majority of Americans as necessities: dishwashers, clothes dryers, central heating and air conditioning, color and cable TV.[8] And back in 1970, there were no microwave ovens, VCRs, CD players, cell phones, fax machines, compact discs, leaf blowers, Xbox games, or personal computers. The use of cell phones has more than doubled the amount Americans spend on phone service in the past ten years.[9] Now, more than half of us take these goods for granted and would feel deprived without them. Well, OK, so maybe you wouldn't feel deprived without Xbox. Meanwhile, consumption of electricity has jumped nearly 50 percent. It takes a lot of energy to run all this stuff.

There always seems to be a "better" model that we've just gotta have. Writing in 2000 about Compaq's then-new iPaq 3600 Pocket PC, *Seattle Times* technology reporter Paul Andrews warned that the iPaq, with its "sleek Porsche-like case and striking color screen," cost $500 more than an ordinary PalmPilot. "But without the color display, music, and photos of the iPaq, life seems pretty dull," he lamented.[10]

And take travel. We drive twice as much per capita as we did a half century ago, and fly an amazing twenty-five times as much.[11] Middle-income Americans seldom ventured more than a few hundred miles from home then, even during two-week summer vacations. Now, many of us (not just the rich) expect to spend occasional long weekends in Puerto Vallarta, or (in the case of New Yorkers) in Paris. Everywhere, humble motels have been replaced by elegant "inns," humble resorts by Club Med. Now, "I need a vacation" means I need to change continents for a few days.

THE CHANGING JONESES

"Greed has infected our society. It is the worst infection," says the real Patch Adams, the doctor portrayed by Robin Williams in a Hollywood film.[12] He's right only to a degree. It may be fear rather than greed that primarily drives our swelling expectations. Fear of not succeeding in the eyes of others. In one magazine ad from the '50s, readers are encouraged to "keep up with the Joneses" by driving what that family is driving: a Chevy. A Chevy sedan at that, not a Corvette. Just about the cheapest car around, even then.

But the mythical Joneses don't drive Chevrolets anymore. And they're no longer your next-door neighbors either, folks who make roughly what you do. Sociologist Juliet Schor studied people's attitudes about consumption in a large corporation and found that most Americans compare themselves with co-workers or television characters when they think about what they "need."

But corporations have become increasingly stratified economically. One frequently comes into contact with colleagues much better paid than oneself. Their cars, clothes, and travel plans reflect their higher incomes, yet set the standards for everyone else in the firm.

Likewise, says Schor, "TV shows a very inflated standard of living relative to what the true standard of living of the American public is. People on television tend to be upper middle class or even rich, and people who watch a lot of TV have highly inflated views of what the average American has. For example, people who are heavy TV watchers vastly exaggerate the number of Americans with swimming pools, tennis courts, maids, and planes, and their own expectations of what they should have also become inflated, so they tend to spend more and save less."[13]

Schor says that as the gap between rich and poor grew during the 1980s, people with relatively high incomes began to feel deprived in comparison to those who were suddenly making even more. "They started to feel 'poor on $100,000 a year' as the well-known phrase puts it, because they were comparing themselves to the Donald Trumps and the other newly wealthy." It happened all the way down the income line, Schor says. "Everybody felt worse compared to the role models, those at the top." By the late '90s, polls showed that Americans believed they needed $75,000 (for a family of four) to lead a "minimum" middle-class life.

I'VE GOT MINE, JACK

In the years just after World War II the super-rich sought to conceal their profli-gacy, but after Ronald Reagan's first inaugural ball many began to flaunt it again. As economist Robert Frank points out, there's been a rush on $15,000 purses, $10,000 watches, even $65 million private jets. Twenty million Americans now own big-screen TVs costing at least $2,000 each. Some buy their children $5,000 life-size reproductions of Darth Vader and $18,000 replicas of Range Rovers, $25,000 birthday parties, and million-dollar bar mitzvahs.[14] Yachts the size of mansions burst their berths in many a marina.

Thus from the hot zones of popular culture and stratified workplaces, our new Joneses—consciously or otherwise—spread the affluenza virus, swelling our expectations as never before. And stuffing us up.

CHAPTER 4

Chronic congestion

A house is just a pile of stuff with a cover on it.

—GEORGE CARLIN

*I*t's nine o'clock at night, and Karen and Ted Jones, a double-income couple in their forties, are peering through a flickering flashlight beam at boxes of stuff, stored a few months earlier at U-Stuff-It, the self-storage facility near their house. He's rooting for a missing report his boss needs the next day, while she's foraging for a painting a friend gave her, because the friend is coming to visit.

"I feel kind of like a burglar," she comments in a low voice, rummaging through a box of Christmas decorations and vaguely familiar objects. "Why?" he asks. "This is OUR stuff. We're just lucky to be able to afford this space, aren't we?" She's not totally convinced. Lucky their stuff can overflow somewhere, with the garage and aluminum shed already popping their nails and rivets. But lucky to be paying $65 a month for 100 square feet of space? Lucky to have so much stuff? She's not sure.

ALL STUFFED UP

Karen and Ted are by no means alone. There are now more than 30,000 self-stor-age facilities in the country, offering over 1.3 billion square feet of relief for a legion of customers starting home businesses, combining households, getting organized after a move, or just unable to stop buying. The industry has expanded fortyfold since the 1960s, from virtually nothing to $12 billion annually, making it larger than the U.S. music industry.[1]

We're all stuffed up, literally! In our homes, workplaces, and streets, chronic con-gestion has settled into our daily lives—chaotic clutter that demands constant main-tenance, sorting, displaying, and replacing.

So which box is that wretched report in?

WHEN HOUSES BECOME LANDFILLS

For Beth Johnson, the acquisition of stuff goes beyond mere frivolity. Like at least two million other Americans who compulsively save everything, she felt overwhelmed by all the excess stuff that clogged her house and her life—from books to clothing to old maps to stacks of phonograph records. "Compulsive savers often have difficulties in their personal relationships because of their excess stuff, although most 'savers' are creative, successful people in their *exterior* lives," she says. "They feel deep shame in their inability to just 'let go' of material possessions."[2] Now on the road to recovery, Beth operates the Clutter Workshop in West Hartford, Connecticut.

She's visited homes jam-packed like warehouses, with only narrow paths from one room to the next. To overcome blockages like these, she helps modify behavior through creative challenges like group garage sales—selling only, no buying allowed! Workshop members are empowered to invite peers into their houses, sometimes for the first time in years.

Do we have stuff, or does it have us? In a world filled with clutter, we too easily become overwhelmed, lose our way, and get swept along in a current that carries us to the mall for more stuff, or to the car dealership for a new car—nothing down.

CAR CLUTTER

Denver resident Dan Berman, like many other Americans, could take his two midsize SUVs to the jagged peak of a mountain, as in the TV ads, but not into his own garage. Neither vehicle would fit in the fifty-year-old brick garage, so he ripped it down and built one suitable for a new millennium. Some of his neighbors in Den-

STUFF WARS AT THE AIRPORT

If American homes crammed with stuff are the metaphorical equivalent of congestion in the lungs, and highways are the plugged arteries, air travel must be the sneeze that propels affluenza carriers (that's us) through the air. Between 1988 and 1998, air travel increased by 35 percent in the U.S., to1,714 passenger miles per capita States, more than four times the 1950 level. At the airport—once our delayed flight is finally ready to go—we plead with the airline attendant to be able to carry on one more bag but are reminded, sternly, of policies designed to protect the passenger. Stuff Wars are in full swing. The airlines have determined that we'll fly no matter how packed the flights and how miniature the complimentary bags of peanuts. Their strategy is "More people, less stuff"—cram passengers in with as little carry-on luggage as possible. (They didn't count on Americans gaining an average 10 pounds in the 1990s, though, which adds an extra $275 million a year in fuel costs, according to the Centers for Disease Control.) Meanwhile, passengers have another agenda—to keep their stuff with them on the plane so they don't have to wait for it at the baggage claim, and so they can access laptops, cosmetics, and emergency rations.

"Please do not leave your baggage unattended . . . " drones the voice on the P.A. as you wait in line to get through security. What's going on here? Everybody's obsessed with stuff! Your carry-on luggage is allowed to be only twenty by forty inches, and they need to X-ray it, label it, inspect it, confiscate your nail clippers, and cross-examine you about it. Why can't they be more understanding? That's your *stuff*, symbolizing who you are. Don't they care who you are? Not really. Remember, you're a passenger, not a person.

The height of Stuff Wars madness can be experienced when the aircraft lands and the captain rings the bell signifying it's time to unfasten your seat belt, jump out of your seat, and scramble for your stuff!

THE SKY *IS* FALLING

In the movie *The Gods Must Be Crazy*, a Coke bottle falls from the sky and disrupts the social structure of a peaceful tribe of Bushmen in Africa's Kalahari desert, unaccustomed to the artifacts of Western culture. In Southgate, California, the detached "nose wheel" of an airplane recently fell from the sky and hit the ground in front of a market, barely missing a woman entering a church.

Even space is jam-packed with stuff. More than seven million pounds of spaceship pieces are hurtling around the planet at 22,000 miles an hour. At that speed, a piece of space debris the size of a small marble has the kinetic energy of a 400-

pound boulder dropped from a hundred feet. To get out beyond the hazards of Earth's space clutter, future astronauts may spend much of their time dodging bullets of space junk.

Meanwhile, back on Earth, space-junk collectors like Jim Bernath of British Columbia anxiously await the descent of more debris, to add to their collections. Bernath already owns chunks of comets and bits of the Canadarm, a device built to retrieve satellites. He's especially hopeful that a piece of the junked MIR space station will fall somewhere in Canada—possibly right into his own backyard.[5]

ANALYZING THE AMERICAN DREAM: WHERE CLUTTER COMES FROM

America's 111 million households—the authors' among them—contain and consume more stuff than all other households throughout history, put together. Behind closed doors, we churn through manufactured goods and piped-in entertainment as if life were a stuff-eating contest. Despite tangible indications of indigestion, we keep consuming, partly because we're convinced it's normal. Writes columnist Ellen Goodman, "Normal is getting dressed in clothes that you buy for work, driving through traffic in a car that you are still paying for, in order to get to the job that you need so you can pay for the clothes, car and the house that you leave empty all day in order to afford to live in it."[6]

Erich Fromm reminds us about the risk of settling for "normal": "That millions share the same forms of mental pathology does not make those people sane."[7] As compared to what a sane society would be—grounded in natural rhythms and social cooperation and trust—the dream we are dreaming is so abnormal that it keeps behavioral anthropologists working overtime, trying to figure out what we think we are doing. The Alfred P. Sloan Foundation recently set aside $20 million to examine the American lifestyle, primarily by carefully observing the daily behavior of *Homo sapiens americanus*.

For example, anthropologist Jan English-Leuck tries to make sense of child behavior as it relates to lifestyle. "When I shadow a three-year-old around, on the surface, that wouldn't seem to be an encapsulation of our culture," she said. "But when that three-year-old turns to his little sister and says, 'Don't bother me, I'm working,' that's worth overhearing."[8] Has the child already made the connection between the hours spent working and all the stuff his parents accumulate at the house?

At the University of Arizona another crew of anthropologists has been studying America's garbage since 1973. Garbologists core-drill Tucson landfills and sort through obsolete naval aircraft carriers, trying to make sense of our everyday artifacts. "We might think of the pattern of modern trash as a tangible record of human consumption," said William Rathje, the program's founder. "Future generations will marvel at the stuff that flows through our lives. The container of a frozen dinner that's cooked and eaten in minutes persists for hundreds of years."[9]

As in a monster movie, more stuff begins to take shape as we sit daydreaming about the perfect living room, the perfect body, or the neighborhood's sexiest lawn mower. Daydreams like these all require a steady stream of products that need to be hunted and gathered. On the vacation after next, maybe we'll hit the ski slopes in Colorado or hike in northern Italy, but before then we'll need to acquire a detailed checklist of expensive ski equipment. In the book *High Tech/High Touch,* John Naisbitt and his coauthors describe some of the items necessary for "adventure travel." "High-tech gear is available for every conceivable need, for every conceivable journey: digitally perfect-fit hiking boots, helmets with twenty-seven air vents, hydration packs, portable water purifiers, bike shorts with rubberized back-spray-repelling seats. . . ."[10]

SHAMEFUL STUFF

Most of us can relate to the dizzying array of technologically correct equipment and apparel. Do you have the right stuff? Does anyone? Some bicycling friends recently asked Dave to ride with them. His cutoff khaki shorts stuck out like a border collie at a greyhound track beside their shiny spandex, but he just kept pedaling. Even more "shameful" was the day his computer crashed and sank, taking years of data down with it. A vandal-generated message appeared suddenly on Dave's computer screen, insulting him by name, and within a few hours a repairman pronounced the computer "toast." Even the emergency floppy disks he fed into the machine were spit out with a growl. The computer was only a few years old, but somehow Dave felt a sense of techno-shame that he wasn't properly equipped to fend off the virus. His penalty for not being state-of-the-art? Two thousand dollars to replace the deceased, useless computer.

Dave's neighbor, eighty-seven-year-old political and social activist Ginny Cowles, appreciates the value of e-mail and the Internet, but she finds she can read the screen well only when she tilts her head up to bring the lower half of her bifocals to the task. "I think I may have to get a new pair of glasses to wear just when I'm on the computer," she said recently, with some frustration in her voice. "It's another example of how stuff always seems to require more stuff."

CHAPTER 5

The stress
of excess

*We hear the same refrain all the time from people:
I have no life. I get up in the morning, day care,
elder care, a 40 minute commute to work. I have
to work late. I get home at night, there's laundry,
bills to pay, jam something into the microwave
oven. I'm exhausted, I go to sleep, I wake up and
the routine begins all over again. This is what life
has become in America.*

—TREND-SPOTTER GERALD CELENTE

*We are a nation that shouts at a micro-
wave oven to hurry up.*

—JOAN RYAN,
The San Francisco Chronicle

Affluenza is a major disease, there's no question about it,"[1] says Dr.
Richard Swenson of Menomonie, Wisconsin, who practiced medicine
for many years before changing his focus to writing and lecturing.
A tall, bearded, deeply religious man, Swenson began over a period of time to conclude that much of the pain in his patients' lives had psychological rather than physical roots. "And after about four or five years, the whole idea of *margin* came to the
surface," he says. He found that too many of his patients were stretched to their
limits and beyond with no margin, no room in their lives for rest, relaxation, and
reflection. They showed symptoms of acute stress.

"It could be physical symptoms," Swenson recalls. "Headaches, low back pain, hyperacidity, palpitations in the heart, unexplained aches and pains. Or it could be emotional problems like depression, anxiety, sleeplessness, irritability, yelling at your boss or at your colleagues or your kids. There were all kinds of behavioral symptoms like driving too fast or drinking too much or screaming too much or being abusive. I recognized that they didn't have any space in their lives, they didn't have any reserves. The space between their load and their limits had just disappeared. I couldn't take an X-ray to find this thing, but nevertheless it was there. And it was a powerful source of pain and dysfunction in people's lives."

POSSESSION OVERLOAD

Swenson observed that many of his patients suffered from what he now calls "possession overload," the problem of dealing with too much stuff. "Possession overload is the kind of problem where you have so many things you find your life is being taken up by maintaining and caring for things instead of people," Swenson says. "Everything I own owns me. People feel sad and what do they do? They go to the mall and they shop and it makes them feel better, but only for a short time. There's an addictive quality in consumerism. But it simply doesn't work. They've gotten all these things and they still find this emptiness, this hollowness. All they have is stress and exhaustion and burnout, and their relationships are vaporizing. They're surrounded by all kinds of fun toys but the meaning is gone."

"Tragedy," observes Swenson, "is wanting something badly, getting it, and finding it empty. And I think that's what's happened."

TIME FAMINE

There's been an almost imperceptible change in American greetings over the past two decades. Remember how when you used to say "how are you?" to the friends you ran into at work or on the street, they'd reply "fine, and you?" Now, when we ask that question, the answer is often "busy, and you?" (when they have time to say, "and you?") "Me too," we admit. We used to talk of having "time to smell the flowers." Now we barely find time to smell the coffee. "The pace of life has accelerated to the point where everyone is breathless," says Richard Swenson. "You look at all the countries that have the most prosperity and they're the same countries that have the most stress."

Tried to make a dinner date with a friend recently? Chances are you have to look a month ahead in your appointment calendars. Even children now carry them. Ask your coworkers what they'd like more of in their lives and odds are they'll say "time." "This is an issue that cuts across race lines, class lines, and gender lines," says African-American novelist Barbara Neely. "Nobody has any time out there."[2] We're all like the bespectacled bunny in Disney's *Alice in Wonderland,* who keeps looking at his watch and muttering, "No time to say hello, goodbye, I'm late! I'm late! I'm late!"

By the early 1990s, trend-spotters were warning that a specter was haunting America: time famine. Advertisers noted that "time will be the luxury of the 1990s." A series of clever TV spots for US West showed time-pressed citizens trying to "buy time" at a bank called 'Time R Us' or in bargain basements. One store offered customers "the greatest sale of all TIME." A weary woman asked where she could buy "quality time." "Now you CAN buy time," the ads promised. "Extra working time with mobile phone service from US West."

More working time. Hmmm.

We thought the opposite was supposed to be true: that advances in technology, automation, cybernation, were supposed to give us more leisure time and *less* working time. Remember how all those futurists were predicting that by the end of the 20th Century we'd have more leisure time than we'd know what to do with? In 1965, a U.S. Senate subcommittee heard testimony that estimated a workweek of from fourteen to twenty-two hours by the year 2000.[3]

We got the technology, but we didn't get the time. We have computers, fax machines, cell phones, e-mail, robots, express mail, freeways, jetliners, microwaves, fast food, one-hour photos, digital cameras, pop tarts, frozen waffles, instant this and instant that. But we have *less* free time than we did thirty years ago. And about those mobile phones: They do give you "extra working time" while driving, but make you as likely to cause an accident as someone who's legally drunk. Progress? And then there are those leaf blowers . . . .

Patience may be the ultimate victim of our hurried lives. David Schenk, the author of *The End of Patience,* says that such things as the speed of the Internet for e-mail and on-line shopping mean that "we're packing more into our lives and losing patience in the process. We've managed to compress time to such an extent that we're now painfully aware of every second that we wait for anything." There are now Internet news monitors in the elevators of a large Northeast hotel chain, and the ability to pedal and surf the Net at the same time at many fitness centers. Gas stations are considering putting in TV monitors on the islands to keep you amused while pumping.

THE HARRIED LEISURE CLASS

We should have paid attention to Staffan Linder. In 1970, the Swedish economist warned that all those predictions about more free time were a myth, that we'd soon be a "harried leisure class" starved for time. "Economic growth," wrote Linder, "entails a general increase in the scarcity of time."[4] He continued, "As the volume of consumption goods increases, requirements for the care and maintenance of these goods also tends to increase, we get bigger houses to clean, a car to wash, a boat to put up for the winter, a television set to repair, and have to make more decisions on spending."[5]

It's as simple as this: increased susceptibility to affluenza means increasing headaches from time pressure.

Shopping itself, Linder pointed out "is a very time-consuming activity." Indeed, on average, Americans now spend nearly seven times as much time shopping as they do playing with their kids. Even our celebrated freedom of choice only adds to the problem.

BRAND A OR BRAND B?

Consider the average supermarket. It now contains 30,000 items, two and a half times as many as it did twenty years ago.[6] Picture yourself having to choose between a hundred types of cereal, for instance (or almost any other item). You can decide by price, grabbing what's on sale; by flavor—sweet sells—or by nutrition—but then, what counts most? Protein? Cholesterol? Calories? Added vitamins? Fat? Dietary fiber? Or you can give in to your child's nagging and buy the Cocoa Puffs. You can reach for tomato juice, confident that you're getting vitamins and antioxidants and only fifty calories per serving. But don't look at the "sodium" column—you won't be able to allow yourself any more salt for the rest of the day without feeling guilty.

Psychologist Barry Schwartz, in his book *The Paradox of Choice*, warns that having so many choices increases our anxiety and is likely to leave us less happy. He points out that many of us are regularly troubled by the sense that we may have made the wrong choice, that we could have gotten a better product or a lower price.

So many choices. So little time. Linder said this would happen, and he warned that when choices become overwhelming, "the emphasis in advertising will be placed on ersatz information," because "brand loyalty must be built up among people who have no possibility of deciding how to act on objective grounds."[7] Ergo, if you're a marketer, hire a battery of psychologists to study which box colors are most associated by shoppers with pleasurable sex. . Or something else you might want.

OVERWORKING AMERICANS

Linder argued that past a certain point, time pressure would increase with growing productivity. But he wasn't sure whether working hours would rise or fall. He certainly doubted they'd fall as much as the automation cheerleaders predicted. He was right. In fact, there seems to be some pretty strong evidence that Americans are actually working more now than they did a generation ago.

Using U.S. Department of Labor statistics, Boston College sociologist Juliet Schor argues that full-time American workers are now toiling 160 hours—one full month—*more*, on average, than they did in 1969. "It's not only the people in the higher income groups—who, by the way, have been working much longer hours," says Schor. "It's also the middle classes, the lower classes, and the poor. Everybody is working longer hours."[8] Indeed, according to the International Labor Organization, in October of 1999 the United States passed Japan as the modern industrial country with the longest working hours. Forty-two percent of American workers say they feel "used up" by the end of the workday. Sixty-nine percent say they'd like to slow down and live a more relaxed life.

NO TIME TO CARE

Moreover, Schor says, "The pace of work has increased quite dramatically. We are working much faster today than we were in the past. And that contributes to our sense of being overworked and frenzied and harried and stressed out and burned out by our jobs." In the fax lane, everybody wants that report yesterday. Patience wears thin rapidly when we get used to a new generation of computers.

Several years ago, Karen Nussbaum, former president of 9 to 5, a clerical workers union, pointed out that "twenty-six million Americans are monitored by the machines they work on, and that number is growing. I had one woman tell me her computer would flash off and on: YOU'RE NOT WORKING AS FAST AS THE PERSON NEXT TO YOU!"[9] Doesn't just thinking about that make your blood pressure rise?

Sometimes the speedup reaches utterly inhumane levels. In late May 2000, evening newscasts across the Northwest showed disturbing footage taken inside the Iowa Beef Processors slaughterhouse in Wallula, Washington. The video showed cattle being struck on the head, electrically prodded, and hoisted in the air as they moved down the slaughtering line, kicking and struggling. Fully conscious cows were skinned alive and had their legs cut off. In a signed affidavit, one employee said, "The chain goes too fast, more than 300 cows an hour. If I can't get the animal knocked out right, it keeps going. It never stops. The cows are getting hung alive or not alive. I can tell some cows are alive because they're holding their heads up. They just keep coming, coming, coming. . . . " The video provides gruesome evidence that the speed of American production, driven by an insatiable desire for more, virtually guarantees us no time to care.

CHOOSING STUFF OVER TIME

Meanwhile, we have less time to recuperate from the work frenzy. A survey by Expedia.com found that Americans gave back an average of three vacation days to their employees in 2003, a gift to corporations of $20 billion. As their reason for doing so, most said they didn't want to be seen as slackers when the next round of layoffs came. Others said they simply couldn't take time off and keep up with the demands of their jobs.

Juliet Schor reminds us that the United States has seen more than a doubling of productivity since World War II. "So the issue is: what do we do with that progress? We could cut back on working hours. We could produce the old amount in half as much time and take half the time off. Or we could work just as much and produce twice as much." And, says Schor, "we've put all our economic progress into producing more things. Our consumption has doubled and working hours have not fallen at all. In fact, working hours have risen."[10]

Europeans made a different decision. In 1970, worker productivity per hour in the countries that make up the European Union was 65 percent that of Americans. Their GDP per capita was about 70 percent of ours because they worked longer than we did back then. Today, EU productivity stands at 91 percent of ours, and several European economies are more productive per worker hour than we are. But real per capita GDP in those countries is still only about 72 percent that of the United States.[11] They have a lot less stuff than we do. So what happened? It's simple: the Europeans traded a good part of their productivity gains for time instead of money. So instead of working more than we do, they now work much less-nearly nine weeks less per year.

As a result, they live longer and are healthier, despite spending far, far less per capita on health care. In fact, the United States ranks dead last in health among industrial nations, and we are now expected to spend 19 percent of our total GDP on health care by the year 2014.[12] Can you say "Mister Yuck?"

Not everyone agrees with Schor about longer working hours. John Robinson, who runs the Americans' Use of Time Project at the University of Maryland, claims that "time diaries" kept by employees (they record how they spend each minute of every workday) actually show a decrease in working hours. But Robinson does agree that most working Americans "feel" more time-pressured than ever.[13] Much of their increased leisure, he says, has been consumed in watching television—and thus by absorbing even more exhortations to consume. He also agrees that Europeans work far less and spend much more time socializing-which has proved to be good for health.

Whether one accepts Schor's numbers or Robinson's, the experience of time famine intensifies, driven by longer, or at least more demanding, working hours, and the competing time requirements associated with the care and feeding of stuff. Something has got to give. For many Americans, it's sleep. Many doctors say more than half of all Americans get too little sleep-an average of an hour too little each night. We average 20 percent less sleep than we did in 1900. And that takes a toll on health (not to mention the 100,000 traffic accidents each year that result from drivers falling asleep at the wheel).[14] So does our urgency about time.

HEART ATTACKS WAITING TO HAPPEN

The intake examination at the Meyer Friedman Institute in San Francisco is like none other in a doctor's office. A nurse runs prospective patients through a series of questions about their relationship to time. "Do you walk fast? Do you eat fast? Do you often do two or more things at the same time?" She also notes their physical responses to her questions. "Something you do a lot," she tells one interviewee, "is what we call expiratory sighing, as if you're emotionally exhausted or don't even want to think about the matter I'm asking you to talk about."

The nurse tabulates the answers provided by patients and gives them a score, putting most squarely in the category that, years ago, the late Meyer Friedman called the Type A personality. While working on the *Affluenza* film, John took the test and asked the nurse how he did. "You're right in the middle," she said, smiling. "You mean, like A minus, B plus?" John quizzed her. "I'm afraid not," she replied. "You're right in the middle of Type A. However, if it's any consolation, you're less Type A than most people in your profession." Unconsoled, John is working on slowing down (is that an oxymoron?). For the first time ever, he's trying to *lower* his grade.[15]

The more Type A someone is, the more likely that person is to suffer from what Dr. Friedman called "time urgency." "We've also called it hurry sickness in the past," Bart Sparagon, the mellow, soft-spoken doctor who now directs Friedman's clinic, says slowly. "It's as if people are struggling against time."

"I have a vivid image of an advertisement for a famous journal about financial affairs," Sparagon adds, with a look of resignation. "It's a picture of men in suits carrying briefcases, leaping over hurdles, with this hostile, tense look on their faces, and it's an ad suggesting that if you buy this magazine, you can win this race. But when I see that picture, I know those men are racing toward a heart attack. I mean, do you *want* to win that race?"[16]

Along with time urgency, the racers usually are afflicted with what Meyer Friedman terms "free-floating hostility." Everything that causes them to slow down—in their pursuit of money or other symbols of success—becomes an enemy, something in their way, an obstacle to overcome. "I think that time urgency is the major cause of premature heart disease in this country," Meyer Friedman once declared.[17] The more Type A a person is, he believes, the greater that person's risk of cardiac arrest.

Affluenza is certainly not the only cause of time urgency. But it is a major cause. Swelling expectations lead to a constant effort to keep up with the latest products, to compete in the consumption arena. That, in turn, forces us to work more, so we can afford the stuff. With so many things to use, and the need to work harder to obtain them, our lives grow more harried and pressured. As one pundit put it, "If you win the rat race, you're still a rat." And you may be a dead one.

In recent years, many scientists have come to believe that viruses and other infections make us more susceptible to heart attacks. Their conclusions have come from studying influenza viruses. But if Meyer Friedman and his theories about Type A personalities are right, they should look more closely at affluenza as well.

CHAPTER 6

Family convulsions

There is a tension between materialism and family values.

—TED HAGGARD,
Pastor, New Life Church, Colorado Springs

ffluenza is a family problem. In a variety of ways, the disease is like a termite undermining American family life, sometimes to the point of collapse. We have already mentioned time pressures. One study found that American couples now find just twelve minutes a day to talk to each other! Others suggest that ten to fifteen minutes of conversation a day would be an *improvement!*[1] Some studies suggest that over the past generation, the time parents spend with their children has declined by as much as 40 percent. Time-diary expert John Robinson convincingly disputes that, but in any case, the time spent together is of a different quality—now much of it consists of parents chauffeuring their children from one event to another, as Dr. William Doherty points out.

Doherty, a family therapist and professor at the University of Minnesota, warns that today's kids are terribly overscheduled, as "market values have invaded the family." Parents often see family life as about instilling competitive values in their children so they can compile the best résumés to get into the best colleges to get the best jobs to earn the most money. Meanwhile, Doherty says, the number of families regularly eating dinner together and taking vacations together has dropped by a third since 1970.

Then, too, the pressure to keep up with the Joneses leads many families into debt and simmering conflicts over money matters that frequently result in divorce. Indeed, the American divorce rate, despite reaching a plateau in the 1980s and declining a bit since then, is still double what it was in the '50s, and family counselors report that arguments about money are precipitating factors in 90 percent of divorce cases.[2]

FOR RICHER . . .

Take, for example, the case of Keaton and Cindy Adams, the couple we introduced you to in chapter 2. They almost let affluenza tear their marriage apart. "Our wedding was so good we almost have it paid off," said Keaton six years after they were married. "And that's where the whole ball started rolling."[3] And so it rolls for many young Americans—thousands shelled out for one big extravaganza, that public pledge of eternal fidelity, "for richer or for poorer."

First, of course, it's for richer. Presents from friends and family—microwaves, blenders, towels, toasters (never out of fashion), dinnerware, Tupperware, tea kettles, and a whole lot more (leaf blowers?). Plus a roomful of wrapping paper, used once and cast aside. Then the wedding bills come due.

After their wedding, Keaton and Cindy began buying lots of other things for their home, all on credit. They bought expensive furniture and the obligatory "home entertainment center." "What's another twenty-five dollars a month?" says Keaton, explaining their thought process at the time, one all too common in American families. "And then we found ourselves making minimum payments all over the place to the point where we couldn't. And we started to get two months behind, three months behind."

In a short time, they were $20,000 in debt, with no hope of paying it off. "The arguments ensued. We started fighting," Keaton recalls. "We were screaming divorce. Finally we ended up reaching a breaking point."

For millions of American families, their story would, no doubt, sound familiar. But it has (so far, at least) a happy ending. The Adamses sought help from Consumer Credit Counseling Service in Colorado Springs, where they lived at the time, and brought their spending and financial crisis under control. Cindy Adams says they've learned a hard lesson. "It's OK not to have the newest thing, the latest style," she now believes. "Our home doesn't have to be in tip-top condition. It lets us focus on things that are more important than stuff."

SOCIALLY SANCTIONED ADDICTION

Mike and Terri Pauly, family counselors in Colorado Springs, say they see many couples who get themselves into situations like that faced by Keaton and Cindy Adams. It starts, Mike says, "with trying to acquire as many things as possible. It's a major stressor right now in couples. There is a real addictive cycle that families get into where they go out and spend money in order to feel good about themselves. I have a number of couples I've worked with recently who are having lots of problems, but who come in on Monday and say, 'We had a great weekend. And it's because we went out and spent a lot of money. We went to the mall and spent five hundred dollars on different things and we had a great time.'"[4] Shopping as therapy. But as a psychotropic drug, it ultimately doesn't work.

The time comes, Mike Pauly points out, "when there's no more money left on the credit card and they get into that position of feeling backed against the wall. They start feeling stress and tension in their relationship." It's a problem, Mike says, "that's a lot like racism. It's all-pervasive, it's everywhere, and people don't realize it."

But unlike racism, the addiction to stuff isn't challenged in our society. In fact, says Terri Pauly, "It's a very socially acceptable way to be addictive, to get a temporary high, to feel good. I'm feeling depressed today—let's go shopping. As far as society goes, it's sanctioned. They get a lot of social reinforcement for it."[5] "And yet," adds Mike, "just like with a drug or with alcohol, when it wears off it's still the same old world and people have to deal with that emptiness inside, which is really what causes people to go out and spend."

FINDING SOMEBODY BETTER

In addition to family conflicts brought on by overspending, Terri and Mike say they see another way in which rampant consumerism or affluenza weakens marriages. "The choices available to people in terms of products are so overwhelming," Terri contends. "Whether you're going to buy a car or a bagel, there's so many choices. There's a feeling when you've bought something that maybe you didn't make the right choice, maybe you missed something. And it can't help but carry over into relationships with people, that there's got to be somebody better out there."

"I see that a lot in my practice," Mike says. "People come in and say they met someone at work or their relationship started at work and they divorced their spouses and got together. But once the wrapping was off it wasn't as new and different and wonderful as it was in the beginning when everyone was dressed up and powdered and looked perfect. So they go back to the company to find some other toy to play with, someone new, someone different." Shopping for partners.

Ted Haggard, pastor of the 11,000-member New Life Church in Colorado Springs, and president of the National Association of Evangelicals, shares the Paulys' concerns. "Everything we watch," he says, "is always promoting dissatisfaction. We need a new stereo, a new upgrade of our computer system, a better car, a bigger house. I think the societal discontent we're seeing is fed by the materialistic society we're living in."[6]

"The whole idea of using a thing and then throwing it away and getting another one is affecting us all as people," Haggard believes. "We start looking at other people and saying that if they don't give us pleasure, they are disposable. I think the trend is dangerous, and I think we need to have old values where we live in the same house as long as we can, where we keep material items as long as we can, and where we be faithful to each other."

In the use-it-once-and-throw-it-away, planned-obsolescence world of American consumer culture, it should not be surprising that attitudes formed in relation to products eventually get transferred to people as well.

Out of sight, out of mind. Moreover, family life strains under the stress of excess. As both parents work full time and more to meet their swelling expectations of the good life, then rush to maintain the frenetic lifestyles those expectations demand, nerves are frayed and tempers boil. In an ironic twist, the degeneration of family life leaves some partners spending *more* time at the office to avoid the friction and turmoil back home, a phenomenon well documented in *The Time Bind,* Arlie Russell Hochschild's study of workers' lives in a large corporation.

As Barbara Ehrenreich puts it in an endorsement of Hochschild's book, it's a "vicious cycle . . . the longer hours we work, the more stressful our home lives become; and the greater the tensions at home, the more we try to escape into work."[7] But the cycle frequently starts not with work, but with affluenza: often we work more because we want more. As a culture, at least, we have chosen money over time.

FAMILY VALUES OR MARKET VALUES?

There is yet another means by which affluenza pulls families apart. Glenn Stanton, the clean-cut director of a conservative family-support organization in South Carolina, calls it "the new homelessness." "We have people living in houses with one another but not connecting with one another," Stanton says.[8] They're not interacting

because, quite simply, they all have their own toys to play with. "Dad is on the Internet," Stanton points out. "Mom's upstairs watching a movie on the VCR. The kids are downstairs playing video games. Everybody is connected to something outside the home even though they are physically within the home.

"The pressure that materialism is bringing to bear on the American family today is woefully underestimated, but it is critically important," he argues. It wasn't something we expected to hear from Stanton. We spoke with him several years ago, when he was a policy analyst for Focus on the Family, the largest Christian conservative organization in the United States.

Founded by Dr. James Dobson, a child psychologist whose radio program is heard by millions of people, FOF is a mini-empire of conservative family advisers based in Colorado Springs. Its operations are housed in palatial hillside headquarters that might embarrass the Parthenon. Inside, the feel is expensive and dynamic. Tour groups learn about Dobson's vision for FOF, while the photographs lining the walls establish his connection to past and present Republican stalwarts, including Ronald Reagan and Newt Gingrich.

Dozens of neatly dressed men and women respond to hundreds of phone callers every day, counseling them and sending out audiotapes, videotapes, and publications geared to teens, single parents, and other readers. "We get thousands of letters every week," said Stanton when we first met him at FOF. "People write to us looking for help to hold their marriage together, their family together."

The ideology at FOF is decidedly free-market capitalist but not without reservations like those expressed by Stanton. "The market in a very real sense is hostile to the family," he contends. "It needs to expand itself. It needs to bring in new consumers. And quite tragically, it brings in new consumers at almost any price. Do we go after a sale even pitting child against parent? We would contend that that is too far."

It may be too far. It is also deliberate. At conferences of children's marketers, it is described as "the nag factor." Increase the nag factor and you increase the chance of a sale—family harmony be damned.

THE CONSERVATIVE CONTRADICTION

Stanton and some other conservatives have begun to look carefully at what they see as an inherent tension between market values and family values. Edward Luttwak, a former Reagan administration official with the Center for International and Strategic Studies, expresses his concerns about the issue rather bluntly. "The contradiction between wanting rapid economic growth and dynamic economic change and at the same time wanting family values, community values, and stability is a contradiction so huge that it can only last because of an aggressive refusal to think about it," says Luttwak,[9] the author of the powerful and critically acclaimed book *Turbo-Capitalism.*

Luttwak calls himself "a real conservative, not a phony conservative." "I want to conserve family, community, nature. Conservatism should not be about the market, about money," he argues. "It should be about conserving things, not burning them up in the name of greed."

Too often, he says, so-called conservatives make speeches lauding the unrestricted market (as the best mechanism for rapidly increasing America's wealth), while at the same time saying we have to go back to old family values; we have to maintain communities. "It's a complete non sequitur, a complete contradiction," Luttwak says. "The two of course are completely in collision. It's the funniest after-dinner speech in America. And the fact that this is listened to without peals of laughter is a real problem."

"America," Luttwak contends, "is relatively rich. Even Americans that are not doing that well are relatively rich, but America is very short of social tranquility. It's very short of stability. It's like somebody who has seventeen ties and no shoes buying himself another tie. The U.S. has no shoes as far as tranquility and the security of people's lives is concerned. But it has a lot of money. We have gone over to being a complete consumer society, a 100 percent consumer society. And the consequences are just as one would predict them. Mainly lots of consumption, lots of goodies and cheap things, cheap flights, and a lot of dissatisfaction."

Indeed, no system seems as effective as the unrestricted free market in delivering the most goods at the lowest prices to consumers. In the Age of Affluenza, such success has become the supreme measure of value. But human beings are more than consumers, more than stomachs craving to be filled. We are producers as well, looking to express ourselves through stable, meaningful work. We are members of families and communities, moral beings with interest in fairness and justice, living organisms dependent on a healthy and beautiful environment. We are parents and children.

Our affluenza-driven quest for maximum consumer access undermines these other values. To produce goods at the lowest prices, we lay off thousands of workers and transfer their workplaces from country to country in search of cheap labor. We shatter the dreams of those workers who are discarded, and often shatter their families as well. The security of whole communities is considered expendable. Lives are disrupted without a second thought. And as we shall see, children are pitted against parents, undermining family life even further.

CHAPTER 7

Dilated pupils

*We are living in a material world,
and I'm a material girl.*

—MADONNA

In 1969, when John was twenty-three, he taught briefly at a Navajo Indian boarding school in Shiprock, New Mexico. His third-grade students were among the poorest children in America, possessing little more than the clothes on their backs. The school had few toys or other sources of entertainment. Yet John never heard the children say they were bored. They were continually making up their own games. And though racism and alcoholism would likely scar their lives a few years later, they were, at the age of ten, happy and well-adjusted children.

That Christmas, John went home to visit his family. He remembers the scene, a floor full of packages under the tree. His own ten-year-old brother opened a dozen or so of them, quickly moving from one to the next. A few days later, John found his brother and a friend watching TV, the Christmas toys tossed aside in his brother's bedroom. The boys complained to John that they had nothing to do. "We're bored," they proclaimed. For John, it was a clear indication that children's happiness doesn't come from stuff. But powerful forces keep trying to convince America's parents that it does.

John tells the story in the first chapter of a new book published by the American Academy of Pediatrics.[1] The book, *About Children*, deals with almost every aspect of childhood in America today—from asthma to violence. The first chapter is about "Childhood Affluenza," making it clear that the medical profession takes affluenza seriously, especially where children are concerned. It does so with good reason.

THE CHILDREN'S MARKETING EXPLOSION

Three ten-year-old girls participate eagerly, punctuating the sound of rolling dice and moving plastic figures with shouts of "Yes!" and "My favorite store!" They're playing the game *Electronic Mall Madness*, from Milton Bradley. They jam their "credit cards" into the plastic ATM and withdraw play money to spend in the mall. The object of the game, which retails for $40, is to buy the most stuff and get back to the parking lot first. It's a good introduction to the happy-go-spending, affluenza-infected, life of today's children.

Spending by—and influenced by—American children recently began growing by a torrid 20 percent a year, stands at about $670 billion today (more than the U.S. military budget of $418 billion), and is expected to reach $1 trillion annually within the next decade. In 1984, kids four to twelve spent about $4 billion of their own money. This year, they'll spend $35 billion. Marketing to children has become the hottest trend in the advertising world.

"Corporations are recognizing that the consumer lifestyle starts younger and younger," explains Joan Chiaramonte, who does market research for the Roper Starch polling firm. "If you wait to reach children with your product until they're eighteen years of age, you probably won't capture them."[2]

From 1980 to 2004 the amount spent on children's advertising in America rose from $100 million to $15 billion a year, a staggering 15,000 percent! In her book *Born to Buy*, Juliet Schor points out that children are now also used effectively by marketers to influence their parents' purchases of big-ticket items, from luxury automobiles to resort vacations and even homes. One hotel chain sends promotional brochures to children who've stayed at its hotels, so the kids will pester their parents into returning. Schor points out that many American kids recognize logos by the age of eighteen months and ask for brand-name products at the age of two. The average child gets about seventy toys a year.

For the first time in human history, children are getting most of their information from entities whose goal is to sell them something, rather than from family, school, or houses of worship. The average twelve-year-old in the United States spends forty-eight hours a week exposed to commercial messages. Yet American children spend only about forty minutes per week in meaningful conversation with their parents.[3] Susan Linn, the author of *Consuming Kids*, writes that "comparing the advertising of two or three decades ago to the commercialism that permeates our children's world is like comparing a BB gun to a smart bomb."[4]

Children under seven are especially vulnerable to marketing messages. Research shows that they are unable to distinguish commercial motives from benign or benevolent motives. One '70s study found that when asked who they would believe if their parents told them something was true and a TV character (even an animated one like Tony the Tiger) told them the opposite was true, most young children said they'd believe what the TV character told them. Both the American Psychological Association and the American Academy of Pediatrics say advertising that targets children is inherently deceptive.

What psychological, social, and cultural impacts are these trends having on children? A recent poll found that 95 percent of American adults worry that our children are becoming "too focused on buying and consuming things."[5]

VALUES IN CONFLICT

In Minneapolis, psychologist David Walsh, the author of *Selling Out America's Children*, teaches parents ways to protect their offspring from falling captive to commercialism. After years spent treating so-called problem children, Walsh worries that childhood affluenza is reaching epidemic levels. He sees a fundamental collision of values between children's needs and advertising. "Market-created values of selfishness, instant gratification, perpetual discontentment, and constant consumption have become diametrically opposed to the values most Americans want to teach their children," says the grandfatherly Walsh, presenting his concerns with gentle passion.[6]

Advertising aimed at children is hardly a new phenomenon. By 1912, boxes of Cracker Jack came with a toy inside to encourage children to ask for more. Long before television, children were saving cereal box tops to send in for prizes. Interestingly, the whole idea of children's TV programming came because advertisers were looking for ways to use the new electronic medium to sell their products. The first TV cartoon shows were created explicitly to sell sugared cereals.

Indeed, nearly 80 percent of food ads on Saturday morning children's programs still hawk high-calorie, sugary, or salt-laden items. With the hours that children spend in front of the tube, it's not surprising that children today are far more likely to be obese than they were in the early days of television. Obesity rates among American children doubled in the 1980s alone and have been increasing even faster since then.[7]

Today's children are exposed to far more TV advertising than their parents were. The average child sees nearly 40,000 commercials a year, about 110 a day. In 1984, deregulation of children's television by the Federal Trade Commission allowed TV shows and products to be marketed together as a package. Within a year, nine of the top ten best-selling toys were tied to TV shows.

But more important, perhaps, is the difference between today's ads and those of a generation ago. In the old ads, parents were portrayed as pillars of wisdom who both knew and wanted what was best for their children. Children, on the other hand, were full of wonder and innocence and were eager to please mom and dad. There was gender stereotyping—girls wanted dolls, and boys wanted cowboys and Indians—but rebelling against one's parents wasn't part of the message.

KIDS AS CATTLE

Now the message has changed. Marketers openly refer to parents as "gatekeepers" whose efforts to protect their children from commercial pressures must be circumvented so that those children, in the rather chilling terms used by the marketers, can be "captured, owned, and branded." At a 1996 marketing conference called Kid Power, held appropriately at Disney World, the keynote address, "Softening the Parental Veto," was presented by the marketing director of McDonald's.

Speaker after speaker revealed the strategy: Portray parents as fools and fuddy-duddies who aren't smart enough to realize their children's need for the products being sold. It's a proven technique for neutralizing parental influence in the marketer/child relationship.

Presenters at Kid Power '96 further revealed how marketers use children to design effective advertising campaigns. Kids are given cameras to photograph themselves and their friends so that marketers can see how they dress and spend their time. They are observed at home, at school, in stores, and at public events. Their spending habits are carefully tracked. They are gathered into focus groups and asked to respond to commercials, separating the "cool" from the "uncool."

The "coolest" contemporary ads frequently carry the message delivered by Kid Power '96 speaker Paul Kurnit, a prominent marketing consultant. "Antisocial behavior in pursuit of a product is a good thing," Kurnit stated calmly, suggesting that advertisers could best reach children by encouraging rude, often aggressive behavior and faux rebellion against the strictures of family discipline.[8] There is, some critics say, a serious danger in this: If rude, aggressive behavior becomes the norm for children as they emulate advertising models, to what level will children have to escalate their aggressive activities to really feel they are rebelling?

SHOOTING YOUR NEIGHBOR'S CAT

None of that seems to matter to the marketers who advertise in *Electronic Gaming Monthly,* a magazine popular with kids who are avid video game players. When her eight-year-old son Arthur first showed her several of the magazine's ads, Caroline Sawe, a Seattle single mother, was shocked. Her son loves video games, but he was disturbed by an ad he saw in the May 1998 issue. It was for a game called "Point Blank." Boldly splashed on the ad in giant print was the headline "MORE FUN THAN SHOOTING YOUR NEIGHBOR'S CAT." "I screamed when I saw it," Sawe recalls. "I think I scared Arthur, but I was so upset."[9]

The ad's copy was equally blunt: "Bang! Meow! Bang! Meow! Come on already. It's time you move up the food chain and take aim at something that sounds better when it explodes. . . . The directions are easy. If it's bigger than a pixel, shoot it." Sawe leafed through the magazine, growing even more horrified. Ad after ad glorified mindless violence. One, for a game called "Vigilante 8," pictured a school bus armed with machine guns and missiles, commandeered by Molo, a "psycho" looking for revenge after being expelled from school. That one was especially disturbing because it was published the same month that Kip Kinkel shot up his high school in Springfield, Oregon, killing two fellow students.

Sawe, a tall, passionate woman who immigrated to the United States from her native Tanzania, shakes her head sadly when she thinks about the ads and Arthur's exposure to them. Is this what she left her tribal homeland on the slopes of Mount Kilimanjaro and came to America for? Are there no limits to what affluenza-afflicted marketers will do in their search for quick profits from children?

GOTTA HAVE THE CLOTHES

The "antisocial" ads are targeted primarily at boys. For girls, the messages are more genteel, but they still place products on a pedestal, above other values. A Sears ad from a few years ago is instructive: In it, actress and singer Maia Campbell tells girls, "You gotta believe in your dreams. You gotta stand up for yourself. You gotta be there for your friends. But, hey, *first* you gotta have something to wear. You *gotta* have the *clothes.*" The ad shows Campbell modeling clothes collectively priced at $267.

Companies selling beauty products are targeting younger and younger girls. By the age of thirteen, 26 percent of American girls wear perfume every day. Christian Dior makes bras for preschoolers. Jeans ads feature preteen girls in sexual poses. Ad critic Laurie Mazur says such images "may have dangerous implications," pointing out that nearly half a million American children are victims of sexual abuse each year.[10]

That didn't stop Abercrombie and Fitch from releasing a Christmas 2003 "field guide" with the teaser headline "Group Sex and More" and articles that essentially encouraged sexual experimentation by teens. The company also paraded teen models in underwear to promote the opening of a new store in Boston and used sexually suggestive slogans to market underwear sized for nine-year-old girls.

TODAY'S LESSON IS BROUGHT TO YOU BY. . .

Not only are the messages different today, but they also aren't limited to print and television. As marketers attempt to get their message through the clutter of advertising aimed at children, they look to put ads in places where ads have never gone before.

In 1998, a student was suspended at Greenbrier High School in rural Georgia. His crime? Wearing a Pepsi T-shirt on "Coke Day in the Schools." It seems the six hundred students at Greenbrier had been instructed to wear Coke T-shirts and to spell out *Coca-Cola* on the school lawn to impress a visiting Coca-Cola executive and give the school a chance to win $500 from the soft drink company. If we had had anything to say about it, it would have been the principal who was suspended, for allowing such a blatant commercial misuse of his school. But the incident at Greenbrier High is only the tip of an iceberg of commercialism that has penetrated deep into America's schools, allowing serious affluenza infections to follow close behind.

BETTER THAN STRAIGHT A'S

In the Age of Affluenza, voters demand tax cuts and reductions in public spending as their personal spending habits leave them with growing credit debt. Then too, affluent families increasingly send their children to private schools, further reducing voter support for public school systems.

As funding for education tightens, school boards all across America have turned to corporations for financial help. In exchange for cash, companies are allowed to advertise their products on school rooftops, hallways, readerboards, book covers, uniforms, and buses.

A walk through the hallways of Colorado Springs high schools reveals a string of mini-billboards informing students that "M&Ms are better than straight A's" and encouraging them to "Satisfy your hunger for higher education with Snickers." The ads, critics say, constitute an endorsement by the schools of the very foods students are warned against in their health classes. School buses in Colorado Springs also carry ads, for 7-Up, Burger King, and the like, boldly painted—by the students!—on their sides. School superintendent Kenneth Burnley (who was chosen National School Superintendent of the Year for his policy allowing advertising in his schools) defends the ads, saying the money they provide is needed because voters in the prosperous, all-American city haven't passed a school bond since 1972. "People say, 'I'd rather buy a boat than give money to the schools,'" Burnley explains.[11]

CASH CROPS?

"Children in our society are seen as cash crops to be harvested," says Alex Molnar, a professor of education at Arizona State University who has been investigating commercialism in the schools for many years.[12] Angry and passionate, Molnar readily displays his collection of "curriculum materials" created by corporations for use in the public schools.

Students find out about self-esteem by discussing "Good and Bad Hair Days" with materials provided by Revlon. They learn to "wipe out that germ" with Lysol, and study geothermal energy by eating Gusher's Fruit Snacks (the "teachers' guide" suggests that each student be given a Gusher to bite and to compare the sensation to a volcanic eruption!). They also learn the history of Tootsie Rolls, make shoes for Nike as an environmental lesson, count Lay's potato chips in math class, and find out why the Exxon Valdez oil spill wasn't really harmful at all (materials courtesy of— you guessed it—Exxon) or why clear-cutting is beneficial—with a little help from Georgia-Pacific. Maybe we could turn around the steady decline of our children's

SAT scores if we just asked them questions about good and bad hair days instead of world geography.

Cover Concepts, a company that bills itself as "America's largest in-school communications partner," claims to reach 30 million students in 43,000 schools by "working in tandem with school administrators to distribute free, advertiser-sponsored materials such as textbook covers, lesson plans, posters, bookmarks, specialty packs, lunch menus, and other fun educational materials." In nearly half a million classrooms, 8.1 million children watch Channel One, a twelve-minute daily news program that includes two minutes of commercials. Viewing is mandatory for students because advertisers, who pay as much as $200,000 for a single thirty-second spot on Channel One, are told they can count on a captive audience.

Fortunately, a parent-teacher backlash is emerging in a few communities. In late 2001, the Seattle School Board voted to create an anticommercial policy, including a ban on Channel One.

CAPTIVE KIDS

As affluenza becomes an airwave-borne childhood epidemic, America's children pay a high price. Not only does their lifestyle undermine the children's physical health, but their mental health seems to suffer too. Psychologists report constantly rising rates of teenage depression and thoughts about suicide, and a tripling of actual child suicide rates since the 1960s.[13]

Much of this stems from the overscheduling of children to prepare them for our adult world of consumerism, workaholism, and intense competition. In some places, this reaches truly ridiculous levels. Since the passage of the No Child Left Behind Act, nearly 20 percent of American school districts have banned recess for elementary school children. The idea, as one Tacoma, Washington, school administrator put it, is to "maximize instruction time to prepare the children to compete in the global economy." This is nuts. We're talking second graders here.

Kate Cashman, a *Seattle Post-Intelligencer* humor columnist, wonders if we don't have it backward. At a time of rising childhood obesity, we're getting rid of recess while inviting junk food into our schools. She thinks we should reverse that—more recess, less junk food. She says she'd call her policy the "No Child Left with a Fat Behind Act." Sign us up to lobby in favor of the act. Let's try to get it passed in every state in the country! It may sound silly, but it makes far more sense than most of the legislation out there these days.

What kind of values do our children learn from their exposure to affluenza? In a recent poll, 93 percent of teenage girls cited shopping as their favorite activity.

Fewer than 5 percent listed "helping others." In 1967, two-thirds of American college students said "developing a meaningful philosophy of life" was "very important" to them, while fewer than one-third said the same about "making a lot of money." By 1997, those figures were reversed.[14] A 2004 poll at UCLA found that entering freshman ranked becoming "very well off financially" ahead of all other goals. Juliet Schor surveyed children age ten to thirteen for their responses to the statement "I want to make a lot of money when I grow up." Of those children, 63 percent agreed; only 7 percent thought otherwise.

Asked about their "highest priority" in a 1999 poll taken at the University of Washington, 42 percent of those surveyed cited "looking good/having good hair." Another 18 percent listed "staying inebriated," while only 6 percent checked "learning about the world."

Jennifer Gailus and Olivia Martin would have been among the 6 percent. In 1996 Gailus, a vivacious former cheerleader, and her best friend, Martin, who is quiet and serious, wrote a play titled *Barbie Get Real*, satirizing the hollow life of appearances and shopping they say had become rampant among their peers at Eastlake High School in affluent Redmond, Washington (the home of Microsoft).

Asked at the time why they wrote the play, Gailus, who is a now a high school math teacher, summed up the pernicious effect affluenza has on children. "The kids in our high school," she said sadly, "take everything for granted. They think they've earned it and the world owes it to them. They'll just take, take, take, and they won't give anything back. And our society's going to crumble if we don't have people that give."[15]

CHAPTER 8

Community chills

Everyplace looks like no place,
and no place looks like home.

—JAMES KUNTSLER, AUTHOR
The Geography of Nowhere

You may have seen the ad. It's a fairly recent one for an SUV. It pictures a suburban street of expensive, identical ranch-style houses with perfect lawns. The SUV being advertised is parked in the driveway of one of them. But in every other driveway is . . . a tank. A real tank. A big, deadly Army tank. It's a chilly ad, meant to remind us of how chilling our communities have become as our war of all-against-all consumer competition continues. Psychologically, it suggests that we need to drive something as strong as a tank to compete with all the other killer vehicles out there. But a classy, comfortable tank. Of course, the ad is an exaggeration. Our communities aren't this cold and hostile. Not yet. But there's a definite chill in the air.

During the 1950s, Dave used to walk with his grandfather four or five blocks to the town square in Crown Point, Indiana, where the older man lived. Everyone knew his grandfather, even the guy carrying a sack of salvaged goods. Forty-five years later, Dave still remembers the names of his grandparents' neighbors, and the summer backyard parties they threw. But a sense of place and the trust that comes with it are disappearing from our towns and neighborhoods.

In 1951, Americans sat together with their neighbors, laughing at Red Skelton. In 1985, we still watched *Family Ties* as a family. But by 1995, each member of a family often watched his or her own TV, as isolation and passivity became a way of life. What began as a quest for the good life in the suburbs degenerated into private consumption splurges that separated one neighbor from another, and one family member from another. We began to feel lost in our own neighborhoods—it wasn't just the "Desperate Housewives" who were ill at ease. Huge retailers took advantage of the confusion, expanding to meet our demand for cheap underwear, hardware, and software.

Many sociologists are concerned about the health implications of our neighborhoods. In a book titled *The Power of Clan*, Dr. Stewart Wolf examines a multi-decade study of a small town near Philadelphia, Roseto, where longevity is legendary. He attributes the town's remarkable health (which has, alas, slipped recently) to three-generation bonding in families, neighborliness, devoted churchgoing, and membership in social organizations. Yet suburban design often turns a cold shoulder on the neighborhood "clan," with garage doors that resemble drawbridges, privacy fences that become castle walls, and private "mini-manors" that encourage exclusive lifestyles. Physical features such as these affect the social and even physical health of suburban residents.

The more we chased bargains and the paychecks that bought them, the more vitality slipped away from our towns. Now, if we want to experience Main Street— the way it was in the good old days—we travel to Disney World, to a faux community where smiling shopkeepers, the slow pace, and the quaintness remind us that our real communities were once close-knit and friendly.

How will Disney portray the good old days of the suburbs, in future exhibits? Will it orchestrate background ambience—highway traffic, leaf blowers, and beeping garbage trucks—to make it more realistic? Will it recreate gridlock as bumper-to-bumper cars, complete with cell phones to tell our families we'll be late for the next ride? Will our tour of the "gated community" require more tickets than rides through the "inner city" do? Will recreational and business opportunities that have sprung up in recent years be dramatized—businesses like Kid Shuttle, a taxi service for kids whose moms aren't home to take them to tae kwon do? Will Disney hire extras to play the roles of other suburbanites who can't drive—elderly, disabled, and low-income residents, peeking out from behind living-room curtains?

BOWLING ALONE

Where can America's stranded nondrivers go, in today's world? There's no colorful café down the block, or bowling alley or tavern, where neighbors can "be apart together, and mutually withdraw from the world," in the words of writer Ray Oldenburg.[1] Such "great good places" or "third places," that are apart from both home and work environments, are now often illegal—violations of zoning codes. The truth is, the term "community life" is perceived as archaic in a world so dominated by business and government.

"We've mutated from citizens to consumers in the last sixty years," says James Kuntsler, the author of *The Geography of Nowhere*. "The trouble with being consumers is that consumers have no duties or responsibilities or obligations to their fellow consumers. Citizens do. They have the obligation to care about their fellow citizens and about the integrity of the town's environment and history."[2]

Harvard political scientist Robert Putnam has devoted his career to the study of "social capital," the connections among people that bind a community together. He observed that the quality of governance varies with the level of involvement in such things as voter turnout, newspaper readership, and membership in choral societies. Recently, he captured the public's imagination by concluding that far too many Americans are "bowling alone" (compared to a generation ago, more people are bowling now, but fewer of them bowl in leagues). Once a nation of joiners, we've now become a nation of loners. Only about half of the nation's voters typically vote in presidential elections. Only 13 percent reported attending public meetings on town or school affairs, and PTA participation has fallen from more than twelve million in 1964 to seven million in 1995. The League of Women Voters' membership is down 42 percent since 1969, and fraternal organizations like the Elks and Lions are endangered species.[3]

Volunteering for Boy Scouts is off 26 percent since 1970, and for the Red Cross, 61 percent. Overall, a record 109 million Americans are volunteering, but many of them do it "on the run," in shorter installments, so the total time volunteered has declined. The "fun factor" is a major stimulant in volunteering. If it's not fun, forget it. A 1998 study on volunteering revealed that 30 percent of young adults volunteered because it was fun; 11 percent said they were committed to the cause.[4]

Putnam concedes that membership has expanded in newer organizations such as the Sierra Club and the American Association of Retired Persons. But most members never even meet, he points out—they just pay their dues and maybe read the organization's newsletter. Internet chat groups, however convenient, are also faceless and fleshless. "Face-to-face connections are clearly more effective for building trust," he says. "Knowing the person you're talking to and taking personal responsibility for your view are crucial to having a conversation about public affairs."[5]

THE CHAINING OF AMERICA

Another symptom of civic degeneration is the disappearance of traditional civic leaders of community organizations. Bank presidents and business owners with long-standing ties to the community are bounced from positions of community leadership when US Bank, Wal-Mart, Office Max, and Home Depot come to town to put them out of business. What do we get when the chains take over? Lower prices, cheaper stuff. But what we lose is the value of community—a nonmaterial value, but more important for a high quality of life. We lose the personal touch.

For example, small businesses give a higher percentage of their revenues to charitable organizations than the big, absentee franchises do, and they offer a lot more in terms of local character and product diversity. At a locally owned coffee shop, you might see artwork from someone who lives down the street. The shop is *your* coffee shop. At your independent bookseller, you stand a much greater chance of finding books from small presses who publish a wider variety of books than mainstream publishers.

The "chaining of America" has happened so quickly that it's hard to believe the statistics. More than 40 percent of independent bookstores failed in the last decade. Barnes & Noble and Borders Books capture half of all bookstore sales.[6] Lowe's and Home Depot now control more than a third of the hardware market, forcing many a neighborhood "Mr. Fixit" to wear corporate apron colors—if he's not "overqualified."[7] Eleven thousand independent pharmacies closed in the last decade, and chain drugstores now account for more than half of all pharmacy sales.[8]

It's the same story in many other retail sectors, such as video rental outlets, grocery chains, and the restaurant industry. More than 4,100 independent video retailers have gone out of business since 1998, leaving Blockbuster and Hollywood Video in control of nearly half the market.[9] Five firms account for 42 percent of all grocery sales, up from 24 percent in 1996,[10] and more than 40 percent of restaurant spending is captured by the top one hundred chains.[11] Even more alarming is the domination of single companies like Wal-Mart, which in 2003 controlled 7 percent of *total* U.S. retail spending. Wal-Mart imports 10 percent of all America's total imports from China, and if it were a country, it would rank ahead of Great Britain and Russia in total imports.[12]

By using economies of scale in purchasing and distribution, and being able to stay in the market even at a loss, these monolithic retailers can drive out competition within a year, and in some cases sooner.[13]

In search of better buys and higher tax revenues, consumers and city council members typically first sacrifice Strip Avenue, then downtown, to the franchise developers, forgetting that much of a franchise dollar is electronically transferred to corporate headquarters, while a dollar spent at the local hardware stays put in towns or neighborhoods. The value of the local dollar is multiplied many times as small businesses hire architects, designers, woodworkers, sign makers, local accountants, insurance brokers, computer consultants, attorneys, advertising agencies—all services that the big retailers contract out nationally. Local retailers and distributors also carry a higher percentage of locally made goods than the chains, creating more jobs for local producers.[14] When we buy from the chains, instead of a multiplier effect, we get a "divider effect."

In 2005 our social defenses are down. Distracted by material things and out of touch with social health, we watch community life from the sidelines. Hurrying to work, we see a fleet of bulldozers leveling a familiar open area next to the river, but we haven't heard yet what's going in there. Chances are good it's Wal-Mart, McDonald's, and Starbucks.

AL NORMAN, SPRAWL BUSTER

"When I'm out of town," says Al Norman, "I come home to as many as a hundred e-mail messages from all over the world. Concerned citizens are asking me for information on how to stop the huge retailers from rolling over their towns like an asphalt roller." Norman spearheaded a Wal-Mart resistance campaign in his own home-town—Greenfield, Massachusetts—and won. After his story appeared in *Time, Newsweek,* the *New York Times,* and *60 Minutes,* "My phone started ringing and hasn't stopped," he says. "I've been to thirty-six states now, teaching hometown activists what tools are available."[15]

Norman's Web site lists about 100 successes, some of which he has personally coached to victory, but he's also very familiar with the defeats and the socioeconomic impacts that follow. "The *Adirondack Daily Enterprise* recently published an account of what has happened to retailers in Ticonderoga, New York, over the past eight months since Wal-Mart came to town," he said. "Business is down at least 20 percent at the drugstore, jeweler, and auto parts stores, but the game's totally over at the Great American Market, the town's only downtown grocery store. First they cut their operating hours, then dropped the payroll from twenty-seven people to seventeen. This January, the grocery closed completely. Many of the people who shopped at the GAM were the elderly, low-income people without access to a car."

"I've been here twenty-five years," a downtown Sunoco station owner told Norman. "On the week before Christmas in prior years, you couldn't find a parking

One nation, divisible...

THE ZONING DISPUTE BETWEEN THE GATED COMMUNITIES OF BONNIE BRAE AND WINSOME WILLOWS CONTINUES TO ESCALATE...

GREAT SHOT, MOM! YOU TOOK OUT A THREE-CAR GARAGE!

EYEWITLESS NEWS

© 2001 SEATTLE POST-INTELLIGENCER • TRIBUNE MEDIA SERVICES

space on this street. This year, you could have landed a plane on it." Everyone's car was parked at the megamall. Norman recalls going into Henniker, New Hampshire, a town actively opposing an 11,000-square-foot Rite-Aid store. "It did my heart good to read a sign at the city limits that, to me, said it all: Welcome to Henniker—the only Henniker on Earth. The problem is, you've got the other side of the American population. They'll stand up in public meetings and insist they have a God-given right to cheap underwear and whipping cream. It seems like their sense of community is no bigger than their own shopping cart."

FORTRESS AMERICA

What happens when affluenza causes communities to be pulled apart (for example, when a company leaves town and lays off hundreds of people), or crippled by bad design? We "cocoon," retreating further and further inward and closing the gate behind us. Including secured apartment dwellers, residents of gated communities, prison inmates, and residential security system zealots, at least a fifth of the country now lives behind bars. "Socially, the house fortress represents a self-fulfilling prophecy," says community designer Peter Calthorpe. "The more isolated people become and the less they share with others unlike themselves, the more they do have to fear."[16]

Sociologist Edward Blakely would agree. "We are a society whose purported goal is to bring people of all income levels and races together, but gated communities are the direct opposite of that," he writes in the book *Fortress America*. "How can the nation have a social contract without having social contact?"[17] If gated enclaves are the final act of secession from the wider community and a retreat from the civic system, twenty thousand such communities, housing almost nine million people, have already seceded. Why have so many retreated from the wider community? Don't we trust each other? In 1958, trust was sky high. Seventy-three percent of Americans surveyed said they trusted the federal government to do what is right either "most of the time" or "just about always." Now only about half feel a strong sense of trust for the feds.

It's the same with trust among individuals. As David Callahan documents in *The Cheating Culture: Why More Americans Are Doing Wrong to Get Ahead,* many are letting their personal ethics slide, whether it's cheating the IRS, fudging the facts as a former *New York Times* reporter did, or injecting steroids, as many athletes have now confessed doing. Sixty percent of Americans now believe "you can't be too careful in dealing with people."[18] It's the same story in the workplace, where the lack of trust is costly. "When we can't trust our employees or other market players," writes Robert Putnam, "we end up squandering our wealth on surveillance equipment, compliance structures, insurance, legal services, and enforcement of government regulations."[19]

If an eight-year-old girl can walk safely to the public library six blocks away, that's one good indicator of a healthy community. For starters, you have a public library worth walking to and a sidewalk to walk on. But more important, you have neighbors who watch out for each other. You have social capital in the neighborhood—relationships, commitments, and networks that create an underlying sense of trust.

Yet in many American neighborhoods, trust is becoming a nostalgic memory. Seeing children at play is becoming as rare as sighting an endangered songbird. A 2000 nationwide poll conducted by the Pew School of Journalism reflected a collective queasiness in America. Compared to the 96 percent who felt safe in their homes, 20 percent did not feel safe in their own neighborhoods, and 30 percent did not feel safe at the mall. What do these results say about the world "out there"? Grab the takeout dinner, survive the commute, just get home. In the poll, a wide sampling of Americans was asked, "What do you think is the most important problem facing the community where you live?" Predictably, crime/violence scored the highest, but surprisingly, it shared top ranking with development/sprawl/traffic/roads. Both are problems that many Americans feel are out of control. And in an effort to regain control, we revert to the primal responses of fight or flight.

We try to fight crime with judicial and enforcement industries that have become 7 percent of the U.S. economy. In recent years we've expanded the number of men and women in police uniforms to control crime and hired three times as many "rent-a-cops" as real cops. And in prisons, taxpayers pick up the tab for costs per prisoner that are comparable to sending a student to Harvard.

In any densely populated area, you'll hear the sounds of insecurity. Car alarms, beeping electronic locks, and police sirens reveal our futile quest to control crime. In reality, despite popular perceptions, living in suburbia may be statistically riskier than living in the inner city, because suburban residents drive three times as much as residents of close-in urban neighborhoods, and three times as many of them die in car crashes. Still, millions continue to take flight to the perceived security of suburbia.

THE SOCIAL COSTS OF PROSPERITY

Since 1950, the amount of land in our communities devoted to public uses—parks, civic buildings, schools, churches, and so on—decreased by a fifth, while the percentage of income we spend for house mortgages and rental payments increased from a fifth to a full half, according to the American Planning Association. The evidence shows that as we've disinvested in the public areas and "privatized" our lifestyles, we've often left citizenship and care at the front door. So many services are now delivered for a profit by the private sector, we seem to have just gotten out of the habit of taking care of each other.

The 1990s were the most continuously prosperous years in the history of America, as measured in economic terms. Yet Marc Miringoff at Fordham University's Institute for Innovation in Social Policy believes that the trends in his Index of Social Health point to a nation in crisis.

"In 1977," Miringoff says, "social health started its long decline, while the GDP continued upward. Since then, the social health index declined 45 percent while the GDP rose by 79 percent."[20]

Far from being just abstract statistics, the trends he cites are about the real people, in your family and mine, who constitute the social wealth and vigor of our communities. More than three million children are reported abused every year—forty-seven cases for every 1,000 children. Miringoff asks, "What will be the impact on marriage, child rearing, education, and employment from all that abuse?" He also points to youth suicide as an unmistakable indicator of underlying discontent. In 1950, the suicide rate among youth aged fifteen to twenty-four was a relatively low 4.5 per 100,000. Today, it's more than double that number. Each suicide resonates far beyond an individual's family, causing serious depression among the victim's friends, schoolmates, and neighbors—not to mention the lost potential of the youth.

A GEOGRAPHY OF NOWHERE?

When affluenza infects our communities, it starts a vicious cycle. We begin to choose things over people, a choice that disconnects us from community life and causes even more consumption and more disconnection. Health scientists have documented that people in relationships outlive single people, and that people who feel the friendship and support of neighbors need less health care. One study also found that residents of neighborhoods in crisis tend to be clinically "socially" depressed, with lower levels of serotonin—what antidepressants stimulate—in blood samples.

Have we become a nation too distracted to care? Like the medium-size fish that eat small fish, we consume franchise products in the privacy of our homes, then watch helplessly as the big-fish franchise companies bite huge chunks out of our public places, swallowing jobs, traditions, and open space. We assume that someone else is taking care of things—we pay them to take care of things so we can concentrate on working and spending. But to our horror, we discover that many of the service providers, merchandise retailers, and caretakers are not really taking care of us anymore. It might be more appropriate to say they're *consuming* us.

CHAPTER 9

An ache for meaning

Man does not live by cheap vacuum cleaners alone.

—CONSERVATIVE ECONOMIST
WILHELM ROPKE

*We are the hollow men.
We are the stuffed men.*

—T.S. ELIOT

CINCINNATI—*The blank, oppressive void facing the American consumer populace remains unfilled despite the recent launch of the revolutionary Swiffer dust-elimination system, sources reported Monday. The lightweight, easy-to-use Swiffer is the 275,894,973rd amazing new product to fail to fill the void—a vast, soul-crushing spiritual vacuum Americans of all ages face on a daily basis, with nowhere to turn and no way to escape.... Despite high hopes, the Swiffer has failed to imbue a sense of meaning and purpose in the lives of its users.*

—FROM THE HUMOR NEWSPAPER, *THE ONION*
FEBRUARY 9, 2000

*T*he road switchbacks up, down, and around precipitous canyons, cross-es raging streams, and winds by glassy lakes offering mirror images of an immense snow-covered volcano, the main attraction in Washington state's Mount Rainier National Park. Each year, two million people drive the road. More than a few stop to admire the beautiful stone masonry, so perfectly in harmo-ny with the natural setting, that forms the guardrails for the road and the graceful arches of its many bridges. This is high-quality work, built to last, built for beauty as well as utility. Built by the Civilian Conservation Corps (CCC).

In the 1930s, during the depths of the Great Depression, hundreds of young men came to Mount Rainier—ordinary, unemployed working men, mostly from cities back East. Living in tent camps or barracks, they built many of the marvelous facili-ties visitors to the park now take for granted. At a time when the dominant notion is that government never does anything well, the work of the CCC at Mount Rainier and many other national parks provides something of a corrective.

The men's work was laborious, performed in snow, sleet, or blazing sun, and their wages barely provided subsistence. Their accommodations were anything but plush, and they had little to entertain them except storytelling and card games. Most could carry all the possessions they owned in a single suitcase. Yet when author Harry Boyte interviewed veterans of the CCC, he found that many looked back on those days as the best of their lives.

They'd forgotten the dirt, the strained muscles, the bite of the mosquitoes. But they remembered with deep fondness the camaraderie and the feeling they had that they were "building America," creating work of true and lasting value that would be enjoyed by generations yet unborn. The sense of pride in their CCC accomplish-ments was still palpable sixty years later.[1]

THE MAN WHO PLANTED TREES

Twenty-five years ago, John Beal was working as an engineer with the Boeing Company when heart problems forced him to take some time off work. To improve his health, he walked frequently near his home. His strolls took him past a stream called Hamm Creek, a tiny rivulet that descends from the hills of southwest Seattle and joins the Duwamish River, an industrial waterway emptying into Puget Sound. Beal knew that in years past, schools of salmon came up the Duwamish to spawning grounds on Hamm Creek.

But in 1980 the creek was barren of fish. The evergreen forests that once lined its banks had all been stripped away. Industries dumped waste into the creek and garbage lined its banks. John Beal set out to change that. "If we could restore

Hamm Creek, in the most polluted part of the city of Seattle," he says he felt at the time, "we could demonstrate that it could be done anywhere."[2]

He worked actively, and successfully, to stop companies from polluting the creek, and hauled out tons of garbage. Then, over the next decade and a half, he planted trees, thousands of them. He restored natural ponds and waterfalls and spawning beds. At first he worked alone, but in time other people began to help. Some newspaper articles and a couple of TV reports attracted more. Beal showed them how to restore the watershed.

The salmon came back, each year a few more until the run is now nearly healthy again. Beal has never been paid for his efforts, though public donations cover his expenses. But he has, he says, been richly compensated by the satisfaction he feels from having made a real difference for Hamm Creek and his community. "That's my reward, that's how I get paid," Beal concludes.

What John Beal, the men of the CCC, and the countless other people who give to their communities have in common is the understanding that meaningful activity matters more than money and that, indeed, it is better to give than receive. They've learned that fulfillment comes from such efforts. But in our consumer society they are becoming exceptions.

The more Americans fill their lives with things, the more they tell psychiatrists, pastors, friends, and family members that they feel "empty" inside. The more toys our kids have to play with, the more they complain of boredom. Two thousand years ago, Jesus Christ predicted they would feel that way. What profit would it bring a person, he asked his followers (Matthew 16:26), were that person to gain the whole world, but lose his soul? In the Age of Affluenza, that question is seldom asked, at least not publicly. It should be.

POVERTY OF THE SOUL

When Mother Teresa came to the United States to receive an honorary degree, she said, "This is the poorest place I've ever been in my life," recounts Robert Seiple, the former director of World Vision, a Christian charity organization. "She wasn't talking about economics, mutual funds, Wall Street, the ability to consume," he adds. "She was talking about poverty of the soul."[3]

Shortly before he died of a brain tumor, Republican campaign strategist Lee Atwater made a confession. "The '80s," he said, "were about acquiring—acquiring wealth, power, prestige. I know. I acquired more wealth, power and prestige than most. But you can acquire all you want and still feel empty." He warned that there was "a spiritual vacuum at the heart of American society, a tumor of the soul."[4]

HUMAN NATURE...

In all the great religious traditions, human beings are seen as having a purpose in life. Stripped to its essentials, it is to serve God by caring for God's creations and our fellow human beings. Happy is the man or woman whose work and life energies serve those ends, who finds a "calling" or "right livelihood" that allows his or her talents to serve the common good. In none of those traditions is purpose to be found in simply accumulating things, or power, or pleasure—or in "looking out for number one."

One seldom hears work described as a calling anymore. Work may be "interesting" and "creative" or dull and boring. It may bring status or indifference—and not in any sense in relation to its real value. Our lives are disrupted far more severely when garbage collectors stop working than when ball players do. Work may bring great monetary rewards or bare subsistence. But we almost never ask what it means and what it serves. For most, though certainly not all of us, if it makes money, that's reason enough. Why do it? Simple. It pays.

Consider, for example, the handsomely compensated professionals who design the hyper-violent video game advertisements that so alarmed Caroline Sawe (described in chapter 7). Undoubtedly, most would describe their jobs as "fun" and certainly "creative," allowing them to continually imagine new ideas for effective promotions (double meaning intended). Nothing rote about such work. Comfortable surroundings? No doubt. Flexible hours? Probably, if long ones. A certain smug self-satisfaction at being smart, effective manipulators, able to come up with oh-so-clever copy like "More fun than shooting your neighbor's cat." "I love my job," they'd be likely to tell you if you asked them.

Then consider the designers of the games themselves. All the same satisfactions apply, plus even higher levels of financial remuneration—enough to purchase Ferraris, Porsches, and mansions. A few admit they would never let their *own* children use the products (or, in the case of purveyors of movie violence, see the films) that they make and market to other people's children. But stop making them? Not when the rewards are what they are.

Gain the world, lose the soul.

That such professionals can "enjoy" their work without the slightest qualms about its ultimate value or consequences surely testifies to the effective repression of questions about meaning and purpose in our modern economy. These privileged workers do not ache—not outwardly, at least. Or perhaps the rewards they receive—money, stimulation, power, status—for their morally dubious products act like morphine to deaden any pangs of regret.

UNDER THE SMILE BUTTONS

But millions of other Americans do hunger for meaning. That's what Dr. Michael Lerner, a rabbi and writer, found when he worked in a "stress clinic" for working families in Oakland, California. Along with his co-workers, Lerner originally "imagined that most Americans are motivated primarily by material self-interest. So we were surprised that these middle Americans often experience more stress from feeling that they are wasting their lives doing meaningless work than from feeling that they are not making enough money."[5]

Lerner and his colleagues brought groups of working people from various occupations together to talk with each other about their lives. "At first, most of the people we talked to wanted to reassure us, as they assured their co-workers and friends, that everything was fine, that they were handling things well, that they never let stress get to them, and that their lives were good." It was, he says, the kind of response that pollsters usually get when they ask people superficial questions about life satisfaction. But in time, as participants in the groups felt more comfortable being honest about their emotions, a different pattern of responses emerged.

"We found middle-income people deeply unhappy because they hunger to serve the common good and to contribute something with their talents and energies, yet find that their actual work gives them little opportunity to do so," Lerner writes. "They often turn to demands for more money as a compensation for a life that otherwise feels frustrating and empty."

"It is perhaps this fear of no longer being needed in a world of needless things that most clearly spells out the unnaturalness, the surreality, of much that is called work today," wrote Studs Terkel in his best-seller *Working*. Perhaps feelings such as those described by Lerner and Terkel have led to one of the most disturbing of contemporary American statistics: The rate of clinical depression in the United States today is *ten* times what it was before 1945. Over any given year, nearly half of American adults suffer from clinical depression, anxiety disorders, or other mental illnesses. By contrast, Old Order Amish, who avoid most of the amenities of our society, suffer from depression less than a fifth as often. Millions of Americans dull their psychic pain with Prozac and other drugs.[6] The use of antidepressants tripled during the past decade.[7] As Americans increasingly fall victim to affluenza, feelings of depression, anxiety, and lowered self-esteem are likely to become even more prevalent. Such a prediction finds scientific support in a series of recent studies carried out by two professors of psychology, Tim Kasser and Richard Ryan. They compared individuals whose primary aspirations were financial with others who were oriented toward lives of community service and strong relationships with other people.

Their conclusions were unequivocal: Those individuals for whom accumulating wealth was a primary aspiration "were associated with less self-actualization, less vitality, more depression and more anxiety." Their studies, they wrote, "demonstrated the deleterious consequences of having money as an important guiding principle in life."[8]

CHANGING STUDENT VALUES

Kasser and Ryan's studies confirm the wisdom of religious traditions that warn about the dangers of preoccupation with wealth. But such wisdom has been falling on deaf ears for quite some time now. In 1962, when Tom Hayden penned the Port Huron Statement, the founding manifesto of Students for a Democratic Society (SDS), he declared, "The main and transcending concern of the university must be the unfolding and refinement of the moral, aesthetic and logical capacities" to help students find "a moral meaning in life."[9]

"Loneliness, estrangement and isolation describe the vast distance between man and man today," Hayden wrote. "These dominant tendencies cannot be overcome by better personnel management, nor by improved gadgets, but only when a love of man overcomes the idolatrous worship of things by man."

During the '60s, calls such as Hayden's for a meaningful life of service to the world—responding in part to John F. Kennedy's inaugural admonition to "ask not what your country can do for you; ask, rather, what you can do for your country"—inspired tens of thousands of students. Oral historian Studs Terkel, while acknowledging some of the youthful excesses of the '60s (the drugs, the foul language, the casual sex), says that what he remembers most about that decade was symbolized by an episode during the 1968 Democratic Convention in Chicago, when police chased antiwar demonstrators through Grant and Lincoln parks, clubbing and gassing them.

Terkel was observing the demonstration with James Cameron, a British journalist, when all of a sudden the police sent a volley of tear gas their way. "We were scurrying away, the tears running down, and as I was stumbling, a canister of tear gas fell at my feet," Terkel recalls. "And I'll never forget this little goofy hippie kid with long blond locks. He kicks the tear gas away from Cameron and me and toward himself. Toward himself. He saves us from the gas! That kid's gesture was really what the sixties was all about. They had causes outside themselves. Civil rights. Vietnam. That's what the sixties was all about."[10]

The dreams of college students have changed markedly since then.

A little more than a decade ago, when Thomas taught at Duke University, he asked students to outline their goals. Above all, they wanted money, power, and things—very big things, including vacation homes, expensive foreign automobiles, yachts, and even airplanes. Their request of faculty members like himself: "Teach me to be a money-making, money-spending machine." The most common thing he remembers Duke students saying to each other was, "I can't believe how drunk I got last night." Alcohol abuse—and particularly binge drinking—is an increasing problem on American campuses. Alcohol-related deaths, injuries, and poisoning are common. Students now spend nearly $6 billion a year on booze, more than they spend on all other beverages and their books combined.[11]

Apparently, it takes a lot of alcohol to fill an empty soul.

WHEN LEFT AND RIGHT AGREED

These days, critics of the emptiness of the consumer lifestyle come most often from the political left. But that wasn't always so. Before Reagan, many conservatives hadn't yet hitched their star completely to libertarian, free-market worship. Prominent conservative philosophers and economists were often as critical of consumerism as were their leftist counterparts, suggesting that it led to lives without meaning.

Wilhelm Ropke was one of the giants of traditional conservative economic thought. "*Homo sapiens consumens* loses sight of everything that goes to make up human happiness apart from money income and its transformation into goods," Ropke wrote in 1957. Those who fall into the "keeping up with the Joneses" lifestyle, he argued, "lack the genuine and essentially non-material conditions of simple human happiness. Their existence is empty, and they try to fill this emptiness somehow."[12]

Long before Enron, WorldCom, and other scandals involving corporate greed, Ropke posed powerful questions about the moral direction of consumer society:

> Are we not living in an economic world, or as R. H. Tawney says, in an "acquisitive society" which unleashes naked greed, fosters Machiavellian business methods and, indeed allows them to become the rule, drowns all higher motives in the "icy water of egotistical calculation" (to borrow from the Communist Manifesto), and lets people gain the world but lose their souls? Is there any more certain way of desiccating the soul of man than the habit of constantly thinking about money and what it can buy? Is there a more potent poison than our economic system's all-pervasive commercialism?"[13]

In *A Humane Economy,* Ropke pointed out that in a capitalist society (which, as a conservative, he strongly supported), it is all the more important for each individual to ask questions about the moral value of his or her activities and not merely be carried along by market currents. Without such vigilance, he suggested, life would become hollow. "Life is not worth living," he wrote, "if we exercise our profession only for the sake of material success and do not find in our calling an inner necessity and a meaning that transcends the mere earning of money, a meaning which gives our life dignity and strength."[14]

STANDARDIZED PEOPLE

Perhaps the best explanation of how the pursuit of material aims leads to meaningless, perpetually bored lives was provided by another conservative, the philosopher Ernest van den Haag.

First, he pointed out, mass production, which makes the universal consumer lifestyle possible, drives large numbers of people out of more varied occupations as artisans and small farmers, and agglomerates them in factories, where the division of labor reduces the scope of their activities to a few repetitive motions. Their work offers neither variety nor control.

In time, their output is sufficient enough, and their organized demands effective enough, that they begin to share in the material fruits of their labor. But to provide the quantity of goods that makes that possible, they must accept mass-produced, and therefore standardized, products. "The benefits of mass production," van den Haag wrote, "are reaped only by matching de-individualizing work with equally de-individualizing consumption." Therefore, he argued, "Failure to repress individual personality in or after working hours is costly; in the end, *the production of standardized things by persons also demands the production of standardized persons* [emphasis ours]."[15]

De-individualization, the result of material progress itself, cannot help but strip life of both meaning and inherent interest. The worker-consumer is vaguely dissatisfied, restless, and bored, and these feelings are reinforced by advertising, which deliberately attempts to exploit them by offering new products as a way out. Consumer products and the mass media—itself made possible only by ads for consumer products—"drown the shriek of unused capacities, of repressed individuality," leaving us either "listless or perpetually restless," declared van den Haag. The products and the media distract us from the soul's cry for truly meaningful activities.

The individual who finds no opportunity for self-chosen, meaningful expression of inner resources and personality, said van den Haag, suffers "an insatiable longing for things to happen. The external world is to supply these events to fill the emptiness. The popular demand for 'inside' stories, for vicarious sharing of the private lives of 'personalities' rests on the craving for private life—even someone else's—of those who are dimly aware of having none whatever, or at least no life that holds their interest."[16]

What the bored person really craves is a meaningful, authentic life. The ads suggest that such a life comes in products or packaged commercial experiences. But religion *and* the science of psychology say it's more likely to be found in such things as service to others, relationships with friends and family, connection with nature, and work of intrinsic moral value.

AFTER AFFLUENZA

Our technologically advanced culture offers opportunities for much more meaningful and creative lives than most of us lead. Our amazingly productive technologies could allow all of us to spend less time doing repetitive, standardized work, or work whose products bring us little pride, by allowing us to trade increased wages for reduced working hours.

Such choices would allow more time for freely chosen, voluntary, often unpaid work that enhances our relationships and communities and/or allows us to express more fully our talents and creativity (like the restoration work of John Beal). And such choices would allow us more time to find meaning and joy in the beauty and wonders of nature, in the delightful play of children, or in the restoration of our damaged environment. They would give us time to think about what really matters to us, and how we really want to use the remaining years of our lives.

CHAPTER 10

Social scars

Today's unfettered celebration of wealth and the things money can buy has created an in-your-face, "I'm rich and you're not" attitude that pigeonholes people as winners or losers, princes or paupers.

—TREND-SPOTTER GERALD CELENTE

I go to Bloomingdale's, to the fourth floor, and I buy 2,000 of the black bras, 2,000 of the beige, 2,000 of the white. And I ship them around between the homes and the boat and that's the end of it for maybe half a year when I have to do it all over again.

—IVANA TRÚMP

Few Americans saw the pictures from Thailand (we have little interest in foreign news, after all), but they were horrifying. In 1993, a Thai toy factory burned to the ground. Unable to escape, hundreds of female workers perished in the flames and smoke. Their charred bodies lay among the ruins of the building, a firetrap similar to many throughout the developing world where millions of plastic toys are made for American children. Here and there amid the blackened rubble were the Bart Simpson dolls and other toys.

Many of the women were mothers whose meager incomes would not allow them to buy for their own children the toys they were making for export. The grisly images from that factory fire, and the facts that lay behind them, speak volumes about the widening canyon that separates the haves and have-nots in the Age of Affluenza.

One fact is simply undeniable: there is no economic system even remotely capable of producing consumer goods as cheaply as the unfettered, deregulated free market. It can, for example (especially with the help of regimes that allow workers little freedom to organize), produce children's toys so cheaply that they can be shipped halfway around the world and still be given away with two-dollar meals at fast-food restaurants like McDonald's and Burger King.

The deregulation of the American economy, which began in the 1980s under Ronald Reagan, coupled with a precipitous decline in the influence of organized labor, has increased domestic productivity. It delivers the goods, but in a manner far less equitable than before.

In contrast to other societies, Americans have long considered theirs a "classless" one, with few citizens who are either very rich or very poor. This notion of a "classless" America has always been suspect. Even in 1981, when all political efforts to counteract or quarantine affluenza were abruptly abandoned, the United States ranked thirteenth among twenty-two leading industrial nations in income equality.[1]

But today we're dead last.[2]

THE OTHER AMERICA

The rising tide of American affluence hasn't lifted all boats, but it has drowned a lot of dreams. A titanic gulf now separates rich and poor in America. "If you look at the big consumer boom since the '80s," says Boston College's Juliet Schor, "one of the things you'll find is that it's fairly heavily concentrated in the upper part of the middle class and above."[3]

Indeed, during the '80s, three-quarters of the increase in pretax real income went to the wealthiest 1 percent of families, who gained an average of 77 percent. Median-income families saw only a 4 percent gain, while the bottom 40 percent of families actually lost ground. Some might argue that these figures reflect overstated inflation estimates, and that, therefore, all sectors gained more than official figures suggest. But what is uncontestable is the astoundingly unequal distribution of the gains.[4]

As the super-rich increased their share of national income during the '80s, they also became stingier. They gave a far smaller share of their incomes to charity than was previously the case. In 1979, people who earned incomes of more than $1 million (in 1991 dollars) gave 7 percent of their after-tax incomes away. Twelve years later, that figure had dropped to less than 4 percent.[5] This, at a time when advocates of sharp cuts in government welfare programs suggested that private charity would make up much of the difference.

Instead, not surprisingly, the percentages of families in poverty, which had been declining, began once again to rise. The number of people who were working (not on welfare) but earning below-poverty wages nearly doubled during the '80s.[6]

In spite of America's image as a cornucopia of plenty, where the shelves of supermarkets are always fully stocked, ten million Americans go hungry each day, 40 percent of them children, and the majority, members of working families. Twenty-one million other Americans keep hunger from the door by turning frequently to emergency feeding programs such as food banks and soup kitchens. On any given night at least 750,000 Americans are without shelter, and nearly two million experience homelessness during the course of the year. That's the bad news. The good news is that nine million Americans own second homes. America's housing shortage might really be a distribution problem.[7]

Increasing concentration of income continued throughout the Clinton economic boom. The top 20 percent of American households now earn nearly as much as the bottom 80 percent (49 versus 51 percent of the national income), a record high rate of inequality. In 1968, the top 20 percent of American households earned about eleven times what the bottom 20 percent did. Today, they earn fifteen times as much.[8] The distribution of wealth is even more skewed. By 1999, 92 percent of all financial wealth (stocks, bonds, and commercial real estate) in America was owned by the top 20 percent of families (and 83 percent of stock was owned by the top 10 percent). Many of the richest Americans find ways to pay little or nothing in the way of taxes. The article "Trillion-Dollar Hideaway" in the November-December 2000 issue of *Mother Jones* magazine shows how the rich evade billions in taxes by sheltering their money in offshore accounts in the Caribbean and elsewhere.[9] Meanwhile, in 2004, the tax share paid by the wealthiest 1 percent of Americans fell by 19 percent while that paid by median-income Americans rose by 1 percent.[10]

THE BIG WINNERS . . .

At one point, before a drop in Microsoft stock prices halved his net worth, Bill Gates held assets worth about $90 billion, nearly as much as the bottom half of the American population (and greater than the gross national products of 119 of the world's 210 nations). By contrast, 40 percent of all Americans own no assets at all.

Nothing better illustrates the extent to which affluenza has been embraced in America than the compensation awarded senior executives of large companies. In a cover package titled "Is Greed Good?", *Business Week,* which seems to think so, reported that in 1998, average total compensation for CEOs of the 365 largest American companies increased by a whopping 36 percent, to $10.6 million each.

By contrast, blue-collar workers got a 2.7 percent raise. Three in five new jobs pay less than the median hourly wage of $13.53.

Average CEO pay has continued to increase at double-digit rates—by 27 percent in 2003. By 2000, CEOs earned 475 times what their average workers made (at financially ailing Delta Airlines, the gap was 1,531 to 1!), up from 40 times as much in 1980 and 84 times as much in 1990.[11] By contrast, until recently, when they began to feel a need to keep up with their American counterparts, Japanese and German CEOs earned only about 20 times as much as average workers.

AND THE LOSERS

Meanwhile, columnist David Broder reports that the people who clean the bathrooms and offices of "the masters of the universe" (as he calls high-tech millionaires) earn poverty-level wages. In Los Angeles in 2000, he found janitors picketing for a pay raise that would bring them $21,000 a year by 2003. Even at that pay scale, it would take 27,380 such janitors to earn as much as a single Los Angeles CEO, Michael Eisner of Disney, made in 1998 ($575 million).

To the affluent, the poor have become invisible. "There are millions of people whose work makes our life easier, from busboys in the restaurants we patronize to orderlies in the hospitals we visit, but whose own lives are lived on the ragged edge

of poverty," writes David Broder. "Most of us never exchange a sentence with these workers."[12] In sight, but out of mind.

Thirty-six million Americans lived in poverty in 2003, up 1.3 million since the year before. Their average income: $12.88 a day. Many worked multiple jobs to make ends meet. In February 2005, one of them, a mother of three named Mary Mornin, told President George W. Bush that she had to work three jobs. "You work three jobs?" the president asked. When she replied in the affirmative, Bush said, "Uniquely American, isn't it? I mean, that is fantastic that you're doing that. Get any sleep?"

Uniquely American? Maybe. Fantastic? What do you think?

One fact Americans used to point to as evidence of a "classless" society was that (compared with, say, the wealthy of Latin America) few American families employed servants to do cleaning and housework. But as we increasingly become a two-tiered society, that's changing. Upper-middle-income Americans are turning to domestic servants in a big way. In 1999, between 14 and 18 percent of American households employed an outsider to do their cleaning, a 53 percent increase from 1995. America's 900,000 house cleaners and servants earned an average of $8.06 an hour in 2003, below the poverty line for three-person families.[13]

"This sudden emergence of a servant class is consistent with what some economists call the 'Brazilianization' of the American economy," wrote Barbara Ehrenreich in *Harper's*. "In line with growing class polarization, the classic posture of submission is making a stealthy comeback," charges Ehrenreich, who worked as a maid for $6.63 an hour to research the story. She points out that one franchise, Merry Maids, even advertises its maid services with a brochure boasting that "we scrub your floors the old-fashioned way—on our hands and knees."[14]

Doing research for her best-seller *Nickel and Dimed*, Ehrenreich went a-scrubbing from McMansion to McMansion in Portland, Maine, working under rules that prohibited her from even taking a drink of water while cleaning a house. She discovered that some homes had hidden video cameras to be sure she stayed on track. She was amazed at what messes people left for her. Especially the children, one of whom exclaimed "Look, Mommy, a white maid!" upon seeing Ehrenreich.

Having "cleaned the rooms of many overprivileged teenagers" as a maid, Ehrenreich concluded that "the American overclass is raising a generation of young people who will, without constant assistance, suffocate in their own detritus."

Whether or not they are literate enough to know what that means.

THE POOR PAY TWICE—AND THEN SOME

Affluenza affects Americans across all income barriers, but its impacts are more destructive for the poor. In the first place, the poor are often the original victims of the environmental consequences of cost-cutting production strategies. They live disproportionately in areas where environmental contaminants and patterns of pollution are most severe—one such area is Louisiana's notorious "Cancer Alley," where petrochemical companies unleash a frightening barrage of carcinogens into the air and water.

At the same time, the vastly inflated wage scales paid to winners in the new "information economy" lead to competitive bidding on housing stock that drives the cost of shelter beyond the reach of average earners. Many are forced to leave communities where they and their families have spent their entire lives.

Finally, the poor are taunted by television programs and commercials that flash before them images of consumption standards that are considered typical of the average American, but which they have no possibility of achieving—except perhaps by robbing a bank or winning the lottery.

Felicia Edwards, an African American mother of two, who lives in a small apartment in a Hartford, Connecticut, housing project, worries about the pressures her children feel to wear the designer-label clothes they see on other children in their school. "These schools tend to be like fashion shows," she says with a shake of her head. "There's a lot of peer pressure that can lead to crime. Kids in school have killed other kids over a pair of sneakers. Parents work two and three jobs to clothe their kids." Felicia's own children rarely pester her for stuff, but when her oldest son begged for a pair of Air Jordans he saw on sale for $90 instead of $120, she relented, after first telling him she couldn't afford them. "Me and his aunt came to a decision that we was going to go half on them," she says. "So he got the sneakers."[15]

And it's not just clothes. Even in the United States, according to the conservative Heritage Foundation, 13 percent of poor families experience hunger at some point during the year. Another million Americans experience some homelessness each year.

In our poorest communities, the sense of deprivation is intense. Trend-spotter Gerald Celente tells of a conversation he had with a man who works with youthful gang members. "I asked him, 'What's the one thing that you see that's causing a lot of these problems?'" Celente says. "Without skipping a beat, he said, 'Greed and materialism. These kids don't feel like their lives would be worth anything unless they have the hottest product that's being sold in the marketplace.'"[16]

Margaret Norris, codirector of the Omega Boys Club in San Francisco, agrees. She says the ethic among the low-income youths she works with is Thou Shalt Get Thy Money On, and by any means necessary. Such desperation often leads to crime.

"Never mind, just lock 'em up" seems to be our response to this situation. Overall crime rates have been falling in the past two decades, a trend that British economist Richard Layard convincingly argues is due, sadly, in large part to the availability of abortion. Another reason is that the United States has already locked more than two million of its people behind prison bars, the largest percentage of any nation in the world, and ten times the rate of most industrial countries.

California alone has more inmates than France, Germany, Great Britain, Holland, Japan, and Singapore combined. In some dying Rust Belt industrial cities, like Youngstown, Ohio, prisons have become the biggest source of jobs. Private companies like the Corrections Corporation of America make millions running lockup facilities. Smart Wall Street brokers play "dungeons for dollars," investing heavily in the new privatized prison industry.[17]

GLOBAL INFECTION

The social scars left by affluenza are being replicated throughout the entire world, as more and more cultures copy the American lifestyle. Each day, television exposes millions of people in the developing world to the Western consumer lifestyle (without showing them its warts), and they are eager to participate. David Korten, the author of *When Corporations Rule the World,* once believed they could and should participate. Korten taught business management at Stanford and Harvard, then worked in Africa, Asia, and Central America for the Harvard Business School, the Ford Foundation, and the U.S. Agency for International Development.

"My career was focused on training business executives to create the equivalent of our high-consumption economy in countries throughout the world," Korten says now. "The whole corporate system in the course of globalization is increasingly geared up to bring every country into the consumer society. And there is a very strong emphasis on trying to reach children, to reshape their values from the very beginning to convince them that progress is defined by what they consume."[18]

Korten now believes that, by pushing consumer values in developing countries, he was spreading the affluenza virus. As he continued to work in the "development" field, the symptoms of that virus became increasingly apparent. He gradually realized that his efforts were causing more harm than good. "I came to see that what I was promoting didn't work and couldn't work," he reflects. "Many people's lives were actually worse off. We were seeing the environment trashed, and we were seeing the breakdown of cultures and the social fabric."

As affluenza, the disease of unbridled consumerism, spreads throughout the world, the gap between rich and poor grows ever wider, and the social scars that still remain somewhat hidden in the United States fester as open sores elsewhere. The grim shantytowns of Rio tumble to the golden sands of Copacabana and Ipanema. The luxurious malls of Manila stand alongside Smoky Mountain, a massive garbage dump where thousands of people live right in the refuse, dependent for their survival on what they can scavenge.

The virus passes easily from Sheraton to slum.

In some ways, a cactuslike plant that grows in the Kalahari Desert of southern Africa may be the metaphor for today's divided world. The razor-thin Bushmen of the Kalahari eat the bitter hoodia plant because it takes away the pangs of hunger. But now a British pharmaceutical company has patented the hoodia's appetite-suppressant properties. The company is creating hoodia plantations and plans to market a diet product containing hoodia to obese Americans and Europeans. When it hits the market, the diet product will stand as a symbol for a divided world where some have too much food, and millions more, far too little.

One-fifth of the world's people—1.2 billion human beings—live in "extreme poverty" (on incomes of less than a dollar day), slowly dying of hunger and disease. Three billion others also desperately need more material goods. Yet, were they to begin consuming as we do, the result, as we learn in the next two chapters, would be an environmental catastrophe.

It is critical that we begin to set another example for the world, and quickly.

CHAPTER 11

Resource exhaustion

*We buy a wastebasket and take it home
in a plastic bag. Then we take the wastebasket
out of the bag, and put the bag in the
wastebasket.*

—LILY TOMLIN,
comedian

WASHINGTON, D.C.—*According to an EPA study conducted in conjunction
with the U.N. Task Force on Global Developmental Impact, consumer-product
diversity now exceeds biodiversity. According to the study, for the first time in
history, the rich array of consumer products available in malls and supermarkets surpasses the number of living species populating the planet.*

*"Last year's introduction of Dentyne Ice Cinnamint gum, right on the heels of
the extinction of the Carolina tufted hen, put product diversity on top for the
first time," study chair Donald Hargrove said. "Today, the Procter & Gamble
subphylum alone outnumbers insects two to one." The sharp rise in consumer-
product diversity—with more than 200 million new purchasing options
generated since 1993—comes as welcome news for those upset over the
dwindling number of plant and animal species.*

"Though flora and fauna are dwindling, the spectrum of goods available to consumers is wider than at any time in planetary history. And that's something we can all be happy about," Hargrove said. University of Chicago biologist Jonathan Grogan said, "Any complex system, whether we are talking the Amazon rainforest or the Mall of America, needs a rich array of species/ products if it is to survive. That is why, in light of the crumbling global ecosystem, it is increasingly vital that we foster the diversification of the global marketplace by buying the widest range of consumer products possible."

—FROM THE HUMOR NEWSPAPER, *THE ONION*
OCTOBER 21, 1998

hough it's a parody, this story from the humor newspaper the *Onion* is painfully close to the truth. The more we buy, the faster natural species disappear. And the damages accelerate every minute. As you read this chapter, at least thirty acres of farmland and open space are being bulldozed to meet a still-burning demand for suburban "starter castles." Each one of these homes typically requires an acre's worth of trees, as well as the equivalent of a house-size hole to provide minerals for concrete, steel, and other construction materials.

Our demand for buildings, fuel, and consumer products sends huge draglines, combines, chainsaws, bulldozers, and oil rigs inexorably into pristine wilderness.

"Industry moves, mines, extracts, shovels, burns, wastes, pumps, and disposes of *four million pounds* of material in order to provide one average middle-class family's needs for a year," write Paul Hawken and Amory and Hunter Lovins in *Natural Capitalism*.[1] According to the United Nations Environment Program, Americans spend more for trash bags than 90 of the world's 210 countries spend for everything! In an average lifetime, each American consumes at least a reservoir of water (forty million gallons, including water for personal, industrial, and agricultural use)[2] and a small tanker of oil (2,500 barrels).[3] Experts at the U.S. Geological Survey predict that world oil production will peak within ten to twenty years, then begin its final, costly decline.

Depressed yet? Facts like these hit us like urgent, middle-of-the-night phone calls. Nature, our mother, is not looking well at all. Virtually unnoticed by the media, she's been admitted to the emergency room, with a critically elevated temperature and hemorrhaging chest wounds. Hours later, distant relatives of Nature (we typical Americans) wait in chilly air-conditioned rooms for news of her condition (or a *Mar-*

"HELP! THIS IS *MOTHER NATURE*...
I THINK I'M BEING *STALKED!*"

ried with Children rerun, whichever comes first). Compulsively, we consume snacks, cigarettes, and electronic games as we wait, somehow oblivious that we are carriers of affluenza—the human disease that strikes Nature like a dozen hurricanes.

ON THE PAPER TRAIL

Most weeklong backpack trips eventually include a weight comparison of the stuff in everybody's pack. On a sixty-mile hike on Vancouver Island's West Coast Trail, Dave's sixteen-year-old son Colin insisted his pack was heavier than his father's, because it contained more of the shared food supplies. Dave maintained that anyone whose pack contained the tent, ground cloth, and cook stove was carrying the lion's share. When your stuff sits on your back, you tend to perform cost/benefit analyses on each object. As they slowly made their way up the coast of Vancouver Island, across suspension bridges and moss-covered logs, the debate about the relative value of the stuff was a recurring topic of conversation. "You shouldn't have brought so many snacks," Colin needled. (Each carried his own energy bars, powdered drinks, and nuts.) Dave countered, "What if the park provided a trailside scale, so hikers could settle these differences of opinion? Then we'd find out who's doing the work."

"Next time pack a scale," Colin suggested, shrugging his shoulders.

That hike was a pivotal experience for both father and son. They "got" the value inherent in unmarketed, pristine nature—in their lungs, and in their senses—especially the sense of being alive. They reaffirmed a lesson that brought Dave to this book and Colin to a first stop as an Outward Bound instructor: *You don't need as much stuff when you genuinely appreciate the value of what's already here.* As their heads cleared, other forms of wealth than money came into focus: the biological abundance of the rain forest and ocean around them, the social and cultural wealth of the indigenous inhabitants of Vancouver Island, and wellness, surely the most valuable wealth of all.

Originally constructed as a survival route for shipwrecked sailors, the West Coast Trail provides spectacular vistas of bright blue ocean and white, pounding surf, often through dark silhouettes of shady rain forest. Tide pools filled with starfish and crabs, families of bald eagles soaring silently overhead, and the breathing spouts of hundreds of humpback whales all speak of nature's abundance.

Yet the beaches were littered with the trunks of dead spruce and fir trees, river-borne escapees from a logging industry that has transformed much of the island's natural capital into barren terrain. One photograph from that trip shows Colin standing on a sawed-off trunk the size of a small stage. He and his father were graphically reminded that many of the products they consumed back home had their beginnings in this particular bioregion, where 10 percent of the world's newsprint comes from.

If asked that week what Vancouver Island was good for, they probably would have said in exhilaration, "Wilderness. Let it regenerate." If the logger whose flatbed-semi can transport three 80-foot tree trunks had been asked the same question, he'd have said, "Timber. Let me harvest it." The issue isn't a simple one, especially since Americans consume a third of the world's wood. After returning home from their travels in Canada, Dave resumed his higher-than-average consumption of paper, being a writer, while the logger probably looked for a great, convenient place to take his kids, being also a father.

Although logging companies leave curtains of trees along the road to hide the damage, Dave and Colin caught glimpses of barren patches of land through the trees, spotlighted by afternoon sun. But less obvious was the fact that operations like these force society to work harder. Though hard to track directly, water utility bills go up when logging sediments pollute rivers that supply drinking water. Taxes go up when roads and bridges are washed out by floodwaters that run off clear-cut land.

The price of lumber and paper goes up as companies feel compelled to advertise how "green" their practices are. In short, we each write checks and work extra hours to smooth over the "out of sight, out of mind" sloppiness.

OUT OF MIND

In the Middle Ages, people carried sticks of burning incense, hoping to ward off the plague, which they believed was caused by foul smells. Seven hundred years later, we still fail to make critical connections—for example, between what we consume and what's happening to the world. We buy plantation-grown coffee, not realizing that each cup of coffee exposes another migratory songbird to potentially lethal pesticides in coffee plantations. Like Rachel Carson, we no longer hear chirps in our own backyards, but we don't make the connection as we take another sip of coffee. The songbirds no longer fly thousands of miles each year from Central or South America to our backyards because they're dead. And if they do survive to return home, chances are good their northern habitats are covered with roads, houses, driving ranges, and parking lots.

When we buy a computer, it doesn't occur to us that 700 or more different materials went into it, converging from mines, oil derricks, and chemical factories all over the world. The sleek, colorful machine purring on each desktop generated 140 pounds of solid and hazardous waste in its manufacture, along with 7,000 gallons of wastewater, and about a fourth of its lifetime energy consumption. Every year, more than twelve million computers—amounting to more than 300,000 tons of electronic junk—are disposed of.[4] According to the Silicon Valley Toxics Coalition and the U.S. Environmental Protection Agency, by 2006, when the market for flat-panel and digital TVs expands, 163,000 TVs and computers will become obsolete every day, and only a small percentage is expected to be recycled. The point is, when we buy a computer, all the rest comes with it, even if it's *out of sight, out of mind.*

What about junk mail? Most of it comes as commercial advertising, but even the nonprofits are guilty on this one. As Donella Meadows wrote, it takes 150,000 direct-mail appeals to garner 1,500 memberships in a given organization. "That means 148,500 will be thrown out. Made from trees, printed with inks by fuel-consuming machines, collated, labeled, sorted by other machines, loaded into pollution-spewing trucks, delivered to mailboxes, loaded into other vehicles headed for (20 percent) recycling stations or (80 percent) landfills."[5] When we toss a piece of junk mail without complaining, we encourage junk mailing.

Every time we eat a fast-food burger, an unseen 600-gallon tank of water comes with it, counting both what the cow and the feed crops drank.[6] And when we ceremoniously open the little jewelry boxes with the glittering gold wedding rings in them, six tons of very drab ore are invisibly connected to the rings—lying in a tailings heap back at the mine, often polluting a stream.[7]

REAL PRICE TAGS

The distinction of being the mother of unseen impacts and hidden costs goes to the automobile. Imagine your sticker shock if the price tag on your new SUV included not only the car's FOB price, but also the full environmental and social costs of the vehicle. The sticker would cover most of the vehicle's windows to list those hidden costs, but here's an executive summary:

THE REAL COST OF YOUR SHINY NEW LIGHT TRUCK

Congratulations! You've just purchased a vehicle that will cost $130,000 by the time it's paid for! (In fact, if you're in your twenties and finance new vehicles like this one every five years for the rest of your life, you'll spend more than a half a million dollars in interest and payments.) That's impressive. As an average American, you'll use your vehicle for 82 percent of your trips, compared with 48 percent for Germans, 47 for the French, and 45 for the British.

The cost of a thirty-mile round-trip commute in this vehicle will be about $15 a day, assuming gas prices remain at current levels. At that rate, you'll spend on average more than $3,500 annually to get to and from work. When insurance, car payments, maintenance, registration, fuel, and other costs are added together, you'll spend more than $8,000 a year to park this vehicle for twenty-two hours a day and drive it for two.

Your vehicle generated 700 pounds of air pollution in its manufacture, and four tons of carbon. It will burn at least 450 gallons of gas every year, requiring more than thirty-five gas station fill-ups. You'll spend three full days every year vacuuming, polishing, and cleaning the windows of the vehicle and waiting for it at the auto shop. When you divide the miles driven by the time spent to buy and maintain your car, you'll be going about five miles an hour—even slower than rush hour in L.A.

Your new vehicle will contribute its fair share to the following national costs:

- 155 billion gallons of gasoline burned annually

- $60 billion spent annually to ensure Middle Eastern oil supplies

- 40,000 fatal car crashes annually, and 6,000 pedestrian deaths

- 250 million people maimed or injured since the days of Charles Olds (1905), and more killed than all the wars in America's history

- 50 million animals killed annually, including at least a quarter million of "extended family": cats, dogs, and horses

- Noise and pollution that inhibit sleep and contribute to radical increases in asthma, emphysema, heart disease, and bronchial infections

- One-fourth of U.S. greenhouse gases, which increase drought, hurricanes, and crop failures

- 7 billion pounds of unrecycled scrap and waste annually

- More than $200 billion annually in taxes for road construction and maintenance, snow plowing, subsidized parking, public health expenditures, and other costs that come directly out of pocket

- A total of more than $1 trillion a year in social costs[8]

Happy motoring!

THE COST OF HIGH LIVING

Alan Durning of Northwest Environment Watch observes, "Everything we use in our daily lives has an ecological wake that ripples out across the ecosystems of the planet." Durning and his colleague John Ryan traced the impacts of everyday products in a book titled *Stuff: The Secret Lives of Everyday Things*. Their coffee, for example, came from the highlands of Colombia, where a hundred beans were picked for each cup. The beans were packed in 130-pound sacks and shipped in a huge ocean freighter to roasting factory, warehouse, supermarket, and coffee cup. At each stage, energy and materials were expended to add value to their morning coffee. The beginning of the story is especially troubling:

> Colombia's forests make it a biological superpower. Though the country covers less than 1 percent of the Earth's land surface, it is home to eighteen percent of the world's plant species and more types of birds than any other nation. . . . In the late 1980s, farm owners sawed down most of the shade trees surrounding the coffee trees and planted high-yielding varieties, increasing their harvests, and also increasing soil erosion and bird fatalities. Biologists report finding just five percent as many bird species in these new, sunny coffee fields as in the traditional shaded coffee plantations. With the habitats of birds and other insect eaters removed, pests proliferated and the growers stepped up their pesticide use. Some of the chemicals they sprayed entered the farm-workers' lungs; others washed or wafted away, to be absorbed by plants and animals. . . . For each pound of beans, about two pounds of pulp was dumped into the river. As the pulp decomposed, it consumed oxygen needed by fish in the river.[9]

"When I first started looking at the real costs of stuff," said Durning, "a friend read my manuscript and said, 'Oh I get it, what you're talking about is guilt trips, not shopping trips.' But it's not really about guilt. It's about creating a lifestyle that doesn't require as much stuff to make us even happier than we are now. Simple things, like buying shade-grown coffee that reduces the use of pesticides. We need to be thinking about what we get, not what we give up."[10]

Because few of us supply our own materials for daily life, almost everything we consume, from potatoes to petroleum to pencils, comes from somewhere else. "The problem is that we're running out of 'somewhere elses,' especially if developing countries try to achieve a Western style of life," says Swiss engineer Mathis Wackernagel.[11]

Dividing the planet's biologically productive land and sea by the number of humans, Wackernagel and his Canadian colleague William Rees come up with 5.5 acres per person. That's if we put *nothing* aside for all the other species. "In contrast," says Wackernagel, "the average world citizen used 7 acres in 1996—what we call his or her 'ecological footprint.'

"That's over 30 percent more than what nature can regenerate. Or in other words, it would take 1.3 years to regenerate what humanity uses in one year." He continues, "If all people lived like the average American, with thirty-acre footprints, we'd need five more planets." (To find out the size of your own ecological footprint, take the quiz at the Redefining Progress Web site: http://www.myfootprint.org/.)

Wackernagel observes, "We can't use all the planet's resources, because we're only one species out of ten million or more. Yet if we leave half of the biological capacity for other species (or if the human population doubles in size), human needs must come from less than three acres per capita, only about *one-tenth* of the capacity now used by Americans."

The solution? No sweat, we'll use the market. We'll just go out and buy five more planets.

DARWIN IN REVERSE

It's bad enough that resource supplies, along with recreational and aesthetic opportunities, are wearing thin as the affluenza-encouraged plundering of the planet continues. But even more distressing is the fact that life on earth becomes far less diverse as habitats disappear. The loss of a key species from an ecosystem is like pulling out the wrong melon from a supermarket display. You create an avalanche of melons thunking to the floor, because each melon was supported by another. To give just one example, when sun heats up a mountain stream because clear-cutting has removed natural shade along the banks, it's a holocaust for the trout population because trout thrive in *cold* water. And when sediment washes off the naked land into that stream, it plugs up the cobbled spaces in rocks that are hiding places for the baby fish. In turn, mammals whose diet includes trout lose an important protein source, so ecological services provided by those mammals are diminished.

Aeons of ecological work are quickly undone. The alarming truth is that hundreds of "melon avalanches" occur every day on the battlefields of resource extraction. Far from being just a rain forest phenomenon, habitat destruction and accompanying extinction are happening right under our noses. "A silent mass extinction is occurring in America's lakes and rivers," says biologist Anthony Ricciardi.[12] His research indicates that freshwater species from snails to fish to amphibians are dying out five times faster than terrestrial species—as fast as rain forest species, which are generally considered to be the most imperiled on earth. Half of America's wetlands are gone, and 99 percent of its tall-grass prairies. As these systems are being destroyed for development, agriculture, and other uses, 935 species in the United States (356 animals, 579 plants) are fighting for their lives.[13]

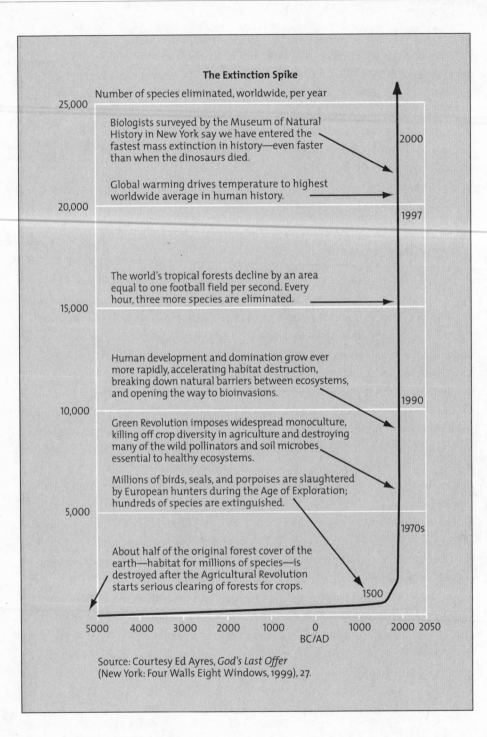

The Extinction Spike

Number of species eliminated, worldwide, per year

Biologists surveyed by the Museum of Natural History in New York say we have entered the fastest mass extinction in history—even faster than when the dinosaurs died.

Global warming drives temperature to highest worldwide average in human history.

The world's tropical forests decline by an area equal to one football field per second. Every hour, three more species are eliminated.

Human development and domination grow ever more rapidly, accelerating habitat destruction, breaking down natural barriers between ecosystems, and opening the way to bioinvasions.

Green Revolution imposes widespread monoculture, killing off crop diversity in agriculture and destroying many of the wild pollinators and soil microbes essential to healthy ecosystems.

Millions of birds, seals, and porpoises are slaughtered by European hunters during the Age of Exploration; hundreds of species are extinguished.

About half of the original forest cover of the earth—habitat for millions of species—is destroyed after the Agricultural Revolution starts serious clearing of forests for crops.

25,000

20,000

15,000

10,000

5,000

2000

1997

1990

1970s

1500

5000   4000   3000   2000   1000   0   1000   2000 2050
BC/AD

Source: Courtesy Ed Ayres, *God's Last Offer* (New York: Four Walls Eight Windows, 1999), 27.

Before nature's health began to slide, we rarely thought about how a product got to us, and what came with it; we just consumed it and threw the leftovers away. We didn't think about the plants, animals, and even human cultures that were displaced or destroyed when the materials were mined. Now, when biologists like Norman Myers and E.O. Wilson tell us we may be in the middle of the most severe extinction since the fall of the dinosaur sixty-five million years ago, many are finally moving beyond denial. We are losing species a thousand times faster than the natural rate of extinction.[14]

What will civilizations of the far future say about our era? Will they somehow deduce the causes of the calamitous decline in species diversity? Or will they shrug their shoulders (if they have shoulders to shrug) the way our scientists do when they ponder extinctions of the past? "It was global warming," the future scientists might conclude. "Inefficient use of land," others will hypothesize. But for the sake of our civilization's dignity, let's hope that none of them uncovers humiliating evidence of our obsessive need for cheap coffee, gasoline, and underwear.

CHAPTER 12

Industrial diarrhea

DDT is good for me!

—1950s jingle

The chemical age has created products,
institutions and cultural attitudes that
require synthetic chemicals to sustain them.

—THEO COLBURN ET AL,
Our Stolen Future

Imagine spotting them through binoculars at a baseball game—the all-stars of advertising, sitting together in front-row seats behind home plate. There's the Marlboro Man and Joe Camel, signing autographs and passing out smokes to the kids. The Energizer Bunny flings handfuls of batteries into the crowd like Tootsie Rolls, while Ronald McDonald argues defensively with an environmentalist about hormones, antibiotics, and pesticide residues now being detected in the Big Mac. The overweight Pillsbury Doughboy giggles as the Jolly Green Giant looks down on the game from the parking lot, ho-hoing every time the home team scores. No one messes with a guy that size, even though chunks of pesticide slough off his green body like gigantic flakes of dry skin. (Look out, here comes another one!)

They all seem so innocent, don't they? So American. We grew up with these guys, and we love their optimism, their goofiness, and their cool. Our demand for their products keeps the U.S. economy cranking at a feverishly giddy pace, and it can't be denied that America's dazzling products make life seem bright, shiny, and convenient. But with a steady diet of this stuff, we risk serious damage to our environment and to our health. Many of the goods we buy contain toxic "bads" such as dangerous chemicals hidden from plain view, but for some reason, we don't want to believe that.

THE GENERATION OF SURPRISES

We don't want to believe that cigarettes now kill more than 430,000 Americans annually, wiping out *five million years of potential life each year*. That radiation from nuclear power—once thought to be "too cheap to meter"—really does destroy DNA and cause cancer and has obliterated a handful of bioregions, effectively forever. That one tiny particle of dioxin transmitted to a fetus at the wrong time could permanently disrupt the unborn child's reproductive system. That between 1940 and 1995 the production of synthetic chemicals increased six hundred times and that we now produce 1,600 pounds a year per capita. And that two out of every five Americans will contract cancer at some point in their lives, including increasing percentages of children.[1]

"Americans have a tradition of trusting manufacturers," said Dr. Suzanne Wuerthele, a toxicologist in the EPA's Denver office. "Ever since the days of the flour mill, the small leather-tanning company, and the blacksmith, products have been assumed innocent until proven guilty—just the opposite of the way it should be. We've worked within an "acceptable risk" strategy. Industry's stance is, 'Show me the dead bodies, or else let me make my product the way I want to.' When a disaster happens, industry begins to respond, and sometimes not even then."

As Wuerthele points out, the track record for synthetic chemicals is laced with unpleasant surprises. "From nuclear radiation and CFCs to the various chlorinated hydrocarbon pesticides, we're always playing catch-up, finding out about health and ecological effects after it's too late. The most recent surprise is that genetically engineered organisms can migrate into the environment, even when they're engineered into the cells of plants. For example, pollen from genetically engineered corn plants migrates to plants like milkweed, where it has been shown to kill the Bambis of the insect world—Monarch butterflies. That shouldn't have caught the corporate and government scientists by surprise—with hundreds of thousands of acres of genetically engineered corn already planted—but it did."[2]

We typically assume that somebody else is minding the shop, making sure all these chemicals are safe. Yet the truth is that out of 75,000 chemicals now in common commercial use, only about 1,200 to 1,500 have been tested for carcinogenicity. In fact, of the 3,000 chemicals produced at the highest volume, 43 percent have no testing data on basic toxicity.[3] Dr. Sandra Steingraber writes in her book *Living Downstream*, "The vast majority of commercially used chemicals were brought to market before 1979, when federal legislation mandated the review of new chemicals. Thus many carcinogenic environmental contaminants likely remain unidentified, unmonitored, and unregulated."[4]

Steingraber, herself a victim of bladder cancer, recalls the advertising blitz for DDT, a product that returned home victorious from World War II after protecting American soldiers from malaria and other diseases overseas. "In one ad," writes Steingraber, "children splash in a swimming pool while DDT is sprayed above the water. In another, an aproned housewife in stiletto heels and a pith helmet aims a spray gun at two giant cockroaches standing on her kitchen counter. They raise their front legs in surrender. The caption reads, 'Super Ammunition for the Continued Battle on the Home Front.'"[5]

. DDT was seen as a harmless pal even though biologists had already documented that the chemical killed birds and fish, disrupted the reproductive systems of laboratory animals, created population explosions of pests with newly evolved resistance, and showed strong signs of causing cancer. By 1951, DDT had become a contaminant of human breast milk and was known to pass from mother to child.

Yet DDT continued to be seen as an "elixir" until Rachel Carson's book *Silent Spring* put the spotlight on birds with convulsions, twitching to death under the elm tree. Since the time of those DDT ads, cancer has become an epidemic in slow motion. Cancers of the brain, liver, breast, kidney, prostate, esophagus, skin, bone marrow, and lymph have all escalated in the past fifty years, as the incidence of cancer has increased by more than 50 percent.

The use of chemicals like DDT seemed justified at first. After all, the use of other pesticides has played a role in the low prices Americans pay for food. (As a percentage of income, we have the world's cheapest food.) But what hidden costs do we pay?

ACCIDENTAL CONCOCTIONS

Ever since the days of alchemy, the field of chemistry has suffered from a tragic flaw: its isolation from the field of biology. Humans were deploying technology long before they understood what causes disease, or how living things interrelate. Sir Isaac Newton may have discovered gravity, but he didn't seem to have a clue that the heavy metals he experimented with could kill him. In a 1692 letter to colleague John Locke, he blamed his insomnia, depression, poor digestion, amnesia, and paranoia on "sleeping too often by my fire." We found out otherwise three hundred years later, when scientists analyzed a lock of his hair, passed along as a family heirloom. The hair was a repository of lead, arsenic, antimony, and mercury molecules from his alchemy experiments. Carefully recorded in his logs were descriptions of the *taste* of each chemical. Little did he know the gravity of his actions.

Even when a toxic cause-and-effect connection was made, our ancestors often adopted a policy of "acceptable risk." Mercury was mined in Spain as far back as 400 BCE, despite severe health effects like chronically bleeding gums, dementia, and eventual death. In that case, the risks were deemed acceptable because convicts and slaves did the mining.

While the benefits accrue only to those who sell or use the products, the risks are often spread among the whole population. Chemicals, if profitable, are deemed innocent until alarming evidence proves otherwise. For example, workers in a pesticide factory didn't realize that their exposure to Kepone was sterilizing them until they sat around the lunch table talking about a common inability to start a family.

BETTER LIVING THROUGH CHEMISTRY?

As America's economy grew at rates never before seen in human history, millions of chemical compounds were brought into the world. Most did not find immediate uses, but a century's worth of tinkering has created an alphabet soup of persistent molecules that hang around in our world like uninvited guests. Many of these ingredients are incorporated into familiar products like detergents, varnishes, plastics, fingernail polish, bug spray, and pharmaceuticals, as well as behind-the-scenes industrial products like degreasers and plasticizers.

A new chemical substance is discovered every nine seconds of the working day, as the "invisible hand of the market" continues to call forth legions of them, like a throng of marching broomsticks straight out of *The Sorcerer's Apprentice*. It's become impossible to call them off, and as a consequence, we're living in a sea of our own waste products. We're exposed to chemicals in consumer products and in the workplace. We're also bombarded by invisible particles that escape into our water, the air in our houses, and the living tissue in our bodies. There is no place on earth that does not contain runaway molecules. "Tree bark sampled from more than ninety sites around the world found that DDT, chlordane and dieldrin were present no matter how remote the area," writes Ann Platt McGinn in *State of the World 2000*.[6] In "toxic body burden" research performed in 2003, medical scientists at the Mount Sinai School of Medicine found an average of fifty or more toxic chemicals in the bloodstreams and urine samples of nine volunteers, most of whom led normal or even environmentally conscious lives. These chemicals, common in consumer products and industrial pollution, are linked to cancer, brain and nervous system diseases, and dysfunction in hormone and reproductive systems. Andrea Martin, a survivor of breast cancer, was one of the volunteers. "I was completely blown away," she says. "There were ninety-five toxins, fifty-nine of which were carcinogens. We're living in a toxic stew, and the manufacturers and polluters are, quite literally, getting away with murder."[7]

If we had microscopic vision, we might get outdoors a bit more—where the air is cleaner—because the horrors we'd see in our own houses would send us running. We'd see microscopic bits of plastics, carpet fibers, and pesticides disappear into the nostrils of family members and never come back out! Because of all the chemicals contained in our everyday products, indoor pollution levels can be two to a hundred times higher than those found outdoors, especially now that homes are more tightly sealed for energy efficiency and air-conditioning.

NOWHERE TO RUN

David and Mary Pinkerton were trusting souls. They were buying a "dream house" in Missouri, and they liked to walk through the construction site after work, to see the house taking shape. On one visit just before moving in, David noticed a health warning printed on the subflooring that had been put in their new house. Irritation of the eyes and upper respiratory system could result from exposure to the chemicals in the plywood. But David trusted the builder. "He makes a living building houses. He wouldn't put anything in there that would hurt anybody."

"Within a month," write the authors of *Toxic Deception*,[8] "the three girls and their parents had grown quite ill. David would sit in an old overstuffed chair until supper was ready; after dinner he would usually go right to bed. . . . One night Mary tried to make dinner and David found her leaning against the wall with the skillet in her hand. . . . All five had bouts of vomiting and diarrhea that would wake them up, almost nightly. Brenda no longer wanted to go to dance classes, even though ballet had been 'her big thing in life,' Mary later recalled."

After the family was forced to evacuate the house within six months of moving in, a state environmental inspector found ten parts per million of formaldehyde in the house, many times higher than the standard.

As many as 40 million Americans may be allergic to their own homes, according to the American Lung Association, and 26.3 million—more than a third of them children—have already been diagnosed with asthma. This chronic disease accounts for millions of sick days from work and school every year, as we continue to bombard ourselves with chemicals in paint fumes, cleaning products, air "fresheners," particleboard, plastics, glues, wallpaper, cosmetics, and a hundred other standard products of the twenty-first century.[9]

DEAD ZONES

Scientists *do* have microscopic vision, and with new-millennium equipment they are finding toxic chemicals wherever they look. The average American hosts up to five hundred chemicals in his or her body. Among the most exotic of the chemicals now being found in waterways are refugees from the American lifestyle: trace amounts of pain relievers, antibiotics, birth control pills, perfumes, codeine, antacids, cholesterol-lowering agents, antidepressants, estrogen-replacement drugs, chemotherapy agents, sunscreen lotions, and hormones from animal feed lots. These compounds survive the assault of sewage treatment's microbes, aeration, and chlorination and eventually show up unannounced in drinking water.[10]

With reports of pesticide, lead, and other industrial compounds gracing the front pages of newspapers across the country, it's no wonder per capita consumption of bottled water increased by more than 1,000 percent between 1997 and 2005, becoming a $35 billion a year industry with annual sales of more than five billion gallons —twenty-four gallons per capita—according to the American Beverage Association. Yet the Natural Resources Defense Council advises that bottled water, at up to a thousand times the cost of tap water, is not only expensive but somewhat suspect. At least a third of the bottled water on the market is just packaged tap water, and another 25 percent contains traces of chemical contaminants.

"In the past we looked for the really toxic actors that have immediate effects like death or cancer," said Edward Furlong, a chemist with the U.S. Geological Survey.[11] "Now we are starting to look more closely at compounds whose effects are more subtle and less easily identified." To his surprise, Furlong discovered what he calls "the Starbucks effect," an indicator that caffeine may be giving aquatic life an unsolicited buzz. In addition to being a basic fuel of the American lifestyle (twenty-four gallons a year per capita), caffeine is a persistent and detectable compound. Just as it often persists in our bodies when we try to sleep, it also lingers in our rivers and streams. These findings are only the most recent in a series of aquatic conundrums presented by our affluent, often oblivious civilization. How long can an economy boom without adequate supplies of drinking water?

A decade or so ago, fishermen began reporting a "dead zone" in the Gulf of Mexico, where their nets always come up empty and their lines never record a strike. By the time the Mississippi River reaches the Gulf of Mexico, it contains enough pesticides, wasted nutrients (from eroded farm soil), and petrochemicals to poison a body of water the size of New Jersey. Luxury cruise ships in the Gulf add insult to critical injury by dumping raw sewage and other waste into open waters. Because of regulatory loopholes, cruise ships can legally discharge "graywater" (graywater is used water that doesn't contain human waste) anywhere, and can dump human waste and ground-up food when they're more than three miles from shore. On a weeklong voyage a typical Carnival or Royal Caribbean cruise ship with three thousand passengers and crew members generates eight tons of garbage, one million gallons of graywater, twenty-five thousand gallons of oil-contaminated water, and two hundred thousand gallons of sewage.[12] Scuba diving, anyone?

DEADLY MIMICRY

The surprises just keep coming, some of them involving other dead zones in the Great Lakes, the Arctic, and, potentially, even the human womb. Like evidence in a gruesome criminal case, the mounting data tell us more than we really want to know. Scientist and author Theo Colburn compiled thousands of data sets spanning three decades. The data report chaos and dysfunction in the natural world: male alligators with stunted sex organs, roosters that don't crow, eagles that don't build nests to take care of their young, "gay" female seagulls that nest together because males aren't interested, whales with both male and female sex organs, and other cases of "sexual confusion."

Though she knew that chemicals were central evidence, Colburn couldn't deduce the mechanism until she began to look beyond cancer, the standard disease of toxicology. She and her colleagues traced persistent chemicals like PCBs, DDT, dioxin, and other pollutants into the human body, where they are stored in fatty tissue, passing from prey to predator, and from mother to breastfed baby. The key finding was that these persistent chemicals fake their way into the endocrine system, masquerading as hormones like estrogen and androgen. It's a deadly case of miscommunication. When hormones, our chemical messengers, are released or suppressed at the wrong time in the wrong amounts, life gets bent out of shape.

For example, ecotoxicologist Pierre Béland began finding dead whales washed up on the shores of the St. Lawrence River in the early '90s, sometimes so toxic they had to be disposed of as hazardous waste. His autopsies typically reveal a devil's brew of breast tumors, stomach tumors, and cysts—all indicators of industrial production gone haywire.

It would be distressing enough if endocrine disruption were taking a toll on the planet's wildlife, but not on humans. However, research is revealing what some scientists have suspected for years: humans are by no means immune, since endocrine systems function similarly throughout the animal kingdom. One experiment studied the health of children whose mothers had eaten PCB-contaminated fish during pregnancy. As compared with a control population, the two hundred exposed children, on average, were born sooner, weighed less, and had lower IQs.[13]

LET THEM EAT VIAGRA

Other research demonstrated that barely detectable molecules of a certain plastic unexpectedly leached off laboratory beakers, mimicked estrogen, and initiated cancerous growth in lab experiments with human breast cells. Perhaps most startling of all is the 1992 study involving fifteen thousand men in twenty countries, indicating up to a 50 percent decline in human sperm production since 1938. "Consider what it might mean for our society if synthetic chemicals are undermining human intelligence in the same way they have apparently undermined human male sperm count," write the authors of *Our Stolen Future*,[14] who also speculate on possible connections between chemicals and the increased incidence of hyperactivity, aggression, and depression—all behaviors regulated by hormones.

The products that cause industrial diarrhea are innocent enough on the surface: plastic packaging, toys, cars, and computer circuit boards. But when we track hazardous chemicals to their sources and end points, we slosh through muck every step of the way. Even the familiar bacon on our plates literally results in industrial diarrhea, as writer Webster Donovan describes:

> Raising hogs used to be a family business, until one enterprising North
> Carolina farmer made it big business. But this booming national industry

is churning out at least one unwelcome by-product—millions of gallons
of pig waste that soil the water and foul the air.

The smell is what hits you first. Like a hammer, it clamps against the
nerve endings of your nose, then works its way inside your head and rat-
tles your brain. Imagine a filthy dog run on a humid day; a long-
unwashed diaper in a sealed plastic bag; a puffed roadkill beneath the
hottest summer sun. This is that smell: equal parts outhouse and musk,
with a jaw-tightening jolt of ammonia tossed in.

In recent years, this potent mix of acrid ammonia, rotting-meat ketones,
and spoiled-egg hydrogen sulfide has invaded tens of thousands of
houses— and millions of acres—across rural America. The vapor billows
invisibly, occasionally lifting off and disappearing for hours or weeks,
only to return while the neighbors are raking leaves, scraping the ice
off their windshield, or setting the table for a family cookout.[15]

Isn't it time to say good-bye to the Industrial Revolution—plagued from the start
with diarrhea—and bring in a new era of ecological design and caution?

CHAPTER 13

The addictive virus

*The urge sweeps over them like a tidal wave.
They go into a kind of trance, an addictive high,
where what they buy almost doesn't matter.*

—PSYCHOTHERAPIST OLIVIA MELLAN

*In my family, money was used to
express love, so I later spent money
to show myself love.*

—Participant in Debtors Anonymous,
a 12-step program

You suspect you may be a coffee addict when you start answering the front door *before* the doorbell rings! But when you can't resist buying a coffee mug with a picture of a coffee mug on it . . . it's official. You're hooked. For you and at least thirty-five million other javaholics (four to five cups a day), coffee is life; the rest is only waiting.

But coffee's not the worst of our addictions, not by a long shot. Fourteen million Americans use illegal drugs, twelve million Americans are heavy drinkers, and sixty million are hooked on tobacco. Five million Americans can't stop gambling away their income and savings. And at least ten million can't stop buying more and more stuff—an addiction that in the long run may be the most destructive of all.[1]

Lianne, a department store publicist in New York City, is a problem shopper. Every year, she uses her employee discount to rack up more than $20,000 in clothing and accessories. She finally suspected she might be addicted when she broke up with her boyfriend and moved her stuff out of his apartment. "Some women tend to shop a lot because they live out of two apartments, theirs and their boyfriend's," she explains. "You never look at your wardrobe as one wardrobe. But when I saw how many things I had that were identical, I began to see that maybe I did have a problem."[2]

Addiction to stuff is not easily understood. It's a bubbling cauldron of such traits as anxiety, loneliness, and low self-esteem. "I'd like to think I shop because I don't want to look like everybody else," Lianne confides, "but the real reason is because I don't want to look like myself. It's easier to buy something new and feel good about yourself than it is to change yourself."

Addicts need to go back for more in order to feel good again. The addictive substance or activity takes away the emotional discomfort of everyday life and also releases the built-up tensions of craving. The goal is to get back to a place of perceived power and carefree abandonment. The drinker suddenly becomes loose and uninhibited, certain he's the funniest man in the world. The gambler feels the elation of risk and possibility—putting it all on the line so Lady Luck can find him. The addicted shopper seeks the high she felt a few days earlier, when she bought a dress she still hasn't taken out of the box.

According to Dr. Ronald Faber, compulsive buyers often report feeling heightened sensations when they shop. Colors and textures are more intense, and extreme levels of focus and concentration are often achieved—literally, altered states of consciousness. Some extreme shoppers compare their highs to drug experiences, while others have compared the moment of purchase to an orgasm.[3]

"I'm addicted to the smell of suede, the smooth texture of silk, and the rustle of tissue paper," admits one shopping addict. She also loves the captive attention she commands when she shops. And because her credit card is always ready for use, she can shop whenever she wants. Now that's power.

NEVER ENOUGH

The thrill of shopping is only one aspect of the addiction to stuff. Many Americans are also hooked on building personal fortresses out of their purchases. Whether it's a new set of golf clubs or a walk-in closet full of sweaters and shoes, having the right stuff and sending the right signal somehow reassures addictive buyers. The problem is that the world's signals keep changing, so addicts never reach a point of having enough. The computer never has enough memory or virus protection, and it's never as fast as everyone else's. The SUV doesn't have a satellite-linked Global Positioning System, so how do we know where we are? The phone system is obsolete without cell phone Internet access, image messaging, and call waiting; the refrigerator doesn't dispense ice cubes, filter water, or have push-button, movable shelves (some now have a flat-screen TV on the door); and the big-screen TV is a good six feet narrower than the living-room wall. Glaring deficiencies like these become unacceptable when affluenza sets in.

Economists call it *the law of diminishing marginal utility*, jargon that simply means we have to run faster just to stay in place. As social psychologist David Myers phrases it, "The second piece of pie, or the second $100,000, never tastes as good as the first."[4]

Yet, despite diminishing returns that are plain to see, affluenza victims get stuck in the *more* mode, not knowing when or how to stop. If eating pie ultimately fails to satisfy, we think we need *more* pie to become satisfied. At this point, the affluenza virus has become an addiction. "Consuming becomes pathological because its importance grows larger and larger in direct proportion to our decreasing satisfaction," says economist Herman Daly.[5]

In terms of the social factors that trigger the addictive virus, our thanks go first to the "pushers" on the supply side. For example, when the highways to which we are addicted become clogged, dealers push *more* highways, which soon become clogged as well. When we get used to a certain level of sexually explicit advertising, the pushers push it a step further, and then further, until preteens pose suggestively on network TV ads in their underwear.

It's the same in restaurants, fast-food outlets, and movie theaters, where portions get bigger, and then get huge. Plates of food become platters, Biggie burgers become Dino-burgers, and boxes of popcorn become buckets. What's next, barrels requiring hand trucks? Our stomachs expand to accommodate the larger portions, which we soon regard as normal (sixty-four-ounce soft drinks and 1,400-calorie Monster burgers, normal?!).

Sometimes more and bigger are not enough. When we can't maintain our consumer highs with familiar products and activities, we search for new highs. Sports become extreme sports or fantasy sports in which thrill seekers bungee-jump off skyscrapers or gamble in Internet fantasy sports leagues. Even real professional athletes, with fantasy salaries, can never get enough. When a bright young baseball prospect signs for $25 million a year, a veteran who makes $12 million suddenly feels dissatisfied. This is the plight of the affluenza addict: even too much is not enough.

SHOPPING TO FILL THE VOID

Similarities among addictions are alarming. When the pathological becomes normal, an addict will do whatever is necessary to maintain a habit. Gamblers and overspenders alike bounce checks, borrow from friends, and go deep into debt to support their habit, often lying to loved ones about their actions. It's not hard to see the connection between addictive behavior and the huge craters in our culture and environment. Just as gamblers sell family heirlooms to continue gambling, so addicted consumers sacrifice priceless natural areas, contentment, and tradition to maintain a steady stream of goods.

Psychologists tell us pathological buying is typically related to a quest for greater recognition and acceptance, an expression of anger, or an escape through fantasy—all connected to shaky self-images. Writes Dr. Ronald Faber:

> One compulsive buyer bought predominantly expensive stereo and television equipment but demonstrated little interest when discussing the types of music or programs he liked. Eventually, it came out that his motivation for buying came mainly from the fact that neighbors recognized him as an expert in electronic equipment and came to him for advice when making their purchases.[6]

Faber reports that anger is often encoded in pathological buying—debt becomes a mechanism for getting back at one's spouse or parent. Or in other cases, extreme shopping is a fleeting getaway from reality:

Buying provides a way of escaping into a fantasy where the individual can be seen as important and respected. Some people indicated that the possession and use of a charge card made them feel powerful; others found that the attention provided by sales personnel and being known by name at exclusive stores provided feelings of importance and status.[7]

WHAT ARE WE THINKING?

If we could read the minds of the busy, intent shoppers at the region's largest mall, wouldn't we be amazed? Certainly we'd feel a little less abnormal, because we'd see that the mall is packed with "shoppers in therapy." (We're all crazy!) At least three in ten flee to the mall when things get out of control at home or work. Others come without a particular purchase in mind, just wanting to be around people, to feel less lonely. One woman resents having to buy a present for her son, who recently stole money from her purse. Several teenagers are desperately hoping their new clothes will facilitate sexual conquests that evening. At least six in ten of the shoppers feel a sense of euphoria from all the stimulation, but it's euphoria with a twist of anxiety. Each shopper knows from past experience that guilt, shame, and confusion—consumer regret—lurk right outside the door.

Still, they'll keep coming back, because they're addicted.

That is, unless they find a way to beat the all-consuming bug, as Thomas Monaghan did. In 1991 the founder of Domino's Pizza suddenly began to sell off many of his prized possessions, including three houses designed by Frank Lloyd Wright and thirty antique automobiles, one of which was an $8 million Bugatti Royale. Construction was halted on his multimillion-dollar home, and he even sold his Detroit Tigers baseball team because it was just a "source of excessive pride." He was quoted as saying, "None of the things I've bought, and I mean none of them, have ever really made me happy."[8]

CHAPTER 14

Dissatisfaction guaranteed

The only chance of satisfaction we can imagine is getting more of what we have now. But what we have now makes everybody dissatisfied. So what will more of it do—make us more satisfied, or more dissatisfied?

—AN INTERVIEWEE OF PSYCHOLOGIST JEREMY SEABROOK

More than ever, we have big houses and broken homes, high incomes and low morale, secured rights and diminished civility. We excel at making a living but often fail at making a life. We celebrate our prosperity but yearn for purpose. We cherish our freedoms but long for connection. In an age of plenty, we feel spiritual hunger.

—PSYCHOLOGIST DAVID MYERS

It's like entering a room and forgetting what you came for, except in this case the whole culture is forgetting. We forget to ask, What's an economy *for?*

En route to a brand-new millennium, we got waylaid. Price tags and bar codes began to coat the surfaces of our lives, as every single activity became a transaction. Eating, entertainment, socializing, health, even religion—all became marketable commodities. To sleep or to jump-start sex, take a pill. To eat, grab some fast food or order "room service" from a three-course store-to-door caterer. To exercise, join a health club. For fun, buy e-products on the Internet. To quit smoking, buy a nicotine patch, or ask your doctor for clinical doses of laughing gas! (No joke.)

To live, we buy. Everything (except "free air" at the gas station, and even that often costs half a buck). But this way of life is not sustainable. You can withdraw only so much money from a trust fund (or fossil fuel and fossil water from underground). You get only so many miles out of a vehicle—even a high-end race car. The American race-car lifestyle is fast approaching burnout because it requires long, stressful workweeks that eat up chunks of life, natural resources, and health. It programs us to substitute consumption for both citizenship and companionship. And it tries to meet nonmaterial needs with material goods, a losing strategy.

GAME OVER

Psychologist Richard Ryan points to scores of studies—his own among them—showing that material wealth does *not* create happiness. "We keep looking outside ourselves for satisfactions that can only come from within," he explains.[1] In the human species, happiness comes from achieving intrinsic goals like giving and receiving love. *Extrinsic* goals like monetary wealth, fame, and appearance are surrogate goals, often pursued as people try to fill themselves up with "outside-in" rewards. Says Ryan, "People with extrinsic goals sharpen their egos to conquer outer space, but they don't have a clue how to navigate inner space.

"We've documented that unhappiness and insecurity often *initiate* the quest for wealth," he continues. Is this surprising, given other evidence that addiction often springs from childhood abuse? In three studies with 140 adolescents, Ryan and colleague Tim Kasser showed that those with aspirations for wealth and fame were more depressed and had lower self-esteem than other adolescents whose aspirations centered on self-acceptance, family and friends, and community feeling.

"The wealth seekers also had a higher incidence of headaches, stomachaches, and runny noses," Ryan says. He believes that while people are born with intrinsic curiosity, self-motivation, and playfulness, too often these qualities are squelched by "deadlines, regulations, threats, directives, pressured evaluations, and imposed goals" that come from external sources of control rather than self-motivated choices and goals. Curious about the origins of extrinsic goals, the psychologists looked at family influences. "When mothers were controlling and cold (based on perceptions of family and friends), individuals were more likely to base their self-worth and security on external sources like money." Their findings do not prove that rich people are always unhappy (some are, some aren't, depending on how they use their money). But they do point out that seeking extrinsic goals can dislodge us from vital connections with people, nature, and community—and *that* can make us unhappy.

Dysfunctions and disconnects seem to disrupt everyone's life these days, rich and poor alike. Donella Meadows cuts to the heart of it in *Beyond the Limits:*

> People don't need enormous cars; they need respect. They don't need closets full of clothes; they need to feel attractive and they need excitement and variety and beauty. People don't need electronic entertainment; they need something worthwhile to do with their lives. People need identity, community, challenge, acknowledgment, love, joy. To try to fill these needs with material things is to set up an unquenchable appetite for false solutions to real and never-satisfied problems. The resulting psychological emptiness is one of the major forces behind the desire for material growth.[2]

Opinion polls reveal that Americans crave reconnection with the real sources of satisfaction, but we can't find our way back through all the jingles, static, broken gadgets, and credit card bills. We adopt a pattern clinically proven to lower our resistance to affluenza when we ask "How much?" rather than "How well?" The inevitable

result can only be dissatisfaction, guaranteed. Quantity can't satisfy the way quality can, and even an infinite supply of virtual reality will never actually be real.

ANOTHER VIEW OF WEALTH

The more real wealth we have—such as friends, skills, libraries, wilderness, and afternoon naps—the less money we need in order to be happy. Throughout history, many civilizations have already discovered this truth, as author Taichi Sakaiya describes in *The Knowledge-Value Revolution*. As the cedars of Lebanon and the topsoil of northern Africa disappeared, people in those areas finally wised up, learning to substitute knowledge, playfulness, ritual, and community for material goods. Their cultures became richer. "Circumstances had changed, and they moved away from a guiding principle that happiness comes from consuming more things. . . . Working oneself into the ground simply to produce and consume more things was not the thing to do. . . . The truly high-class lifestyle was one that allowed free time in which to enrich one's heart and soul—and this led to a groundswell of interest in religion. The people of the medieval era stressed the importance of loyalty to and faith in a communally held vision."[3]

During resource-scarce periods, the Japanese culture developed *kenjutsu* (fencing), *jujitsu* (martial arts), *saka* (tea ceremony and flower arrangement), *go* (Japanese "chess"), and many other cultural refinements. The culture became so highly evolved, according to Sakaiya, that the firearm was banned as too crude and destructive a method of settling differences.

When humanist psychologist Abraham Maslow observed the Canadian Blackfoot Indian culture in the 1930s, he too found evidence that the concept of wealth is a social construct, based partly on instinct and partly on the strategic pursuit of such socially laudable goals as equity, diversity, and resourcefulness. In short, wealth is far more than just money. "The rich men of the tribe accumulated mounds of blankets, food, bundles of various sorts, and sometimes a case of Pepsi-Cola. . . . I remember the Sun Dance ceremony in which one man strutted and, we would say, boasted of his achievements. . . . And then, with a lordly gesture of great pride but without being humiliating, he gave his pile of wealth to the widows, to the orphaned children, and to the blind and diseased. At the end of the ceremony, he stood stripped of all possessions, owning nothing but the clothes he stood in."[4]

Maslow contended that this concept of wealth is based on higher values than material gratification. "It would seem that every human being comes at birth into society not as a lump of clay to be molded by society, but rather as a structure which society either suppresses or builds upon."

LOWER ON THE HIERARCHY?

Everyone knows a few unique individuals—usually elderly—who are healthy, wise, playful, relaxed, spontaneous, generous, open-minded, and loving: people who focus on problems outside themselves and have a clear sense of what's authentic and what's not. They are people for whom life gets in the way of work, on purpose. For them, work is play, because they choose work they love. Abraham Maslow termed these people "self-actualized" individuals. He placed a lot of faith in the human potential to meet basic needs and then progress—under one's own guidance—up a hierarchy of needs toward fulfillment. Before he died in 1969, Maslow concluded that most Americans had met the basic physical (the only ones that are primarily material) and security needs, and had progressed to at least the "love and belongingness" rung of the hierarchy. Many individuals were higher than that.

MASLOW'S HIERARCHY OF NEEDS

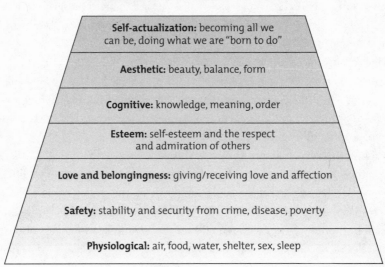

Self-actualization: becoming all we can be, doing what we are "born to do"

Aesthetic: beauty, balance, form

Cognitive: knowledge, meaning, order

Esteem: self-esteem and the respect and admiration of others

Love and belongingness: giving/receiving love and affection

Safety: stability and security from crime, disease, poverty

Physiological: air, food, water, shelter, sex, sleep

The question is, has America—weakened by affluenza—slipped *down* the hierarchy in the last thirty years? It seems the rungs of Maslow's ladder have become coated with slippery oil, as in a cartoon. According to polls, we're more fearful now. We're more insecure about crime, the possible loss of our jobs, and catastrophic illness. More than fifty thousand Americans die every year from medical malpractice, making us all the more insecure about our health.

How can we meet intrinsic community needs when sprawl creates distances between people? How can we feel a sense of beauty, security, and balance if beautiful open spaces in our communities are being smothered by new shopping malls and rows of identical houses? (Sometimes the only way to find your new house is to push the "house finder" button on your garage door opener, and watch which door opens.) How can we have self-respect in our work if it contributes to environmental destruction, social inequity, and isolation from living things? (The highest incidence of heart attacks is on Monday morning; apparently some would rather die than go back to work.)

Since America became a nation of consumers spoon-fed by automated products, fewer of us are now able to use our hands, or a sense of craft, in our work. As a result, creative satisfaction gets lost in the shuffle, along with knowledge, meaning, beauty, and balance—all higher rungs on Maslow's ladder.

Psychologists, anthropologists, artists, and the distant voices in our own heads tell us that both the potential and the urgency exist for a new definition of wealth in America. If we enrich our own nonmaterial sources of wealth, how much less money—and less paid labor—will be necessary? If we "produce" our own entertainment, perhaps by learning to be musicians, master gardeners, or woodworkers, informed conversationalists, or sports participants rather than ticket-purchasing fans, we'll reduce our financial needs substantially. If we provide some of our own transportation (and exercise) needs on foot—by living closer to work, stores, and recreation—we carve a large chunk out of the $7,500 spent annually by the average car owner. In effect, instead of working from January 1 to March 10 just to cover transportation costs, we can knock off in February.

Good diet, satisfying work, and regular exercise will keep our shopping carts free of side effects from expensive medicines we don't need (as well as preventing some of the more than thirty thousand deaths in America annually from fatal reactions to prescription drugs). Cooking with healthy ingredients can make our taste buds, synapses, and white blood cells happy enough for us to raise our health insurance deductibles and lower our premiums. Living in an energy-efficient home will shave at least $300 off a utility bill and make the home more comfortable. Changes like these are not about deprivation but about *increasing* the richness of our lives— and decreasing bills, stress, and waste. Quality satisfies more deeply than mere quantity.

Maslow termed the basic physical needs *deficiency needs* and assumed that as long as you ate, your food needs were being met. If you lived in a house or an apartment (as opposed to the street), your shelter needs were being met, and so on. However, his concept of deficiency didn't explore the *quality* of the food or shelter, or whether the needs were being supplied in a way that preserved the systems— the farms, forests, and fisheries—that met those needs. Individual satisfaction ultimately banks on the stability of the system.

Maslow didn't consider *sufficiency* and the implications of overconsumption of the basic needs. Nor did he really get into *efficiency* in meeting needs—the technologies and pathways of production and use. If technologies are wasteful and destructive, they can't deliver overall satisfaction, because they leave scars in nature. In our free market, waste itself has become an important product, and it's hard to feel proud of that. Loans and incentives offered by bankers, tax-policy makers, and regulators guide us toward wasteful designs and approaches, further frustrating our search for self-actualization. In summary, our economic system is programmed for dissatisfaction!

'MAY THE FORK BE WITH YOU'

Even with its shortcomings, Maslow's hierarchy is still widely used as a tool to explore personal and cultural growth. We use it here to look at how affluenza gets in the way of satisfaction. Imagine carrying a bulging sack of groceries from the supermarket to your car. What kind of value does the sack contain? What kind of health does the food provide? Between 1950 and 2000, America attained the lowest cost per unit of food in the world, as a percentage of income, but also the highest health care costs per capita. What's the connection? Are the items in our grocery sacks toxic? Are our habits—and the habits of industry—also toxic?

In America, obesity is a greater health threat than starvation. Because the typical diet is too high in fats and sugars and too low in unrefined, slow-release carbohydrates, 71 percent of Americans are overweight by an average of ten pounds. An estimated four hundred thousand Americans die each year from unhealthy diets in combination with chronic inactivity. The GDP swells in proportion to our waistlines, since at least $150 billion is spent to control obesity and to treat related diseases. While we continue to gorge, the contents of our grocery sacks deliver diabetes, gallbladder disease, hypertension, cancer, and higher risks of stroke.

The weight-control and health care industries in particular grow large as America tries, unsuccessfully, to grow lean. Our grocery sacks are filled with brightly packaged frustration! On average, we gulp about a 55 gallon drum of soft drinks every year, eat 150 fatty pounds of meat annually, and ingest the equivalent of 53 teaspoons of sugar *every day*.

Much of our dietary dissatisfaction comes from the lack of vitality that processed food delivers. The loss of control about food choice is also dissatisfying. Sugar is a good example. In 1997, Americans consumed three-fourths more sugar per capita than a hundred years ago, when most of the sugar produced went directly into our homes. In those days, we prepared most of our own meals and determined the amount of sugar that went into them. In today's world, we've lost control, in many ways! More than three-quarters of the sugar produced today goes into the prepared, processed foods in our grocery sack.

Our high-protein diet is a prime example of meeting needs imprecisely. Livestock eat 70 percent of the grain produced in America, yet if humans ate more grain directly, our diet would be seven to eight times more efficient per pound. Essentially, we wouldn't waste the grain's energy in the production of mountains of concentrated cow, hog, and chicken manure that pollute our waterways.

As Japan and China adopt a Western diet, previously rare Western diseases like arteriosclerosis and coronary heart disease come with it, explains health guru Andrew Weil. "Japanese women on traditional diets have one of the lowest rates of breast cancer in the world, but when they move to America and eat like Americans, their breast cancer risk quickly rises."[5]

Weil notes that there's far more to eating than the well-known consumer food groups (are those greasy, crunchy, sweet, and salty?). Food has always been a medium of social activity, he explains. The word *companion* means literally "with bread." High-quality food delivers satisfaction and contentedness, but low-quality food delivers poor health, irritability, pesticide residues, cancer, farm erosion, and the loss of rural communities as agribusiness giants take over. Simply put, junk food reduces our chances of reaching the top of Maslow's ladder. Sadly, our excessive diet too often produces lethargic and hyperactive humans who lack the energy and motivation to climb toward peak potential.

IS THE OBJECT SEX?

Monetary wealth is not a prerequisite for self-actualization, but authentic, vital connections are. In our culture, sex is another physical need that sometimes becomes an obstacle, rather than a stepping-stone, to self-actualization. Because sex is so instinctively compelling, it has become one of affluenza's most virulent carriers. Sex sells. But like food, it's also a fundamental social bond. Writes Erich Fromm, "The experience of sharing keeps the relation between two individuals alive. . . . Yet the sexual act—the prototype of shared enjoyment—is frequently so narcissistic, self-involved, and possessive that one can speak only of simultaneous, but not of shared pleasure."[6]

How much more self-involved can sex be than "cybersex," an emerging icon of isolation and unreality? "The affordability, accessibility and anonymity of the Internet have spawned a new psychological disorder among men and women who seek sexual stimulation from their computers. Some of these addicts spend hours each day masturbating to online pornographic images or having online sex with someone they have never seen, heard, touched, felt, or smelled."[7] We might call cybersex gratification, but in no way can it be termed satisfaction.

CULTURE CRUNCH

An old story about a native Pacific Islander rings true in the Age of Affluenza. A healthy, self-motivated native relaxes in a hammock that swings gently in front of his seaside hut, as he plays a wooden flute for his family and himself. For dinner, he picks exotic fruits and spears fresh sunfish. He feels glad, and lucky to be alive. (Think of it—he's on "vacation" most of the time!) Suddenly, without warning, affluenza invades the island. Writes Jerry Mander, "A businessman arrives, buys all the land, cuts down the trees and builds a factory. He hires the native to work in it for money so that some-day the native can afford canned fruit and fish from the mainland, a nice cinderblock house near the beach with a view of the water, and weekends off to enjoy it."[8]

Like Pacific Island natives, we've been cajoled into meeting most of our needs with products brought to us courtesy of multinational corporations—what you might call take-out satisfaction. "Almost every facet of American life has now been franchised," observes writer Eric Schlosser, "from the maternity ward at a Columbia/HCA hos-pital to an embalming room owned by the Houston-based Service Corporation Inter-national—which today handles the final remains of one of every nine Americans."[9]

What's good for America is good for the world—that's what the CEOs will tell you. One of the seven modern wonders of the world, the Golden Arches of McDon-ald's now grace thirty thousand restaurants in 119 countries, an empire on which the sun never sets. A friend of Dave's recently returned from China, where he observed a culture clash beneath the arches. "McDonald's missionaries spread the gospel of high-volume, low-cost fast food," he says, "but the Chinese don't really seem to want fast food—although they're intrigued with American burgers. They want to sit and leisurely drink tea. They don't get that they're supposed to be in a hurry. And they can't go out and sit in their cars to eat, because many came on their bikes."[10]

Yet even McDonald's occasionally makes concessions. In 2001, the company intro-duced seafood soup, and in 2004, sales jumped when stores modified their generic look and feel with large wall-mounted Chinese characters signifying "happiness." Affluenza continues to infect Chinese culture, with a hundred new McDonald's restaurants every year. (In fact, as Lester Brown of the Earth Policy Institute docu-ments, "Among the five basic food, energy, and industrial commodities—grain and meat, oil and coal, and steel—consumption in China has eclipsed that of the United States in all but oil.")[11]

Now that the Great Wall has cracked, can the Taj Mahal be far behind? Will India's sacred cow become the sacred burger? Culture crunchers have already scored a huge victory in Spain, with a surgical procedure to remove the siesta. In her book, *Leap,* Terry Tempest Williams describes a conversation she had on an airplane with a Procter & Gamble executive who boasted to her of his role in squeezing out the Spanish siesta. For a thousand years or more, the Spanish had enhanced their quality of life with a luxurious midday break that doesn't cost a single peseta. Yet in the eyes of commerce, siestas are a complete waste of time. What the world needs is more production, more consumption, less relaxation, and more money. Wake up and get rich! An English friend informs us that the British afternoon tea is also vanishing, along with the traditional sit-down dinner.

However, commerce's most successful culture coup to date has taken place in the once-fertile frontiers of the American mind. Accounts of North America in the 1600s speak of a forest so vast that a squirrel could travel from what is now Virginia to Illinois "without ever touching the ground." Today, by virtue of a media-happy free market, it may now be possible for a person to travel from one week to the next without thinking an original thought unshaped by manipulative messages! Much of the territory between our ears has now been commercially "colonized." The question is, if we get evicted from our own minds, who are we?

WANTING WHAT WE HAVE

Let's assume you've somehow satisfied physical, safety, and security needs, and even Maslow's "higher" needs for giving and receiving love. You've avoided junk food, the carelessness of the health care industry, and the battlefields of wounded relationships that stifle love and belongingness needs. Watch out, because the next rung, esteem, is teeming with viruses. Better wear gloves when you get to the esteem trap. How much of our consumer behavior is dictated by needs for self-esteem and peer approval? In our search to fulfill these needs, we often contort ourselves into human doings rather than human beings.

We look outside ourselves for approval, talking loudly about what we have rather than what we know or what we believe in. Having what we want becomes a more important goal than wanting what we have. And appearance too often becomes more important than reality. Partly as a spin-off from TV programs like *Extreme Makeover* and *The Swan,* plastic surgery is now seen by many as an escalator to higher self-esteem. In 2003, plastic surgeons performed just under three million cosmetic procedures, and the number of girls under 18 who received breast implants *tripled* from 2002 to 2003. Sadly, many of these media victims received cosmetic surgery as a graduation or birthday gift—yet another example of how we try to purchase happiness instead of experiencing it.[12]

As we identify ourselves with the social species "consumer," our sense of confidence becomes dependent on things largely out of our control. For example, we suffer mood swings with the rising and falling of economic tides. As of this writing, our "consumer confidence" is bobbing up and down from month to month, down slightly from its peak that preceded the 2001 stock market bust. Our current "poker face" is a bit hard to read. Tellingly, the same issue of the newspaper that reported our highest-ever level of consumer confidence featured an article explaining "Why the Ignorant Are Blissful."[13] David Dunning, a professor of psychology at Cornell, demonstrated that people who do things poorly usually appear more confident and self-assured than those who do things well. "Not only do they reach erroneous conclusions and make unfortunate choices," wrote Dunning, "but their incompetence robs them of the ability to realize it." The study documented that subjects who scored the lowest on logic, English grammar, and humor tests were also the most likely to overestimate how well they had done.

As a culture, are we blissfully ignorant? Are we erroneously confident we'll find peer approval, self-esteem, and meaning in material things, if we just keep looking?

PART TWO

Causes

CHAPTER 15

Original sin

Empty-handed we came into the world, and empty-handed, beyond question, we must leave it; if we have food and clothing to last us out, let us be content with that. Those who would be rich fall into temptation, the devil's trap for them; all those useless and dangerous appetites which sink men into ruin here and perdition hereafter. The love of money is a root from which every kind of evil springs.

—FIRST TIMOTHY 6:7–10

Now that you've been introduced to affluenza and its multiple symptoms, you may be asking yourself how we got to where we are today. What was the genesis of affluenza? Is it a bug that's always been there, just part of human nature? Is it culturally conditioned? Could it result from both nature and nurture? Those are the questions we'll attempt to answer in the next section of this book. We'll examine early efforts to contain or quarantine the disease and attempt to understand how the virus mutated and grew more virulent over time in response to the forward march of history.

We believe it's necessary to understand the epidemiology of affluenza in order to begin to fight it effectively. As we researched this aspect of the issue, we became convinced that affluenza is not a new disease. But during the last few decades, it has been spreading faster than ever before, as cultural values that once kept it in check have eroded under modern commercial pressures and technological changes.

THE SEARCH FOR PATIENT ZERO

When epidemiologists trace the evolution of a disease, they look for the first individual known to have contracted it, who is given the inglorious label "Patient Zero." For example, the official Patient Zero for the AIDS epidemic was a South African man who died in 1959 (though it is suspected that the disease originated as early as the 1920s).

So who was affluenza's Patient Zero? In the Judeo-Christian-Islamic tradition, there were two: Adam and Eve. While they had everything they needed in the Garden of Eden, they transgressed God's limits to eat the forbidden apple. So the first lesson in the Bible is an admonishment against coveting more than we need. Greed was, in fact, the original sin.

Some evolutionary biologists suggest that the uncertainties of primitive life meant that a hoarding orientation became part of human nature. Those folks who stored food in good times had it to sustain them in lean times, They survived and passed their hoarding genes on to their offspring.

Ergo, amassing stuff is as human as apple pie.

But on the other hand, for 99 percent of the time we *Homo sapiens* have existed on earth, we have been hunter-gatherers. Our problem was that our food-seeking activities quickly depleted the areas we lived in of fruits, nuts, animals, and other edibles. So we often had to move on to allow those areas to rebound. Mobility was

the name of the primitive game. And mobility didn't allow one to carry a whole lot of cargo. Hence a simpler, stuff-free life was a requirement for survival. A genetic propensity toward hoarding would have been downright deadly.

ORIGINAL AFFLUENCE

Life for hunter-gatherers was fraught with danger—from wild animals, accidents, disease, and an occasional enemy. Infant mortality was high, as were infirmities. Broken bones didn't heal well. Modern medicine might have been a godsend.

But the Stone Age wasn't as miserable as most of us believe. Some anthropologists who have observed contemporary "Stone Age" cultures call them "the original affluent societies."[1] Studies of such groups as the !Kung Bushmen of the Kalahari Desert indicate that before modernization confined them in smaller regions and destroyed the biological habitats from which they found subsistence, these hunter-gatherers were able to provide for their basic needs on as little as three or four hours of work a day. So-called Stone Age life apparently included more leisure time than does our own.

UCLA anthropologist Allen Johnson and his family spent two years living with a Stone Age tribe called the Machiguenga, hunter-gatherers who also practice some subsistence agriculture and inhabit the upper regions of the Amazon rain forest in Peru. He says he came to Machiguenga country loaded down with a huge footlocker full of possessions. "One of the lessons we learned over a period of just a few months, actually, was to dispense with most of our possessions," Johnson recalls.[2] "This kind of minimalist existence became quite comfortable to us after a while and we began to feel that all these other possessions were completely superfluous. I learned from the Machiguenga that we could be comfortable living a much simpler life."

Johnson found the Machiguenga not quite originally affluent enough to get by on a four-hour workday. "Anthropologists," he says, "may have gone a little bit overboard in describing how easy it is to be a hunter-gatherer, but the Machiguenga are certainly able to meet all their needs with six to eight hours of work. And that leaves a lot of time. The Machiguenga struck me as people who always have enough time. They're never in a hurry."

He came to admire their gentle ways and kind interactions with each other, the pleasure they found in quiet observation of their surroundings, the fact that they never seemed to get bored.

"There seems to be a kind of general satisfaction in the things that they do," Johnson says. "It's just a pleasure to be around the Machiguenga when they're working. They're calm. They're physically comfortable. They're sewing or weaving, or making a box or a bow and arrow. And there's a sense of them enjoying it as we might enjoy a hobby or a craft. No time pressure."

"One of the things they do in the evening," he observed, "is sit around telling stories. And as you go by a Machiguenga house in the evening, you'll see through the slats of the walls of the house. You'll see the fire glowing and hear people's voices softly telling stories. If a man went hunting, he'll tell the story with the sights and the sounds and the smells. They also tell folktales. I've translated a lot of them and they're absolutely beautiful, a real literature."

BACK IN THE U.S.A.

Like many travelers who return from time spent with so-called underdeveloped or primitive cultures, Johnson had trouble returning to the fast-paced, possession-laden life in the United States. Culture shocked, he walked through a supermarket aisle that was entirely filled with cake mixes and wondered, "Where's the affluence? Is this really progress?"

Life in Los Angeles seemed surreal when Johnson first returned. His children complained regularly of boredom despite a plethora of toys and activities. People he met seemed constantly busy but unsatisfied with their lives, working and consuming frantically as if to fill "some kind of hole or emptiness," an emotional state he never encountered among the Machiguenga.

Johnson doesn't romanticize Machiguenga existence. Their life expectancy was short, as they often fell victim to jungle diseases. But they hadn't a hint of affluenza.

So it's not "human nature." But it's easy to find evidence of early infection among societies that achieved agricultural surpluses sufficient to allow long-term settlements, class divisions, and the beginnings of city life. In such cultures, political and economic hierarchies flourished and, as they strove for greater riches, members of the upper echelon began to oppress the poor and subjugate their neighbors. Without naming it as such, prophetic traditions in all civilizations, East and West, challenged those who had been infected by affluenza. "Beware an act of avarice; it is a bad and incurable disease," warned an ancient Egyptian proverb.[3] Buddha taught that the way to happiness and enlightenment lies in reducing desire, which he thought to be the cause of suffering.

MORAL ANTIDOTES

The Hebrew prophets railed against those who amassed riches by oppressing the poor and the weak. Moderation was the key: "Give me neither poverty nor riches, but only enough," reads the book of Proverbs. One day each week, the Sabbath, was to be kept completely free of money-making and thereby remain holy. Of the Sabbath, the great Jewish scholar Rabbi Abraham Heschel writes, "He who wants to enter the holiness of the day must first lay down the profanity of chatter-ing commerce . . . and fury of acquisitiveness."[4] The Book of Deuteronomy, writ-ten about 700 BCE, admonishes against wasting things, the natural corollary to a life of material desire. As Rabbi Daniel Schwarz puts it, "when you waste creation, it's like spitting at God."[5]

The ancient Greeks, too, warned against affluenza. "Simplicity is an ancient, even a primordial, ideal," says historian David Shi, the author of *The Simple Life* and now president of Furman University. "The Greeks," Shi says, "spoke of the 'Middle Way,' that midpoint between luxury and deprivation."[6] Aristotle warned against those "who have managed to acquire more external goods than they can possibly use and are lacking in the goods of the soul."

By contrast he suggested that happiness would come to "those who have cultivat-ed their character and mind to the uppermost and kept acquisition of external goods within moderate limits." "Aristotle was the first to maintain the diminishing marginal utility of money," writes philosopher Jerome Segal. "His belief was that each addi-tional increment of money is of progressively less benefit to its possessor, and beyond a certain point, having more is of no value, and may even be harmful."[7]

"Unlimited wealth," Aristotle wrote, "is great poverty." Two groups of Greek non-conformists, the Stoics and the Cynics, were even more critical of materialism. By the time of the birth of Christ, their ideas were widespread. The Roman philosopher Seneca, a Stoic, challenged his own culture: "A thatched roof once covered free men; under marble and gold dwells slavery."[8]

According to New Testament scholar Burton Mack, early Christian teachings bore a strong resemblance to those championed by Epictetus, Diogenes, and other followers of the Cynic tradition in Greece. Living simply, the Cynics mocked the conventional culture of their affluent peers. Their ideas were widely known through-out the Mediterranean region two millennia ago.

But perhaps the strongest rebuke to incipient affluenza came from Jesus him-self. He continually warned of the dangers of wealth, declaring it the major impedi-ment to entry into the kingdom of heaven. It would be easier for a camel to pass through a needle's eye than for a rich man to enter heaven, he told his followers. The rich man who wished to follow Jesus was told he would first have to sell his possessions and give the money to the poor. "He went away unhappy for he had great wealth."[9]

Don't store up treasures on earth, Christ commanded. Rather be like the birds and flowers who possess nothing. God takes care of them, and their beauty is not matched by Solomon in all his glory. The earliest of Jesus's disciples and believers lived in simple communities where they shared all things in common and preached that "the love of money is the root of all evil."

"I think one of the most riveting passages in the New Testament is where Christ warns about Mammon, which is the power of wealth, the power of money," says Dr. Richard Swenson, a physician who lectures widely in evangelical churches. "Christ says you cannot serve both God and Mammon. He didn't say it's hard, it's difficult, it's tricky. He said it's impossible."[10]

In fact, one of Jesus's final public acts was a stinging rebuke to the affluenza that had begun to permeate his society. By chasing the money-lenders from the temple and overturning their tables, he challenged physically (one might even say, violently) a profane commercialism that had crept into even the holiest of places.

Christian theologian (and environmental scientist) Calvin DeWitt says our modern consumer philosophy turns scriptural teachings on their head: "Consume more, then you'll be happy. Remain discontented with everything so that you'll continue to strive for more and more. That's the message we hear. But the biblical teaching is to be content with what you have, honor God, take care of creation, give your bread to the hungry. Then joy comes as a by-product of service. If you take those teachings and just write their antithesis, you find yourself describing our current consumer society."[11]

A CLASH OF CULTURES

In the spring of 1877, the famous leader of a tribe of hunter-gatherers addressed a council of his people, gathered around him on the windswept plains of South Dakota. The Lakota Sioux chief Tatanka Yotanka (Sitting Bull), gave thanks for the change of seasons and the bounty that the earth freely provided. But he warned his people about "another race, small and feeble when our fathers first met them, but now great and overbearing." He described the pale-faced men and women who had come to mine and till the earth, carrying with them (and seeking to convert the Indians to) the words of a man who preached brotherhood, peace, and goodwill among all, a preference for the poor, and a life free from the encumbrances of worldly possessions.

Something, apparently, had gotten lost in the translation because, as Sitting Bull observed, "These people have made many rules which the rich may break but the poor may not. They take tithes from the poor and weak to support the rich who rule. They claim this mother of ours, the earth, for their own and fence their neighbors away; they deface her with their buildings and their refuse. Their nation is like a spring freshet that overruns its banks and destroys all who are in its path. We cannot dwell side by side."[12]

Of the white invaders, Sitting Bull said, one thing was certain: *"The love of possession is a disease with them."* Today he might have called that disease "affluenza." Back then, he would have found that even among the whites, there were many who shared his fears of the virus in their midst.

An ounce of prevention

The devaluation of the human world increases in direct relation to the increase in value of the world of things.

—KARL MARX,
Economic and Philosophical
Manuscripts of 1844

ear of affluenza has been part of the American tradition since some of the first colonists arrived here from Europe. It was a mixed bunch that risked life and livelihood to cross the Atlantic on small wooden ships. The first came seeking riches. The Spanish wanted gold; the French, furs. The Dutch sought new trade routes to the fabled Indies.

But among the early arrivals from England were refugees seeking to escape what they had come to view as a godless materialism taking root in Europe. "When the Puritans arrived in the New World, one of their major premises was their desire to try to create a Christian commonwealth that practiced simple living," explains historian David Shi.[1]

In the Massachusetts Bay Colony, the Puritans adopted what were known as sumptuary laws, forbidding conspicuous displays of wealth. They required colonists to wear simple clothing, for example. But because they were never applied fairly, the laws failed to stem a growing trade in luxury goods arriving in the New World from Europe. Wealthier, politically powerful Puritans could effectively ignore the laws and wear whatever they chose, while their poorer brethren were punished for transgressions of the dress code. In effect, the sumptuary laws exacerbated the visible class differences.

In Pennsylvania, the Quakers, under the leadership of John Woolman, were more successful in their efforts to keep affluenza at bay. "My dear friends," Woolman preached, "follow that exercise of simplicity, that plainness and frugality which true wisdom leads to."[2] "Among Quakers," writes philosopher Jerome Segal, "the restrictions on display and consumption became more widely applicable. Most important, the pursuit of luxurious consumption was linked to a broad range of injustices and social problems, including alcoholism, poverty, slavery and ill treatment of the Indians."[3]

YANKEE DOODLE DANDIES—NOT!

In some respects, the American Revolution itself was a revolt against affluenza. British colonial masters bled their American colonies in order to support a lifestyle of luxury approaching decadence. The English lords often spent half the day dressing, much of it on their ever-more-elaborate headpieces (this is the origin of the term "bigwigs"). Then they stuffed themselves on dinners that took hours to consume.

The American colonists, meanwhile, grew angry at the taxes imposed on them to keep British coffers full. But at the same time, colonial leaders were troubled by unbridled pursuit of wealth on the part of some of their own countrymen. "Frugality, my dear, must be our refuge," wrote John Adams to his wife, Abigail, during the revolution. "I hope the ladies are everyday diminishing their ornaments, and the gentlemen, too. Let us drink water and eat potatoes rather than submit to unrighteous domination."[4]

At the end of the eighteenth century, as the world changed politically with the triumph of the American and French revolutions, it was also changing economically. The Industrial Revolution's "dark, satanic mills" (in William Blake's phrase) brought steam power and assembly-line techniques, making possible the production of textiles and other goods in a fraction of the time previously required. Benjamin Franklin argued that with such productive tools at humanity's disposal, it was possible to reduce the work time needed to produce all the "necessaries" of life to three or four hours a day.[5]

But in fact, the opposite occurred. During the early Industrial Revolution, working hours were roughly doubled, rather than reduced. The medieval workday, scholars now estimate, averaged about nine hours, more in summer, fewer in winter.[6] Moreover, the pace of work was quite slow, with frequent breaks for rest. And in some parts of Europe, workers enjoyed nearly 150 religious holidays, when they didn't work at all. Pieter Brueghel's sixteenth-century paintings of peasants dancing, feasting, or napping in their wheat fields in the afternoon were accurate portrayals of the life he witnessed.

THE SPIRIT OF SAINT MONDAY

But with the Industrial Revolution, factory workers—driven into desolate, Dickensian industrial cities as the land they once farmed was enclosed for sheep raising—were working fourteen, sixteen, even eighteen hours a day. In 1812, one factory owner in Leeds, England, was described as humane and progressive because he wouldn't hire children under ten years of age and limited children's working hours to sixteen a day.

But factory workers did not readily comply with the new industrial discipline. Stripped of their old religious holidays, they invented a new one: Saint Monday. Hung over from Sunday nights at the tavern, they slept in late or failed to show up to work at all. Workers were paid on a piece-rate basis, and at first they only worked as long as they needed to subsist. If an employer paid them more as an incentive to work more, he soon found that his strategy backfired. As Max Weber put it, "The opportunity of earning more was less attractive than that of working less."[7]

This was obviously a pre-affluenza situation.

Consequently, as Karl Marx repeatedly pointed out, employers sought to pay the lowest wages possible so that workers would have to keep working long hours simply to survive. But while such miserliness was rational behavior for individual employers, it undermined capitalist industry as a whole. Workers' lack of purchasing power led to overproduction crises that periodically destroyed entire industries.

"In these crises," Marx and Engels wrote in *The Communist Manifesto* of 1848, "a great part not only of the existing products but also of the previously created productive forces are periodically destroyed. . . . Society suddenly finds itself put back into a state of momentary barbarism. . . . And how does the bourgeoisie get over these crises? On the one hand, by enforced destruction of a mass of productive forces; on the other, by the conquest of new markets, and by the more thorough exploitation of old ones."[8]

MARX ON AFFLUENZA

So just how is this "more thorough exploitation" accomplished? In effect, by exposing one's potential customers to affluenza, though, of course, Marx never used the term. But in a brilliant passage from *The Economic and Philosophical*

Manuscripts of 1844, worth quoting from at length, he describes the process. "Excess and immoderation" become the economy's "true standard," Marx wrote, as

> the expansion of production and of needs becomes an ingenious and always calculating subservience to inhuman, depraved, unnatural and *imaginary* appetites. . . . Every product is a bait by means of which the individual tries to entice the essence of the other person, his money. Every real or potential need is a weakness which will draw the bird into the lime. . . . The entrepreneur accedes to the most depraved fancies of his neighbor, plays the role of pander between him and his needs, awakens unhealthy appetites in him, and watches for every weakness in order, later, to claim the remuneration for this labor of love.[9]

That passage, written 161 years ago, accurately describes much of modern advertising, which, indeed, stimulates "imaginary appetites," consistently uses sex to sell products, and certainly, in cases such as the video game promotions described in chapter 7, "Dilated Pupils," "accedes to the most depraved fancies."

Ultimately, though, Marx believed that market expansion would always be inadequate and that overproduction crises could be prevented only if the workers themselves gained ownership of the factories and used the machinery for the benefit of all. That didn't mean an ever-growing pie of material production simply shared more equitably. Marx's goal was never a materialistic one. Indeed, he stressed that to simply increase the purchasing power of workers "would be nothing more than a better remuneration of slaves and would not restore, either to the worker or to the work, their human significance and worth."[10]

WEALTH AS DISPOSABLE TIME

Neither would "an enforced equality of wages," made law by a socialist government, lead to happiness, which, Marx believed, was to be found instead in our relationships with other people and in the development of our capacities for creative expression. "The wealthy man," he wrote, "is one who needs a complex of human manifestations of life and whose own self-realization exists as an inner necessity." He suggested that "too many useful goods create too many useless people."[11]

Of course, Marx understood that human beings must have enough wholesome food, decent shelter, and protective clothing. Mass production, he believed, made it possible for everyone to achieve these ends. And to do so each person would have to perform a certain minimum amount of repetitive, noncreative labor. Marx called this time, which he and Engels estimated could be reduced (even in the mid-1800s) to as little as four hours a day, "the realm of necessity."

The work time necessary to satisfy real material needs could be reduced further by increases in productivity, "but it always remains a realm of necessity. Beyond it begins that development of human power, which is its own end, the true realm of freedom," when self-chosen activity prevails. Of this realm of freedom, Marx added, "the shortening of the working day is its basic prerequisite."

"A nation is really rich if the working day is six hours rather than twelve," Marx wrote, quoting approvingly the anonymous author of a British article written in 1821: "Wealth is liberty—liberty to seek recreation, liberty to enjoy life, liberty to improve the mind: it is disposable time and nothing more."[12]

SIMPLY THOREAU

Meanwhile, across the Atlantic, an American movement offered a similar critique of industrialization and the acquisitiveness it engendered. The transcendentalists, as they called themselves, idealized the simple life close to nature, and they started intentional communities (none destined to last very long) such as Brook Farm and Fruitlands, based on their principles.

Better remembered, if similarly short-lived, was Henry David Thoreau's 1845 sojourn to a one-room cabin he built on the shore of Walden Pond, near Boston. "Simplicity, simplicity, simplicity," wrote Thoreau in *Walden*. "Most of the luxuries and many of the so-called comforts of life, are not only not indispensable, but positive hindrances to the elevation of mankind."[13]

In *Life without Principle*, Thoreau was even more damning of the acquisitive industrial personality, already in need of antibodies for affluenza. Like Marx, Thoreau believed that true wealth meant sufficient leisure for self-chosen creative activity, suggesting that half a day's labor should be enough to procure real material necessities. "If I should sell both my forenoons and my afternoons to society as most appear to do, I am sure that for me there would be nothing left worth living for," Thoreau wrote.

> Let us consider the way in which we spend our lives. The world is a place of business. What an infinite bustle. . . . There is no sabbath. It would be glorious to see mankind at leisure for once. It is nothing but work, work, work. I cannot easily buy a blank book to write thoughts in; they are commonly ruled for dollars and cents. . . . I think there is nothing, not even crime, more opposed to poetry, to philosophy, ay, to life itself than this incessant business.[14]

"If a man should walk in the woods for love of them half of each day, he is in danger of being regarded as a loafer, but if he spends his whole day as a speculator, shearing off those woods and making earth bald before her time, he is esteemed an industrious and enterprising citizen,"[15] Thoreau wrote, in words all the more relevant today, when corporate speculators shear off entire forests of old-growth redwoods to pay for junk bonds.

For Marx, Thoreau, and many other oft-quoted, but more often ignored, philosophers of the mid-nineteenth century, industrial development could only be justified because, potentially, it shortened the time spent in drudgery, thereby giving people leisure time for self-chosen activity.

Given a choice between more time and more money, these philosophers chose the former. For precisely a century following Thoreau's retreat to Walden, that choice, as our next chapter suggests, would engage Americans in a broad and energetic debate. Then, suddenly, it would be resolved—in favor of more money. But it would not be forgotten.

CHAPTER 17

The road not taken

*We want bread, but roses, too
[and time to smell them].*

—Female textile workers in Lawrence,
Massachusetts, 1912

After the horrors of the Civil War, a new, quieter conflict, ultimately more powerful in its impact, emerged in the United States. Two roads, as Robert Frost put it in his lovely poem "The Road Not Taken," presented themselves to Americans, and after a period of indecision that lasted nearly a century, we chose one of them, "and that has made all the difference."

Nineteenth-century Americans still had more respect for thrift than for spend-thrifts, and the word *consumption* meant something different then. As Jeremy Rifkin explains, "If you go back to Samuel Johnson's dictionary of the English language, to consume meant to exhaust, to pillage, to lay waste, to destroy. In fact, even in our grandparents' generation, when somebody had tuberculosis, they called it 'consumption.' So up until this century, to be a consumer was not to be a good thing; it was considered a bad thing."[1]

Yet the factory system had made possible a tremendous efficiency in the time required to produce products. And herein lay the roots of the new conflict: what to do with all that time? One side suggested that we make more stuff; the other believed we should work less. Luxury or simplicity. Money or time.

THE RIGHT TO BE LAZY

Across the Atlantic, a similar argument was brewing. In 1883, while in a French prison, Paul Lafargue, a son-in-law of Karl Marx, wrote a provocative essay called "The Right to Be Lazy," challenging the make more, have more ethic. Lafargue mocked industrialists who "go among the happy nations who are loafing in the sun" and "lay down railroads, erect factories and import the curse of work."[2]

Lafargue deemed laziness "the mother of arts and noble virtues" and suggested that factories were so productive even then that only three hours a day of labor should be required to meet real needs. Like Marx, he pointed out that Catholic Church law had given workers many feast days honoring the saints when work was forbidden. It was no surprise, he suggested, that industrialists favored Protestantism (with its work ethic), which "dethroned the saints in heaven in order to abolish their feast days on earth."

At the same time in England, William Morris, a poet, artist, essayist, and the designer of the Morris chair, claimed that under the factory system, "the huge mass of men are compelled by folly and greed to make harmful and useless things."[3] "An immensity of work" wrote Morris, was expended in making "everything in the shop windows which is embarrassing or superfluous." "I beg of you," Morris pleaded,

> to think of the enormous mass of men who are occupied with this miserable trumpery, from the engineers who have had to make the machines for making them, down to the hapless clerks who sit day-long year after year in the horrible dens wherein the wholesale exchange of them is transacted, and the shopmen, who not daring to call their souls their own, retail them . . . to the idle public which doesn't want them but buys them to be bored by them and sick to death of them.

"The good life of the future," said Morris, would be totally unlike the life of the rich of his day. "Free men," he maintained, "must live simple lives and have simple pleasures." Morris defined a decent, wealthy life as requiring "a healthy body, an active mind, occupation fit for a healthy body and active mind, and a beautiful world to live in."

THE SIMPLE LIFE

Back in the United States, new institutions like the department store helped promote a life of conspicuous consumption. "Urban department stores came in during the 1880s," says historian Susan Strasser, "basically to create the sort of place where people go and lose themselves and meanwhile spend their money."[4] By the 1890s, wealthy Americans proudly displayed the material signs of their success, wearing affluenza on their sleeves, you might say. But not everyone was impressed.

"In the late nineteenth century, there was a major revival of American interest in simple living," says historian David Shi. "Theodore Roosevelt was one of the foremost proponents of a simpler life for Americans during that period. Roosevelt was quite candid in saying that for all his support for American capitalism, he feared that if it were allowed to develop unleashed it would eventually create a corrupt civilization."[5] Shi provides other examples of this turn-of-the-century interest in simplicity in his wonderful book *The Simple Life*. Even America's best-selling magazine, *The Ladies' Home Journal*, promoted simplicity during that era.

THE SHORTER HOURS MOVEMENT

Organized labor, too, had not yet then accepted the definition of the good life as a goods life, in which the marker of progress was the making of stuff. Indeed, for more than half a century, the demand for shorter hours topped labor's agenda. In 1886, hundreds of thousands of workers filled American cities, demanding that an eight-hour workday be made America's legal standard. That didn't happen until 1938, when the Wagner Labor Relations Act made the eight-hour day and forty-hour week the law of the land. And by then, labor leaders were fighting for a six-hour workday. It was needed, they argued, as much for spiritual as economic reasons.

"The human values of leisure are even greater than its economic significance," wrote William Green, president of the American Federation of Labor, in 1926. Green claimed that modern work was "meaningless, repetitive, boring," and offered "no satisfaction of intellectual needs." Shorter working hours were necessary "for the higher development of spiritual and intellectual powers," Green claimed. His vice president, Matthew Woll, charged that modern production ignored "the finer qualities of life. Unfortunately, our industrial life is dominated by the materialistic spirit of production [affluenza?], giving little attention to the development of the human body, the human mind or the spirit of life."[6]

Juliet Stuart Poyntz, education director of the International Ladies Garment Workers Union, declared that what workers wanted most of all was "time to be human." "Workers," she observed, "have declared that their lives are not to be bartered at any price." "No wage, no matter how high" was more important than the time that workers needed.[7]

TIME TO KNOW GOD

Behind them, as Benjamin Hunnicutt of the University of Iowa points out in his book *Work without End,* rallied prominent religious leaders, who worried that workers had no time for reflection and spiritual matters, no "time to know God." Jewish leaders challenged Saturday work as violating their Sabbath, and led the fight for a five-day work week. Catholic leaders backed Pope Leo XIII's call (in his encyclical *Rerum Novarum,* 1891) for a "living wage" or family wage that would guarantee the breadwinner in working families sufficient income for a life of *"frugal* comfort." But beyond that, they believed that more time was more important to workers than more money.

During the '20s, Monsignor John Ryan, editor of the *Catholic Charities Review,* pointed to St. Augustine's claim that natural law demanded a "maximum" standard of living as well as a minimum one. "The true and rational doctrine," Ryan wrote, "is that when men have produced sufficient necessaries and reasonable comforts, they should spend what time is left in the cultivation of their intellects and wills, in the pursuit of the higher life." They should, he said, "ask what is life for?"[8] Jewish scholar Felix Cohen pointed out that in the biblical tradition, work was a curse visited upon Adam for his sin in Eden, and suggested that with the abolishment of wasteful and unnecessary production, it would soon be possible to reduce the workweek to ten hours![9]

THE GOSPEL OF CONSUMPTION

But industrial leaders in the 1920s had their own religion, the gospel of consumption. A reduction in working hours, they believed, might bring the whole capitalist system to its knees. Increased leisure, Harvard economist Thomas Nixon Carver warned, was bad for business:

> There is no reason for believing that more leisure would ever increase
> the desire for goods. It is quite possible that the leisure would be spent
> in the cultivation of the arts and graces of life; in visiting museums,
> libraries and art galleries, or hikes, games and inexpensive amusements

. . . it would decrease the desire for material goods. If it should result in more gardening, more work around the home in making or repairing furniture, painting and repairing the house and other useful avocations, it would cut down the demand for the products of our wage paying industries.[10]

It would, you might say, reduce affluenza. He had a problem with that.

After the Model T began rolling from Henry Ford's assembly lines in 1913, a cornucopia of material products followed. Businesses sought ways to sell them—and the economic gospel of consumption—giving rise to an advertising industry that looked—and still looks—to psychology for help in pushing products.

"Sell them their dreams," a promoter told Philadelphia businessmen in 1923. "Sell them what they longed for and hoped for and almost despaired of having. Sell them hats by splashing sunlight across them. Sell them dreams—dreams of country clubs and proms and visions of what might happen if only. After all, people don't buy things to have things. They buy hope—hope of what your merchandise will do for them. Sell them this hope and you won't have to worry about selling them goods."[11]

People's wants, the captains of American industry declared, were insatiable, and business opportunities therefore boundless. During the '20s, their gospel of wealth had plenty of believers. The world's first mass-consumption society came in dancing the Charleston. Cash registers were ka-chinging, and the stock market soared—higher, higher, higher—as it did in the 1990s. There were those who thought it would never go down.

SHORTER HOURS DURING THE DEPRESSION

Then on Black Friday in October 1929, it all collapsed. "Wall Street Lays an Egg," declared the headline in *Variety*. Millionaires suddenly became paupers and leaped out windows. Breadlines formed. Millions were out of work and "buddy" couldn't spare a dime. With so many people out of work, the idea of shortening work hours, "work sharing," was back in vogue. Even Herbert Hoover called shorter hours the quickest way to create more jobs.

Once again, labor leaders like William Green were demanding "the six-hour day and the five-day week in industry." Imagine their delight when word came from the Capitol in Washington on April 6, 1933, that the U.S. Senate had just passed a bill that would make thirty hours the official American workweek. Anything over that would be overtime. Thirty hours. That was nearly seven decades ago.

But the bill failed in the House by a few votes. President Franklin D. Roosevelt opposed it because he was convinced that federal job creation programs—the New Deal—offered a better way to both reduce unemployment and keep industry strong.

But some businesses had already adopted thirty-hour workweeks, with excellent results. Cereal tycoon W. K. Kellogg took the lead, in December 1930. Kellogg was a paternalistic capitalist who ran his company with an iron hand. But he had a certain radical vision. In Kellogg's view, according to Benjamin Hunnicutt, leisure time, not economic growth without end, represented the "flower, the crowning achievement, of capitalism."[12] The vision came to Kellogg because he mourned his rigid childhood and his own addiction to long hours of labor. "I never learned to play," he once told his grandson, regretfully.

Kellogg offered his workers thirty-five hours' pay for a thirty-hour week, and he built parks, summer camps, nature centers, garden plots, sports fields, and other recreational facilities for them. The plan immediately created 400 new jobs in Battle Creek, Michigan, where Kellogg's plants were located. Productivity rose so rapidly that within two years Kellogg could pay his thirty-hour workers what he had previously paid them for forty hours. Polling of Kellogg's workers during the '30s showed overwhelming support for the thirty-hour week; only a few single males wished for more hours and higher pay.

OLD EIGHT HOURS HAS GOT US ALL

But after Kellogg died, the company waged a long campaign to return to the forty-hour week. The reason: benefits. As benefits increasingly became a larger part of the wage package, it made more sense to hire fewer workers and keep them on longer. But the thirty-hour week at Kellogg's wasn't fully abandoned until 1985, when the company threatened to leave Battle Creek if the remaining thirty-hour workers (about 20 percent of the company, and nearly all women) didn't agree to work longer. The women held a funeral (complete with a casket) for the thirty-hour week at Stan's Place, a local bar, and one, Ina Sides, wrote a eulogy:

> Farewell good friend, oh six hours
> 'Tis sad but true
> Now you're gone and we're all so blue.
> Get out your vitamins, give the doctor a call
> 'Cause old eight hours has got us all.[13]

While writing his book *Kellogg's Six-Hour Day*, Hunnicutt spent time with many former Kellogg workers in Battle Creek. Most remembered the thirty-hour week with deep fondness. They remembered using their leisure well—to garden, learn crafts, practice hobbies, exercise, and share in a vibrant community life. "You weren't all wore out when you got out of work," said one man. "You had the energy to do something else."

Chuck and Joy Blanchard, a married couple who both worked at the plant, remembered that Chuck took care of the kids and was a "room parent" at their school "long before anyone heard about women's liberation."[14] They also remembered that after the return to forty hours, volunteering in Battle Creek went down and crime went up. The Blanchards say they *had* little, but their lives, blessed with abundant leisure, were happier than those of young families today, who have so much more stuff but never seem to have time.

Never before or since in America had ordinary industrial workers traveled so far down that "other road"—the road of time instead of money. In that sense, the Kellogg's workers were, as Hunnicutt sees them, explorers in a new and wondrous land that all Americans might have come to had World War II not intervened, and—in demanding a vast national outpouring of labor—locked the gate. Today, we meet people who cannot quite believe that more than half a century ago, in a corner of the United States, full-time workers were spending only thirty hours a week on the job. But it happened. And it can happen again when we get a grip on affluenza.

CHAPTER 18

An emerging epidemic

Man today is fascinated by the possibility of buying more, better, and especially, new things. He is consumption hungry.... To buy the latest gadget, the latest model of anything that is on the market, is the dream of everybody, in comparison to which the real pleasure in use is quite secondary. Modern man, if he dared to be articulate about his concept of heaven, would describe a vision which would look like the biggest department store in the world.... He would wander around open-mouthed in this heaven of gadgets and commodities, provided only that there were ever more and new things to buy, and perhaps, that his neighbors were just a little less privileged than he.

—PSYCHOANALYST ERICH FROMM, 1955

During World War II, Americans accepted rationing and material deprivation. Wasteful consumption was out of the question. In every city, citizens gathered scrap metal to contribute to the war effort. Most grew some of their own food, in so-called victory gardens. Driving was limited to save fuel. Despite the sacrifices, what many older Americans remember most from that time was the sense of community, of sharing for the common good and uniting to defeat a common enemy.

But shortly after the war, pent-up economic demand in the form of personal savings, coupled with low-interest government loans and mushrooming private credit, led to a consumer boom unparalleled in history. The G.I. Bill sparked massive construction of new housing at the edge of America's cities, beginning with the famous Levittown development on Long Island. The average size of a Levittown bungalow was only 750 square feet, but its popularity encouraged other developers to build sprawling suburbs with larger homes.

New families filled the new homes as the baby boom began. Each family needed lots of new appliances and—because transit service in the suburbs was nonexistent—cars. It's fascinating to watch the many corporate and government films produced during that period, both documenting and extolling the new mass-consumption society.

THE GOODS LIFE

"The new automobiles stream from the factories," the narrator cheers, in one late-forties film. "Fresh buying power floods into all the stores of every community. Prosperity greater than history has ever known." In the same film, we see a montage of shots of people spending money and hear more peppy narration: "The pleasure of buying, the spreading of money, and the enjoyment of all the things that paychecks can buy are making happy all the thousands of families!"[1] Utopia had arrived!

Another film proclaims that "we live in an age of growing abundance" and urges Americans to give thanks for "our liberty to buy whatever each of us may choose" (the words come with a heavenly chorus humming "America the Beautiful" and shots of the Statue of Liberty). A third reminds us that "the basic freedom of the American people is the freedom of individual choice" (of which products to purchase, of course).

One film appeals to women to take up where the soldiers of World War II left off and fight "the age-old battle for beauty." We've been told "you can't buy beauty in a jar," the narrator says, "but that old adage is bunk. We have the money to spend and we want all the lovely-smelling lotions, soaps, and glamour goo we can get with it." Joy in a jar. As women try on perfumes in an upscale department store, the narrator continues: "Our egos are best nourished by a well-placed investment in real luxury goods—what you might call discreetly conspicuous waste."[2] "Waste not, want not," Benjamin Franklin once admonished. But the new slogan might have been Waste More, Want More. Almost overnight, the good life became the *goods* life.

PLANNED OBSOLESCENCE

"The immediate postwar period does represent a huge change in the kinds of attitudes that Americans have had about consumption," says historian Susan Strasser, the author of *Satisfaction Guaranteed*.[3] "Discreetly conspicuous waste" got another boost from what marketers called "planned obsolescence." Products were made to last only a short time so that they would have to be replaced frequently (adding to sales), or they were continually upgraded, more commonly in style than in quality. It was an idea that began long before World War II with Gillette disposable razors, and it soon took on a larger life.

Henry Ford, who helped start the '20s consumer boom by paying his workers a then-fantastic five dollars a day, was a bit of a conservative about style, once promising that consumers could have one of his famous Model T's in any color as long as it was black. But just before the Great Depression, General Motors introduced the idea of the annual model change. It was an idea that took off after World War II. Families were encouraged to buy a new car every year. "They were saying the car you had last year won't do anymore, and it won't do anymore because it doesn't look right," Strasser explains. "There's now a new car and that's what we want to be driving."[4]

INSTANT MONEY

Of course, none but the richest Americans could afford to plunk down a couple thousand dollars on a new car every year, or on any of the other new consumer durables that families wanted. Never mind. There were ways to finance your spending spree. "The American consumer! Each year you consume fantastic amounts of food, clothing, housing, amusements, appliances, and services of all kinds. This mass consumption makes you the most powerful giant in the land,"[5] pipes the narrator in a cute mid-'50s animated film from the National Consumer Finance Association.

"I'm a giant," boasts Mr. American Consumer, as he piles up a massive mountain of stuff. And how does he afford it? Loans, says the film: "Consumer loans in the hands of millions of Americans add up to tremendous purchasing power. Purchasing power that creates consumer demand for all kinds of goods and services that mean a rising standard of living throughout the nation." You can probably already hear the drum roll in your mind.

A TV ad for Bank of America made about the same time shows a shaking animated man and asks, "Do you have money jitters? Ask the obliging Bank of America for a jar of soothing instant money. M-O-N-E-Y. In the form of a convenient personal loan." The animated man drinks from a coffee cup full of dollars, stops shaking, and jumps for joy.[6]

It was a buy now, pay later world, only to become more so with the coming of credit cards in the sixties.

AMERICA THE MALLED

During the 1950s and 1960s, the rush to suburbia continued (it hasn't stopped yet). In 1946 a government program, the G.I. Bill, spurred it along. Ten years later, another government program did the same. President Dwight D. Eisenhower announced the beginning of a vast federal subsidy to create a nationwide freeway system. In part the system was sold as national defense—roads big enough to run our tanks on if the Russians invaded. The new freeways encouraged a mass movement to even wider rings of suburbs. All were built around the automobile and massive shopping centers, whose windows, according to one early '60s promotional film, reflected "a happy-go-spending world."[7]

"Shopping malls," the film continues, "see young adults as in need of expansion [interesting choice of words]. People who buy in large quantities and truck it away in their cars. It's a big market!" The narrator continues gushingly: "These young adults, shopping with the same determination that brought them to suburbs in the first place, are the goingest part of a nation of wheels, living by the automobile." Going to the mall was, for these determined consumers, an adventure worthy of Mount Everest, at least according to the film, which later describes the consumers' hardest challenge as finding their cars again in the mall's giant parking lots.

By 1970, Americans were spending four times as much time shopping as were Europeans. The malls encouraged Sunday shopping, then as rare in the United States as it still is in Europe. To its everlasting credit, the Sears, Roebuck Company opposed opening its store on Sunday, on the grounds that it wanted "to give our employees their Sabbath." But by 1969 it caved to the competition, opening on Sundays "with great regret and some sense of guilt."[8]

THE BOX THAT ENLIGHTENED

The big economic boom wasn't the result of any one thing. A series of synchronous events made it possible: pent-up demand, government loans, expanded credit, suburbanization, longer shopping hours, and mallification. But perhaps no single cause was more responsible for the emerging postwar epidemic of affluenza than the ubiquitous box that found its way into most American homes by the 1950s.

Television showed everyone how the other half (the upper half) lived. Its programs were free, made possible only because of the sale of time to advertisers who hawked their wares during and between the features. Crude at first, the ads became increasingly sophisticated—both visually, because of improving technologies, and psychologically, as batteries of experts probed the human mind to find out how to sell most effectively.

The early TV ads relied a great deal on humor—"Any girl can find a good husband, but finding the right man to do your hair, now that's a problem." Like many print and radio ads before them, they played on anxieties about personal embarrassment, warning of horrors like "B.O." (body odor). But mostly, they just showed us all the neat stuff just waiting to be bought.

On TV, convenience was the new ideal, disposability the means. "Use it once and throw it away." Out of sight, out of mind. TV dinners in disposable aluminum trays. "No deposit, no return" bottles. Dinnertime, and the livin' is easy. People danced onscreen with products. The airwaves buzzed with jingles. John still can't stop singing one that must have been on the tube every night when he was a kid: "You'll wonder where the yellow went, when you brush your teeth with Pepsodent."

AFFLUENZA'S DISCONTENTS

Of course, not everyone wanted Americans to catch affluenza. "Buy only what you really need and cannot do without," President Harry Truman once said on TV. By the early '50s, educational films were warning schoolkids about overspending. But they were, in a word, boring. No match for TV's wit and wizardry. In one, a nerdy-looking character called Mr. Money teaches students to save. One can imagine the collective classroom yawns it produced. In another, the voice of God says, "You're guilty of pouring your money down a rat hole. You forget that it takes a hundred pennies to make a dollar." The visuals are equally uncompelling: a hand puts a dollar in a hole in the dirt labeled—you guessed it—"Rat hole."[9]

Meanwhile, far-sighted social critics from both left and right warned that America's new affluence was coming at a high price. Conservative economist Wilhelm Ropke feared that "we neglect to include in the calculation of these potential gains in the supply of material goods the possible losses of a non-material kind."[10] Centrist Vance Packard lambasted advertising (*The Hidden Persuaders,* 1957), keeping up with the Joneses (*The Status Seekers,* 1959) and planned obsolescence (*The Waste Makers,* 1960). And the liberal John Kenneth Galbraith suggested that a growing economy fulfilled needs it created itself, leading to no improvement in happiness. Our emphasis on "private opulence," he said, led to "public squalor"—declining transit systems, schools, parks, libraries, and air and water quality. Moreover, it left "vast millions of hungry and discontented people in the world. Without the promise of relief from that hunger and privation, disorder is inevitable."[11]

The affluent society had met its members' real material needs, Galbraith argued at the end of his famous book. Now it had other, more important things to do. "To furnish a barren room is one thing," he wrote. "To continue to crowd in furniture until the foundation buckles is quite another. To have failed to solve the problem of producing goods would have been to continue man in his oldest and most grievous misfortune. But to fail to see that we have solved it, and to fail to proceed thence to the next tasks, would be fully as tragic."[12]

YOUNG AMERICA STRIKES BACK

During the following decade, many young Americans sensed that the critics of consumerism were right. Raised in the suburbs, they rejected the suburban lifestyle with its "little boxes made of ticky-tacky" (as songwriter Malvina Reynolds called them), where everyone grew up to be "just the same." During Berkeley's tumultuous Free Speech Movement of 1964, its leader, Mario Savio, attacked a school system that wanted students to be "well-behaved children in a chrome-plated consumer's paradise."[13] A new "counterculture" arose, rebuking materialism. Thousands of young Americans left the cities for agricultural communes practicing simple living, the most successful of which still survive.

Many of the young questioned American reliance on the growth of the gross national product as a measure of the nation's health. In that they were supported by the popular senator Robert F. Kennedy. During his 1968 campaign for president (which ended when he was assassinated) Bobby Kennedy stressed that

> we will find neither national purpose nor personal satisfaction in a mere continuation of economic progress, in an endless amassing of worldly goods. . . . The gross national product includes the destruction of the redwoods and the death of Lake Superior.[14]

By the first Earth Day, April 22, 1970, young Americans were questioning the impact of the consumer lifestyle on the planet itself. Leading environmentalists like David Brower, founder of Friends of the Earth, were warning that the American dream of endless growth was not sustainable.

Then, in 1974, a nationwide oil shortage caused many people to wonder if we might run out of resources. Energy companies responded as they still do today, by calling for more drilling. "Rather than foster conservation," writes historian Gary Cross, "President Gerald Ford supported business demands for more nuclear power plants, offshore oil drilling, gas leases and drilling on federal lands," as well as "the relaxation of clean air standards."[15]

CARTER'S LAST STAND

But Ford's successor, Jimmy Carter, disagreed, promoting conservation and alternative energy sources. Carter went so far as to question the American dream in his famous "national malaise" speech of 1979. "Too many of us now tend to worship self-indulgence and consumption," Carter declared. It was the last courageous stand any American president ever made against the spread of affluenza.

And it helped bring about Carter's defeat a year later. "Part of Jimmy Carter's failure," says historian David Shi, "was his lack of recognition of how deeply seated the high, wide, and handsome notion of economic growth and capital development had become in the modern American psyche."[16]

The Age of Affluenza had begun.

CHAPTER 19

The age of affluenza

Advertising separates our era from all earlier ones as little else does.

—CONSERVATIVE ECONOMIST
WILHELM ROPKE

Any space you take in visually, anything you hear, in the future will be branded.

—REGINA KELLY,
DIRECTOR OF STRATEGIC PLANNING,
SAATCHI AND SAATCHI ADVERTISING

It's morning in America," announced the 1984 TV commercials for Ronald Reagan, whose message that Americans could have their cake and eat it too had overwhelmed the cautious conservationist Jimmy Carter four years earlier. And indeed, it was morning, the dawning, you might say, of the Age of Affluenza. Despite economic ups and downs, the last twenty years of the twentieth century would witness a commercial expansion unparalleled in history. Those Reagan commercials, small towns and smiling people in golden light, seem quaint now, more like the sunset of an old era than the morning of a new one. For one thing, there are no ads to be seen anywhere in the America pictured in those political commercials, no billboards, no product being sold except Reagan. That's not America anymore.

Reagan's decade may have been that of supply-side economics, but it was also the decade of demand creation. Yuppies were made, not born. "Greed is good," chirruped Wall Street's Ivan Boesky. The message of Reagan's first inaugural ball and Nancy's $15,000 dress was clear: It's cool to consume and flaunt it. The tone of '80s advertising echoed the sentiment: "Treat Yourself. You *Deserve* a Break Today. You're Worth It." Look out for number one.

Since 1980, few industries have grown as fast as advertising. Its importance is underscored by a little-known fact: Madison Avenue real estate is the priciest on the planet. A mere ten square feet of space there—smaller than the size of a single bed—now rents for an astonishing $6,500 a year!

ADFLUENZA

That advertising's prime purpose is to promote affluenza is hardly a secret, as even its prime proponents have frequently stated that in different words. As Pierre Martineau, marketing director for the *Chicago Tribune*, put it back in 1957, "Advertising's most important social function is to integrate the individual into our present-day American high-speed consumption economy."[1] "The average individual doesn't make anything," wrote Martineau in his classic text *Motivation in Advertising*. "He buys everything, and our economy is geared to the faster and faster tempo of his buying, *based on wants which are created by advertising in large degree*" (emphasis in original). This was no critic of advertising expressing himself, but one of its most prominent practitioners.

"Our American level of living is the highest of any people in the world," Martineau went on to say, "because our standard of living is the highest, meaning that our *wants* are the highest. In spite of those intellectuals who deplore the restlessness and the dissatisfaction in the wake of those new wants created by advertising and who actually therefore propose to restrict the process, it must be clear that the well-being of our entire system depends on how much motivation is supplied the consumer to make him continue wanting." Were Pierre Martineau still alive, he would doubtless be proud to see how much motivation is now supplied to keep consumers "wanting."

If, as the old saying goes, "a man's home is his castle," then Madison Avenue has battering rams galore. Two-thirds of the space in our newspapers is devoted to advertising. Nearly half the mail we receive is selling something.

THE HIGH COST OF MOTIVATION

You could call it Couch Potato Blight. The average American will spend nearly two years watching TV commercials over a lifetime.[2] A child may see a million of them before reaching the age of twenty. More time is devoted to them now—the average half hour of commercial TV has ten minutes of commercials, up from six minutes two decades ago. And there are more of them—faster editing (to beat the remote-control clicker) and the increasing cost of commercial time has shortened the length of the average ad.

Ads are phenomenally expensive: a typical thirty-second national TV commercial costs nearly $300,000 to produce—that's $10,000 per second! By contrast, production costs for an entire hour of prime-time public television are about the same—$300,000, or $83 a second. Commercial network programming is somewhat more expensive but can't hold a candle to the cost of the ads. Is it any wonder that some people say they're the best thing on TV?

Moreover, it costs a company hundreds of thousands of dollars every time its ads are broadcast during national prime-time programming. In fact, thirty-second slots during the Super Bowl have sold for as much as $1.6 million each. Advertising, the prime carrier of the affluenza virus, is a $217-billion-a-year industry, and it is growing at a rate more than twice the average rate of the economy as a whole.[3]

It's paying off. In 1997, when NPR's Scott Simon asked teenagers at a Maryland mall what they were buying, they ran off a list of brand names: Donna Karan, Calvin Klein, Tommy Hilfiger, American Eagle. A recent study showed that the average American can identify fewer than ten types of plants but recognizes hundreds of corporate logos.

WELCOME TO LOGOTOPIA

In the effort to create demand, marketers seek to place commercial messages everywhere. Today, outdoor advertising is a $5-billion-a-year industry (and it's growing at a rate of 10 percent a year), with more than a billion spent on billboards alone. "Outdoor advertising is red-hot right now," says Brad Johnson in *Advertising Age.* "There's a shortage of space available."[4]

Thirty-five years after Lady Bird Johnson's Beautify America campaign, our landscape is filled with more billboards than ever. Ad critic Laurie Mazur calls them "litter on a stick." "From a marketer's perspective, billboards are perfect," she says. "You can't turn them off. You can't click them with remote control."[5]

Mazur points out that marketers themselves say the ad environment has become "cluttered," so smart sellers look for ever-newer places to put ads. Schools, as discussed in chapter 7, "Dilated Pupils," are one target, reached in a myriad of ways, including corporate logos in math text books: "If Joe has thirty Oreo™ cookies and eats fifteen, how many does he have left?" Of course there's a big picture of Oreo cookies on the page. The publisher might want to add another question: How many cavities does Joe have?

Hollywood films offer sliding scales for product placements, as Mazur points out: "$10,000 to have the product appear in the film, $30,000 to have a character hold the product. In *Other People's Money*, Danny DeVito holds a box of doughnuts, looks into the camera, and says, 'If I can't depend on Dunkin' Donuts, who can I depend on?'"[6]

"Advertising is just permeating every corner of our society," says Michael Jacobson, coauthor with Mazur of *Marketing Madness*. "When you're watching a sports event, you see ads in the stadium. You see athletes wearing logos. You see ads in public restrooms. Some police cars have ads. There are ads in holes on golf courses. And there are thousands of people who are trying to think of one more place to put an ad where nobody has yet put the ad."[7]

Daniel Schifrin has found such a place. He started a Silicon Valley company called Autowraps. Drivers make their cars available as rolling billboards, sporting advertising logos. Schifrin pays their owners $400 a month but tracks them by satellite to make sure they drive to the sorts of places where target audiences will see the ads. They are required to drive at least a thousand miles a month. Hucksters, start your engines.[8]

THE MARKETER'S MOON

The extreme idea for advertising placement, says Michael Jacobson, "is the bill-board that was proposed for outer space that would project logos about the size of the moon that would be visible to practically everyone on earth."[9]

When the moon fills the sky like a big pizza pie, it's—Domino's! Imagine a romantic walk at night in the light of the full . . . logo.

For now, the idea of logos in outer space is still a marketer's pipe dream, but, says Jacobson, "what is the limit? Maybe outer space. But down here on earth we're will-ing to accept just about everything."

Perhaps the biggest expansion of commercialism in the Age of Affluenza is occur-ring on the Internet. Ads are popping up like mushrooms on the information high-way. While still small compared to total advertising dollars, spending on Internet ads rose 43 percent from the second quarter of 2003 to the second quarter of 2004, according to the Interactive Advertising Bureau and PricewaterhouseCoopers. And of course, this doesn't even consider the phenomenal increase in e-mail spam that all of us tear our hair out over. What was hailed as an educator's Eden has become a seller's paradise instead, as e-commerce attracts billions of investment and adver-tising dollars.

There is, admittedly, a bright spot in this grim scenario. We don't know about you, but since President George W. Bush signed the Do Not Call legislation in 2003, and we signed on, we've stopped getting those irritating dinnertime calls from peo-ple who want to clean our carpets or sell us something we don't need. For this, Mr. President, we thank you! Apparently, even market-worshipping legislators were tired of having their dinners interrupted. Now, if they could only ban Internet spam!

HYPERCOMMERCIALISM

Our hypercommercial era is one in which images are everywhere and "image," as tennis star Andre Agassi says in the sunglasses commercial, "is everything." The daily bombardment of advertising images leaves us forever dissatisfied with our own appearance and that of our real-life partners. "Advertising encourages us to meet nonmaterial needs through material ends," Mazur says. "It tells us to buy their product because we'll be loved, we'll be accepted. And also it tells us that we are not lovable and acceptable without buying their product."[10] To be lovable and acceptable is to have the right image. Authenticity be damned.

We live in what Susan Faludi calls an ornamental culture, which "encourages peo-ple to play almost no functional public roles, only decorative and consumer ones."

The Consumption Spike

Gross world product or purchasing equivalent, in trillions of dollars

The amount of money spent on advertising and marketing in 1997 (close to $1 trillion) exceeds the total GDP of the world just a little more than a century earlier. **1998**

The average individual in a German, Dutch, or American household uses up 45 to 85 tons of natural resources per year—the equivalent of 300 shopping bags per week. Much of it ends up as industrial waste or pollution.

The global economy expands as much in each year now as it did in any century prior to 1900. **1990**

In the 1980s and 1990s, Americans shift from keeping up with the Joneses to keeping up with the wealthy. The rest of the world tries to keep up with the Americans.

1980

1970

Explosion of global media and advertising drives up per-capita demand faster. Number of TVs in the world leaps from under 5 million in 1950 to 900 million in the mid-1990s.

Americans strive to "keep up with the Joneses" in the 1950s; in 1958, John Kenneth Galbraith's *Affluent Society* is published. **1960**

As human population begins to spike, consumption follows—at first in parallel, then even steeper, as industrialization spreads and increases per-capita demand. **1950**

1925

1900

1820

Year

Note: Values are in 1997 dollars.

Source: Courtesy Ed Ayres, from the book *God's Last Offer* (New York: Four Walls Eight Windows, 1999). 39.

"Constructed around celebrity and image, glamour and entertainment, marketing and consumerism," writes Faludi, ornamental culture "is a ceremonial gateway to nowhere. Its essence is not just the selling act but the selling of self, and in this quest every man is essentially on his own, a lone sales rep marketing his own image."[11]

Back in 1958, a prominent conservative economist and staunch defender of the free enterprise system warned that the twentieth century might well end up being known as "the Age of Advertising." Wilhelm Ropke feared that if commercialism were "allowed to predominate and to sway society in all its spheres," the results would be disastrous in many ways. As the cult of selling grows in importance, Ropke wrote, "every gesture of courtesy, kindness and neighborliness is degraded into a move behind which we suspect ulterior motives."[12] A culture of mutual distrust arises.

"The curse of commercialization is that it results in the standards of the market spreading into regions which should remain beyond supply and demand," Ropke added. "This vitiates the true purposes, dignity and savor of life and thereby makes it unbearably ugly, undignified and dull. Think of Mother's Day. The most tender and sacred human relationship is turned into a means of sales promotion by advertising experts and made to turn the wheels of business."

Only by limiting the scope of its reach, claimed Ropke, could the free market system be expected to continue to serve the greater good. Extreme commercialization, the very sine qua non of our era, would, if not kept in check, "destroy the free economy by the blind exaggeration of its principle."

CHAPTER 20

Is there a (real) doctor in the house?

We have transformed information into a form of garbage.

—NEIL POSTMAN

In the public relations industry, the idea is to manage the outrage, not the hazard.

—SHARON BEDER, GLOBAL SPIN

What happens when we ignore the symptoms of a disease? It usually gets worse. That's why affluenza is steadily spreading around the planet. Although symptoms like the stress of excess, resource exhaustion, and social scars are right in our faces, we tend to look the other way—told over and over again that the market will provide. But will it?

Author and "adbuster" Kalle Lasn tells a tale about a large wedding party that takes place in a spacious suburban backyard. The party oozes affluence and "the good life": the live music is great, and everyone dances with abandon. The problem is that they're dancing on top of an old septic system, which causes the pipes to burst. "Raw sewage rises up through the grass," writes Lasn, "and begins to cover everyone's shoes. If anyone notices, they don't say anything. The champagne flows, the music continues, until finally a little boy says, 'It smells like shit!' And suddenly everyone realizes they're ankle deep in it."[1]

How many million Americans are wheezing with affluenza, yet remain stubbornly in denial? "Those who have clued in apparently figure it's best to ignore the shit and just keep dancing," Lasn concludes. Meanwhile, the companies liable for the damages admit the pipes have cracked but try to convince us there's nothing to worry about.

According to some trend watchers, at least forty million Americans are ready for recovery programs to beat affluenza. But where can we turn for the advice we'll need? There seem to be as many quacks and spin doctors out there as real doctors. With a strict policy of concealing their funding sources (as well as their planets of origin), the quack scientists do their best to make the world "safe from democracy." The first step is to encourage us to do nothing, to just keep ignoring the symptoms. They tell us in voices that sound self-assured, "Go back to sleep, the facts are still uncertain, everything's fine. Technology will provide. Just relax and enjoy yourself."

'TOXIC SLUDGE IS GOOD FOR YOU'

We all know how pervasive advertising is. But in fact, *we* pick up the tab for advertising in the products we buy—at least $600 a year per capita. Yet as John Stauber, the coauthor of *Toxic Sludge Is Good for You,* comments, "Few people really understand the other dimension of marketing—an undercover public relations industry that creates and perpetuates our commercial culture."[2] (In other words, our affluenza.) What is PR, exactly? According to Stauber, it's covert culture shaping and opinion spinning. Not only do PR professionals alter our perceptions, but they also finesse the political and cultural influence that ushers those perceptions into the mainstream. Unreported by the blindfolded eyes of the media, PR-managed initiatives are often signed into law and adopted as standard operating procedures while the public's civic attention is diverted by the most current scandal, crime, or catastrophe.

"The best PR is never noticed" is an unwritten slogan of an industry whose arsenal includes backroom politics, fake grassroots activism, organized censorship, and imitation news. The weapon of choice is a kind of stun gun that fires invisible bullets of disinformation. You can't remember how you formed a certain opinion or belief, but you find yourself willing to fight for it. For example, a popular corporate strategy staged by contracted PR firms is to form citizen advisory panels. This technique makes people feel included rather than polluted. Citizens are carefully chosen to attend catered lunches around the corporate conference table to discuss community issues.

Predictably, familiarity can breed content. One community advisory panel was content to approve a new waste incinerator and defend it vocally at a local hearing. "You can't buy that kind of help at any price," comments Joel Makower, editor of the *Green Business Letter*.[3]

Similarly, on the advice of contracted PR experts, many corporations fund and sponsor the very environmental groups that have dogged them for years. This "absorb the enemy" tactic accomplishes several things at once. It gives the company a buffed-up, green-washed image, and it distracts the environmental opponent/partner. Said one corporate partner, "We keep them so busy they don't have time to sue us."

"Another basic tactic is what I call book burning," Stauber says. "PR firms are hired to cast dark shadows on certain books. They often obtain book tour itineraries from inside sources and use a variety of tactics to sabotage the tours." For example, Jeremy Rifkin's tour for *Beyond Beef*, a critique of the meat industry, was derailed by fake phone calls, allegedly from the author's publicist, canceling each speaking appearance.

Conversely, sometimes PR firms are hired to infiltrate the ranks of everyday life and "talk up" products in casual conversation. A classic case is the campaign orchestrated by camera-phone pioneers at Sony Ericsson, which hired sixty actors in ten cities to appear in public places and ask strangers, "Would you mind taking my picture?" Then, of course, the actors pointed out the various features of the camera phone that made their new gadget so special, and so hip—converting a "chance" meeting into guerrilla marketing.[4]

Proctor & Gamble uses similar tactics to peddle soaps, toothpaste, and diapers. Somehow, this company has enrolled a volunteer army of 240,000 or more enthusiastic teenagers (a battalion called Tremor) who advertise and influence by word of mouth. Why do they do it? Apparently because it gives them a sense of being in the forefront—knowing about a new product, for example, before others do. They like having access, being influential, being part of the "shaping" of opinion, and they like the free samples.

The founder of another word-of-mouth agency, BzzAgent, has also discovered the awesome power of personal persuasion. "Our goal was to find a way to capture honest word of mouth," says David Balter, BzzAgent's founder, "and to build a network that would turn passionate customers into brand evangelists." His agents (who can redeem points to get prizes but typically don't) just like to tell others what they are reading and what restaurant they've discovered and what gizmo they just bought. The company has more than 60,000 in its eager, enthusiastic ranks, and for a typical twelve-week campaign involving a thousand agents, it rakes in $95,000 or more.[5]

Who can you trust, now, when your best friend, or your mother, might be a covert commercial agent?

HOW MONEY TALKS

One of the most effective and powerful PR tactics is to fund "front groups" and give them very friendly, responsible-sounding names, like the American Council on Science and Health, whose experts defend petrochemical companies, the nutritional value of fast foods, and pesticides. The mission of front groups is to supply the "right" information on a product or industry and debunk the "wrong" information. As Sharon Beder writes in *Global Spin*,

> The American Council on Science and Health is funded by Burger King, Coca-Cola, NutraSweet, Monsanto, Dow, and Exxon, among others. As in other front groups, the organization's scientists pose as independent experts to promote the corporate causes. The group's members portray themselves as moderates, often using words like 'reasonable,' 'sensible,' and 'sound.' They downplay the dangers of environmental problems while emphasizing the costs of solving them.[6]

Front groups are staunch defenders of the rights of Americans, such as the right to smoke (the National Smokers Alliance); the right to have employee accidents (Workplace Health and Safety Council, an employer organization that lobbies for the weakening of safety standards); the right to pay more for less health care (the Coalition for Health Insurance Choices); the right to choose large, fuel-inefficient cars (the Coalition for Vehicle Choice); and the right to dismantle ecosystems for profit (the Wise Use Movement). Front groups portray themselves as champions of free enterprise—strongholds of fairness and common sense—an image that helps their PR products get circulated in influential circles.

Stauber, a director of the organization PRWatch, first became involved in watch-dogging the public relations industry when he was researching biotechnology through internal documents and interviews with industry insiders. "We saw strong evidence of collusion between Monsanto, a manufacturer of biotech products, and various government agencies and professional organizations," he said. "The *Journal of the American Medical Association* urged doctors to wave the flag for genetic engineering and pump up the new industry. Government agencies like the FDA and USDA did their part by working with Monsanto to overcome farmer and consumer opposition to the emerging products. Government agencies are supposed to be watchdogs, but too often they are more like lap dogs."[7]

INVASION OF THE MIND-SNATCHERS

In effect, America's PR professionals create stage sets in which the rest of us play-act our lives. Like the main character in the movie *The Truman Show,* we've never doubted that the sets are real. Corporations alone contract $15 billion to $20 billion in PR campaigns annually—campaigns that create consumer culture, buy political agendas, and "spin" scientific opinion. As the average underpaid journalist knows, public relations—not journalism—is the profession to be in if you want to live in one of "those" neighborhoods. "Journalism students—even at the best colleges and universities—are more likely to graduate and work in PR and business communications than as journalists," Stauber says. "The schools combine PR and journalism classes as if they were one and the same." Fact is, the kids are going where the money is.

The PR industry cut its teeth in the 1920s on campaigns that promoted tobacco and leaded gasoline—products whose health effects badly needed to be swept under the carpet. Mark Dowie describes a classic perception coup executed by PR pioneer Edward Bernays in 1929: "On the surface it seemed like an ordinary publicity stunt for 'female emancipation.' A contingent of New York debutantes marched down Fifth Avenue in the 1929 Easter Parade, each openly lighting and smoking cigarettes, their so-called 'torches of liberty.' It was the first time in the memory of most Americans that any woman who wasn't a prostitute had been seen smoking in public."[8]

Bernays made sure publicity photos of the models appeared in the worldwide press, and the tobacco industry quickly added sex appeal to its glorious if deadly parade through the twentieth century. Responding to the "1954 emergency"— involving medical disclosures on the hazards of smoking—the tobacco industry hired PR firm Hill & Knowlton to launch a smoke-and-mirrors campaign to meet the enemy head-on. Among many other tactics, the firm combed 2,500 medical journals for any inconclusive or contrary findings about tobacco's health effects and then showcased these gleanings of doubt in a booklet sent to more than 200,000 doctors, members of Congress, and news professionals.[9] Tactics like these became standard procedures of the PR industry. "In a world of manufactured reality, the *perception* of a hazardous product or accident is what needs to be managed, not the hazard itself,"[10] Beder explains.

GETTING THE LEAD IN

A similar tactic was used in the 1920s to promote leaded gasoline (ethyl). The mission was to boost both automobile performance and the profits of General Motors, DuPont, and Standard Oil. These allies soothed and massaged the American public's justified fear of leaded gasoline by performing health-effects research in-house, with precedent-setting approval from the federal government. Word from the corporate labs was "no problem," even as factory workers making ethyl were dying by the dozens. A 1927 ad in *National Geographic* urged, "Ride with Ethyl in a high-compression motor and get the thrill of a lifetime." The overt message was "Don't let others pass you by," but the hidden tag line was ". . . even if it kills you."[11]

FLASHFLOODS OF INFORMATION

There's no shortage of information in America. Search for just about any keyword on the Internet and the cyber-hounds will retrieve gigabytes of "matches" of all shapes and flavors. It's true that a search for "art depicting the Madonna" may yield a colorful, profanity-spiked quote from a pop singer-actress by the same name—but hey, isn't that information too? Every day, on average, Americans dodge 3,000 commercial messages, each of them shouting louder or purring more seductively than the last. Sound bites, fun facts, and bad-news nuggets also compete for our attention, along with the million words a week some of us process at work. Getting just the information we need is like trying to take a sip of water from a fire hose.

Even more disturbing than the flood of information is its *quality*. We try to base intelligent civic, family, and marketplace decisions on vested-interest information. No wonder we can't shake our affluenza—the economy is programmed for sickness. Drug companies teach us how to overcome depression, and pesticide companies tell farmers how much pesticide to use. In the mania of media, good news is no news because it doesn't "work" on TV. The quality of our information is spiked throughout all sectors of our society, but we're forced to drink it anyway because it's the only information we can get.

'GREENING THE EARTH WITH GLOBAL WARMING'

If the true facts about global warming are thought of as the flow of a mighty river, the average American ends up with only a cupful. The complexity of global warming makes a third of the information unavailable even to scientists, who tell us they don't know enough yet about the relationships among oceans, biomass, and atmospheric physics. They do know without any doubt that CO_2 levels have already increased by about 30 percent since the Industrial Revolution began, and that the decade from 1990 to 2000 was the warmest on record. They've known for a hundred years that a blanket of greenhouse gases like CO_2 can warm the planet the same way a car with rolled-up windows overheats in a parking lot.

However, PR firms and the PR environmental offices of oil, mining, and automobile companies have a different story to tell—a story that sends a large portion of the information flow into a calculated whirlpool. Their mission is to craft "customized" information to create doubt, confuse the public, and protect the client's profits. Scientists are found whose skeptical views support the fossil-fuel industry. These "third-party experts" have an appearance of objectivity that sometimes fades when the scientists reveal, under oath, that their research funding comes from utilities and fossil-fuel consortiums. Even if the earth *is* warming, they maintain, it could be a natural occurrence. In a recent *Frontline-Nova* program, *What's Up with the Weather?*, one fossil-fueled scientist summarized his stance on global warming: "Americans are moving to the Sun Belt by the millions," he said, "which proves we like warm climates." The question is, do we also like the spread of tropical diseases, drought, hurricanes, and economic disruption, and a rising sea level?

A video titled *Greening the Planet Earth* exposed many a congressional staff office to fantasy science. Produced by the Greening Earth Society, the industry-funded

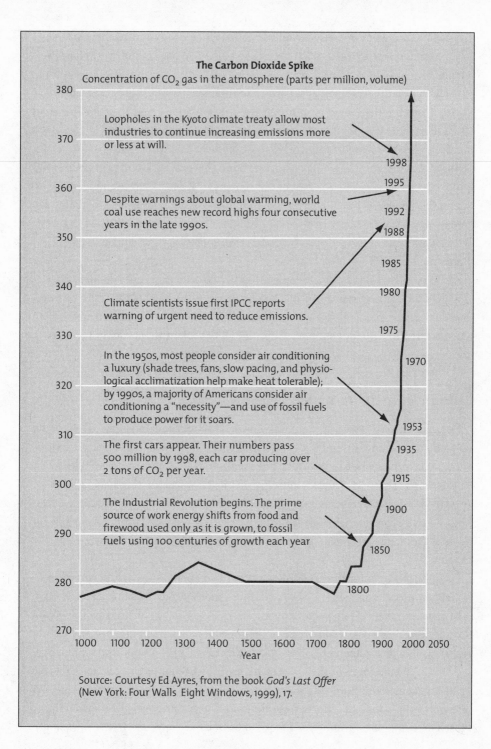

The Carbon Dioxide Spike
Concentration of CO_2 gas in the atmosphere (parts per million, volume)

Loopholes in the Kyoto climate treaty allow most industries to continue increasing emissions more or less at will.

Despite warnings about global warming, world coal use reaches new record highs four consecutive years in the late 1990s.

Climate scientists issue first IPCC reports warning of urgent need to reduce emissions.

In the 1950s, most people consider air conditioning a luxury (shade trees, fans, slow pacing, and physiological acclimatization help make heat tolerable); by 1990s, a majority of Americans consider air conditioning a "necessity"—and use of fossil fuels to produce power for it soars.

The first cars appear. Their numbers pass 500 million by 1998, each car producing over 2 tons of CO_2 per year.

The Industrial Revolution begins. The prime source of work energy shifts from food and firewood used only as it is grown, to fossil fuels using 100 centuries of growth each year

Year

Source: Courtesy Ed Ayres, from the book *God's Last Offer*
(New York: Four Walls Eight Windows, 1999), 17.

program begins with dramatic narration: "The year 2085. The atmospheric level of carbon dioxide has doubled to 540 parts per million. What kind of world have we created?"

"A better world," answers a corporate-funded scientist. "A more productive world. Plants are the basis for all productivity on earth. . . . And they're going to be much more effective, much more efficient when the earth is warmer".[12] (Never mind that two thousand of the world's most eminent scientists signed a statement saying global warming will be a catastrophe and that a 2004 UN report projects a temperature rise of up to 10 degrees Fahrenheit by 2100.) With pseudoscience like that of the Greening Earth Society in hand, fossil-fueled politicians are equipped to create happy-face scenarios about abundant cotton fields and prolific citrus trees. Who knows, maybe ferns three stories tall and, someday, the reappearance of dinosaurs—wouldn't that be cool?

Well, no, not really. Street theater recently performed in Australia illustrates why: melting ice sculptures of kangaroos and koalas are symbols that the warmest decade in recorded history is taking a heavy toll on the world's ecosystems, with more in the forecast. But somehow, despite all the scientific research, the message doesn't seem to be getting through.

GOOD NEWS IS NO NEWS

Journalists simultaneously supply and divert the information stream. Depending on a journalist's sources and biases, we may come away from a newspaper article knowing less than when we started (but thanks to the adjacent ads, we'll know where brassieres are on sale!). On perpetual deadline, and with a mandate for objectivity as well as controversy, journalists present both fabricated science-for-sale and its exaggerated, Chicken Little opposite. Effectively, they stage a "media clash of the titans." (Which expert will *you* root for, the kept professor or the chicken?)

Marching orders for the news media come from one of the half dozen or so remaining media conglomerates—including Time Warner, Viacom, Disney, GE's NBC Universal, and Comcast Corporation—whose CEOs dictate what's newsworthy and what's not (when you're one of them you buy newspaper companies like the rest of us buy newspapers). As recently as the 1980s, fifty corporations still had a slice of the media pie, but that elite clan has shrunk to an incestuous handful that invest in each other's companies, are fattened by the same group of mega-advertisers, and get in-the-field reports from the same large wire services. Alarmingly, these companies are pushing for the privatization—as opposed to the licensing—

of the airwaves. When these invisible yet very tangible wavelengths are controlled by a few multibillionaires, George Orwell's *1984* prophecies will be nearly complete: "The special function of certain Newspeak words . . . was not so much to express meanings as to destroy them."[13]

Because journalists are usually short on time, they are tempted to interview and quote experts conveniently supplied by PR firms through services like Profnet. PR shadow-journalists also supply press releases, video news releases, and radio scripts by the thousands. One company, PR Newswire, pumps out 100,000 news releases every year for fifteen thousand private clients. RadioUSA supplies broadcast-quality scripts to five thousand radio stations, and MediaLink distributes more than five thousand "video news releases" to TV stations every year, ready to be aired as is, free of charge.[14]

According to the former managing editors of the *Washington Post*, the *New York Times*, and the *Wall Street Journal*, at least 40 percent of the news in those papers is generated by "spin doctor" PR journalists.[15] Because newspaper, magazine, and many Internet writers must also compress their stories into a given number of inches, they have little room for context and complexity. The same is true of TV news, sandwiched between the commercials and crime reporting that make up a third of network news content. In 1968, the average interview sound bite was forty-two seconds; in 2000, the standard is eight seconds. Instead of political process, we get isolated events. Instead of context, we get vignettes about novelty and conflict. Information about change and reform takes too long to explain, so we are fed high-speed chases and newborn zoo animals instead. The goal is to keep us watching, not to keep us informed.

After journalists dumb down and abbreviate the remnants of the information stream, deep-pocketed advertisers divert more of the flow, often exerting enough pressure on editors to mop up a story altogether. Some advertisers issue policy statements to editors and news directors, requesting advance notice on stories that may put their products in an unfavorable light. Phone calls from CEOs of advertising companies are like delete buttons on editors' computers: There goes a story from the front page of tomorrow's paper, or the six o'clock news.

By the time the truth about global warming reaches the American citizen, it's been siphoned and filtered down to a trickle of questionable pop science.

DELAYED, DISCOUNTED, AND DILUTED FEEDBACK

Scientists like Donella Meadows have argued that we need to be sensitive to scientific signals—"feedback"—or we risk crashing our civilization into a brick wall.

Meadows compared our world to a speeding automobile on a slippery road: "The driver goes too fast for the brakes to work in time."[16]

At the scale of an entire society in overdrive, she observed that "decision makers in the system do not get, or believe, or act upon information that limits have been exceeded." Part of our dilemma is from insufficient feedback: We don't even realize that caution is necessary. Another part of the problem is the speed we're traveling: Our "pedal to the metal" economy is based on beliefs that resource supplies are limitless and that the earth can continually bounce back from abuse. These beliefs are in part scripted by public relations and advertising experts, just doing their jobs. What the heck, no harm done, right? Not exactly. Because of low-quality, incomplete information, we may be overlooking an obvious, and ominous, concept: The car will still achieve racecar speeds as always, even if the tank is almost empty.

PART THREE

Treatment

CHAPTER 21

The road to recovery

This situation imagined by *Affluenza* coproducer Vivia Boe has not occurred. Not yet.

Y ou're watching TV, in the middle of a program, when the screen goes black for a moment. The scene cuts to a breaking news story. A large crowd is gathered outside an expensive home with some equally pricey cars parked out front. A well-dressed family of four stands on the stairs, looking grim. One of the children is holding a white flag. The reporter, in hushed tones, speaks into his microphone: "We're here live at the home of the Joneses—Jerry and Janet Jones—the family we've all been trying to keep up with for years. Well, you can stop trying right now, because they have surrendered. Let's eavesdrop for a moment."

The shot changes, revealing a tired-looking Janet Jones, her husband's hand resting on her shoulder. Her voice cracks as she speaks: "It's just not worth it. We never see each other anymore. We're working like dogs. We're always worried about our kids, and we have so much debt we won't be able to pay it off for years. We give up. So please, stop trying to keep up with us." From the crowd someone yells, "So what will you do now?" "We're just going to try to live better on less," Janet replies. "So there you have it. The Joneses surrender," says the reporter. "And now for a commercial break."

The Joneses haven't really surrendered. Not yet. But millions of Americans are looking for ways to simplify their lives. And in the rest of this book, you'll learn about some of those ways, and how people are coming together to help create a more sustainable society, free from the clutches of affluenza. We suggest that you start by taking our affluenza self-test, an admittedly unscientific, but we think useful, means of determining whether you've got affluenza, and if so, how serious your case is.

OK, now the moment of truth. In the privacy of your own home, without anyone looking over your shoulder, take the following diagnostic quiz to see if you have affluenza or are susceptible to it. If you have it, reader, you're not alone! There's help available in this part of the book, so read on. If you don't have it, read on anyway to stay healthy.

AFFLUENZA SELF-DIAGNOSIS TEST

YES NO

❏ ❏ 1. Do you get bored unless you have something to consume (goods, food, media)?

❏ ❏ 2. Do you try to impress your friends with what you own, or where you vacation?

❏ ❏ 3. Do you ever use shopping as "therapy"?

❏ ❏ 4. Do you sometimes go to the mall just to look around, with nothing specific to buy?

❏ ❏ 5. Do you buy home-improvement products in a large chain store rather than the neighborhood hardware store?

YES NO

❏ ❏ 6. Have you ever gone on a vacation primarily to shop?

❏ ❏ 7. In general, do you think about things more than you think about people?

❏ ❏ 8. When you pay utility bills, do you ignore the amount of resources consumed?

❏ ❏ 9. Given the choice between a slight pay raise and a shorter workweek, would you choose the money?

❏ ❏ 10. Do you personally fill more than one large trash bag in a single week?

❏ ❏ 11. Have you ever lied to a family member about the amount you spent for a product?

YES NO

❏ ❏ 12. Do you frequently argue with family members about money?

❏ ❏ 13. Do you volunteer less than five hours a week to help other people?

❏ ❏ 14. Do you routinely compare the appearance of your lawn or home with others in your neighborhood?

❏ ❏ 15. Does each person in your house or apartment occupy more than 500 square feet of personal space?

❏ ❏ 16. Do you routinely gamble or buy lottery tickets?

❏ ❏ 17. Do you check your investments at least once a day?

❏ ❏ 18. Are any of your credit cards maxed out?

❏ ❏ 19. Do worries about debt cause you physical symptoms like headaches or indigestion?

❏ ❏ 20. Do you spend more time shopping every week than you do with your family?

❏ ❏ 21. Do you frequently think about changing jobs?

❏ ❏ 22. Have you had cosmetic surgery to improve your appearance?

❏ ❏ 23. Do your conversations often gravitate toward things you want to buy?

❏ ❏ 24. Are you sometimes ashamed about how much money you spend on fast food?

❏ ❏ 25. Do you sometimes weave back and forth in traffic to get somewhere faster?

❏ ❏ 26. Have you ever experienced road rage?

❏ ❏ 27. Do you feel like you're always in a hurry?

YES NO

❏ ❏ 28. Do you often throw away recyclable materials rather than take the time to recycle them?

❏ ❏ 29. Do you spend less than an hour a day outside?

❏ ❏ 30. Are you unable to identify more than three wildflowers that are native to your area?

❏ ❏ 31. Do you replace sports equipment before it's worn out in order to have the latest styles?

❏ ❏ 32. Does each member of your family have his or her own TV?

❏ ❏ 33. Is the price of a product more important to you than how well it was made?

❏ ❏ 34. Has one of your credit cards ever been rejected by a salesperson because you were over the limit?

❏ ❏ 35. Do you receive more than five mail-order catalogs a week?

❏ ❏ 36. Are you one of those consumers who almost never take a reusable bag to the grocery store?

❏ ❏ 37. Do you ignore the miles per gallon of gasoline your car gets?

❏ ❏ 38. Did you choose the most recent car you bought partly because it enhanced your self-image?

❏ ❏ 39. Do you have more than five active credit cards?

❏ ❏ 40. When you get a raise at work, do you immediately think about how you can spend it?

❏ ❏ 41. Do you drink more soft drink, by volume, than tap water?

❏ ❏ 42. Did you work more this year than last year?

YES NO

❑ ❑ 43. Do you have doubts that you'll be able to reach your financial goals?

❑ ❑ 44. Do you feel "used up" at the end of your workday?

❑ ❑ 45. Do you usually make just the minimum payment on credit card bills?

❑ ❑ 46. When you shop, do you often feel a rush of euphoria followed by anxiety?

YES NO

❑ ❑ 47. Do you sometimes feel as though your personal expenses are so demanding that you can't afford public expenses like schools, parks, and transit?

❑ ❑ 48. Do you have more stuff than you can store in your house?

❑ ❑ 49. Do you watch TV more than two hours a day?

❑ ❑ 50. Do you eat meat nearly every day?

SCORING YOUR RESULTS (GULP!)

Each "yes" answer carries a weight of two points. If you're uncertain as to your answer, or it's too close to call, give yourself one point. If you score:

0–25   You have no serious signs of affluenza, but keep reading to stay healthy

26–50   You are already infected—keep reading to boost your immune system.

51–75   Your temperature is rising quickly. Take two aspirin and read the next chapters very carefully.

76–100 You've got affluenza big time! See the doctor, reread the whole book, and take appropriate actions immediately. You may be contagious. There's no time to lose!

The Surrender of the Joneses

CHAPTER 22

Bed rest

Are you making a living or making a dying?

—JOE DOMINGUEZ

O K. You've taken the affluenza self-test and you're admitting to yourself you've got a few of the symptoms, maybe more than a few. You sit back in your chair, wipe the sweat from your brow, cough a couple of times, sneeze mightily, and rummage around for a thermometer. You're wondering, "What do I do now?"

Remember what the doctor once told you when you had a bad case of the flu? "Go home and go to bed, take some aspirin, and call me in the morning." (They don't want you to call them anymore in this age of HMOs, but that's a different issue.) Well, a case of affluenza calls for bed rest, too. We just define it a little differently. But the point is the same: Stop what you're doing. Stop now. Cut back. Take stock. Give yourself a break.

FORCED TO REASSESS

Sometimes we have to hit bottom to do that. Fred Brown was once upwardly mobile, the personnel director of a large company. He was earning $100,000 a year. On the outside, it looked as if he had everything—a great job, a big home, and a beautiful family. But on the inside, Fred felt like a prisoner in golden handcuffs. He worked long hours and found little time for his wife and two daughters. Then his marriage broke up. His job was stressful: It was his responsibility to tell other employees they'd been laid off. Then he got a frightening phone call. His own job had been eliminated. "It's a different experience on the receiving end than on the giving end," he says, remembering that call.[1]

Though he was forced into involuntary simplicity, it wasn't the loss of income that hit Fred hardest. It was the loss of security, "letting go of what I thought I was supposed to do with myself." At first, Fred sought other opportunities in his field, but to find them, he'd have to move to another part of the country. He was suddenly forced to stop and take stock of his life, and the more he thought about it, the more he realized his work hadn't been making him happy. "There came a point," he says, "when I realized I simply had to take the step off the cliff into the unknown."

In a stunning reversal of occupation and lifestyle, Fred went back to school and became a massage therapist. He earns about $20,000 a year and lives in a small apartment instead of the big house he once owned. But he is, he says, a much more contented man. And despite an 80 percent drop in income, he manages to save a little money and to pay off debts he ran up when he was making five times as much! More important, he has more free time and has renewed his relationship with his daughters. And he's doing work he finds intrinsically satisfying. "It turns out that for me living simply seems to be leading to more happiness. What a concept!" Fred says with a smile. "I'm thankful now that I was laid off, because I'm doing something that I love. It's what the Buddhists call *right livelihood*. It feels to me like I've found my right livelihood."

ONE LIFE TO LIVE

Sometimes the shock that forces us to reexamine our lives is even more devastating than the loss of a job, as Evy McDonald found out. A feisty, cheerful woman, Evy was determined early on to make her mark. "My goal," she remembers, "was to become the youngest female hospital administrator in the country." By 1980, she was close to success. Promotions and pay raises were coming her way often, and so was a lavish lifestyle. She bought a new house with each promotion, and a bigger car. "I talked about wanting to help people who were less fortunate than myself, but

I had seventy pairs of shoes and a hundred blouses. I had so much more than I needed."[2]

Then disaster struck. During an unusual bout of illness, Evy went to the doctor. Tests were done, and the doctor pronounced a grim verdict: Evy had a fatal disease—one from which there were no known survivors. She had, perhaps, only months to live. Stunned, she returned home, only to find that her house had been broken into and practically everything she owned had been stolen. And she had no insurance. Suddenly, both sick and possessionless, Evy was confronted with questions about the meaning of her life.

"Who did I want to be when I died?" she asked herself. "And what I discovered was that I didn't want to have the most things. What I wanted my life to be about was understanding love, understanding service, and feeling whole and complete." Miraculously perhaps, Evy's disease went into remission, and she recovered her strength and energy, though doctors have warned her that the disease could always come back.

"And on my road to health," she says now, "I saw that I needed to integrate my life. I needed to become a whole person, and part of that was bringing my financial life, how I spent my money, what I did with it, into alignment with my values and life purpose." It was then that she met a couple whose ideas moved her so deeply she spent most of the next two decades working with them.

YOUR MONEY OR YOUR LIFE

Joe Dominguez was a former stockbroker, Vicki Robin a former actress. Believers in frugality and simple living, they taught others to get out of debt, save money, and work on saving the world. John got to know Joe Dominguez and had a chance to interview him less than a year before Dominguez died in 1997. By that time, Joe was a frail man, weak from fighting cancer for many years. But he had not lost any of the passion, moral courage, and biting sense of humor that had helped him influence the lives of thousands of people.

During one interview, Joe described the turnaround in his thinking that occurred while he was still a stock market analyst. "When I was on Wall Street," he said, "I saw that people who had more money were not necessarily happier and that they had just as many problems as the folks that lived in my ghetto neighborhood [in Harlem] where I grew up. So it began to dawn on me that money didn't buy happiness, a very simple finding."[3] Simple indeed, but mighty rare in the Age of Affluenza.

Dominguez tried frugality. He found he enjoyed life more and he found a way to save so much that he was able to retire at the age of thirty-one and live on his interest (when he died, he was living on $8,000 a year). "A lot of people would ask me,

How did you do it?" Joe recalled. "How did you handle your finances so you're not an indentured slave like the rest of us?"

So with his newfound time, he set out to teach other people how to cut their spending sharply. He soon met Vicki Robin, who became his partner for the rest of his life. Says Robin, "I found that I needed to learn how to fix things, and I became fascinated with living life directly and developing my skills and capacities and ingenuity, rather than just earning more money and throwing money at problems."[4]

Together, Dominguez and Robin resettled in Seattle and went from conducting workshops in people's homes to producing an audiotape course that thousands of people ordered. "Then the publishing industry came to us to write a book," Joe remembered, "and the rest is history." The book, *Your Money or Your Life*, was published in 1992 and soon became a best seller that has sold nearly a million copies. If the letters from readers that Joe and Vicki have received are to be believed, *Your Money or Your Life* has transformed countless lives.

Dominguez contrasted *Your Money or Your Life* with the plethora of financial self-help books on the market. "It's not about making a killing in the stock market. It's not about how to buy real estate with no money down or anything of that sort. It's just the opposite. It's about how to handle your existing paycheck in a much more intelligent way that creates savings instead of leading you deeper and deeper into debt. It's the stuff our grandparents knew but we've forgotten or been taught to forget."

NINE STEPS TO FINANCIAL INTEGRITY

The book offers a nine-step "new frugality" program by which readers can get their financial feet back on the ground. When all the steps are followed, many higher-income readers find that they can achieve "financial independence" in a decade or so, allowing them to devote their time to work they find more meaningful than their current jobs. But even lower-income readers have found they can cut their expenses sharply. "In fact, the steps will be most useful to low-income people," Dominguez said, "because they're the ones who really need to know how to stretch a buck." Even following a few of the initial steps makes a big difference for many readers, who, on average, cut their spending by about 25 percent.

The initial steps include these four practices:

1. *Making peace with your past.* Calculate how much money you've earned in your life, and then what you have to show for it, your current net worth. You may be shocked at the total you've squandered, what we might call the toll of affluenza.

2. *Tracking your life energy.* Calculate your real hourly income by adding the hours spent in commuting and other work-related activities to your total work-week, and subtracting money spent on things needed for work (for example, business clothing and commuting). Your working time is an expenditure of your essential life energy. What are you getting for it and using it for?

3. *Tabulating all of your income and spending for one month.* Then keep track of every cent that comes into or goes out of your life.

4. *Asking yourself whether you've received real fulfillment for the life energy you have spent.* Joe and Vicki recommend plotting a "fulfillment curve," which rises as you spend for essential needs, then begins to fall as you spend on luxuries that aren't that important to you. The top of the curve is the point called "enough"—the point when you should stop spending and start saving.[5]

Doing these things means stopping your regular routine of activity to take stock. When you've got the flu, go to bed. When you're walking off the edge of a cliff, step back. When you've got affluenza, stop and think it over.

Joe Dominguez and Vicki Robin gave away all the money they earned from their popular book. Though she still lives extremely frugally, no one who knows Vicki Robin would ever consider her poor. Money can most certainly be a blessing, not a curse, she would argue, most of all when it is used to make the world a better place.

DOWNSHIFTING

Of course, the "Your Money or Your Life" model isn't the only bed to rest in. Thousands of Americans have found other helpful ways to slow down, cut back, and reassess. They've taken personal steps to live better on less income. *U.S. News & World Report* correspondent Amy Saltzman calls them "downshifters." A 1995 poll found that 86 percent of them say they are happier as a result. Only 9 percent report feeling worse.[6] People choosing to downshift can find tips for living more simply and less stressfully from dozens of journals and books, many of which are included in our bibliography. You can find others at your library or local bookstore. Web sites offer many more resources. Among the best are www.newdream.org (the Center for a New American Dream) and www.simpleliving.net (the Simple Living Network).

CHAPTER 23

Aspirin and chicken soup

Study circles are beginning to develop, newsletters, magazines, Internet resources on the computer and so on, and that is now beginning to create a culture of simplicity, a culture of ecological living.

—DUANE ELGIN,
author, *Voluntary Simplicity*

Think, for a moment, back to your childhood. You were sick in bed with the flu and mom came in with a little TLC. Words of comfort and maybe some medicine—aspirin for your fever, lozenges for your cough. And a bowl of hot chicken soup just to make you feel better. But the most important thing was having mom there with her sympathy, so you wouldn't have to suffer alone.

The same goes for affluenza. To conquer it, most of us need to know we're not all by ourselves in the battle. We need support from others who are fighting the disease as well. Every addiction nowadays seems to have support groups for its victims, and conquering affluenza, the addictive virus, may require them even more, because there isn't any social pressure to stop consuming—just the opposite. But there is, you might say, an AA for affluenza—the voluntary simplicity movement.

VOLUNTARY SIMPLICITY

"In our seventeen years of trend tracking," Gerald Celente of the Trends Research Institute said in 1996, "never have we seen an issue that's gaining such global acceptance as voluntary simplicity." He estimated that 5 percent of American baby boomers were practicing a "strong form of voluntary simplicity" and expected that number to reach 15 percent by the year 2000. "They're finding a cure for affluenza," Celente declared. "They get rid of their stress and they say, 'You know, I like living this way a lot better. How did I ever live like that before?'"[1]

Voluntary simplicity took a bit of a hit from the prosperity of the late 1990s. Nonetheless, millions of Americans are still attracted to the idea of simpler, more environmentally friendly living. The voluntary simplicity "movement," if one wants to call it that, is alive, well, and still growing, if not quite as quickly as Celente predicted. It's a movement that's centered in discussion groups of many varieties, beginning with the kind Cecile Andrews first started nearly a decade ago.

STUDY CIRCLES CAN SAVE THE WORLD

Andrews, a Seattle teacher with a childlike sense of awe and wonder, and an ability to make people laugh that any stand-up comedian would envy, was promoting adult education classes as a community college administrator in 1989, when she read a book called *Voluntary Simplicity,* by Duane Elgin. "I was really excited about it," she says, "but no one else was talking about it." She decided to offer a course on the subject. "But only four people signed up, so we had to cancel," she says with a laugh. "Then we tried it again three years later for a variety of reasons, and that time we got 175."[2]

Afterward, participants told Andrews that her voluntary simplicity workshop had changed their lives. It wasn't the kind of thing a community college administrator hears every day, she says, "so I ended up resigning my full-time position and devoting myself to giving these workshops."

She also remembered an idea she'd learned in Sweden. There, neighbors and friends organize discussion groups, called *study circles*, that meet in people's homes. Andrews began to organize her would-be voluntary simplicity students into such groups. Participants started with a short reading list, but most of the discussion focused on their personal experiences. People began to tell their own stories, "why they were there: that they have no time, they are working too much, they have no fun, they're not laughing anymore."

Some of the groups that Andrews began in 1992 continue today. Participants give each other advice and build networks for tool sharing and other activities that increase their sense of community. They find ways to help each other out that reduce their need for high incomes. They meet frequently in each other's homes and share tips, stories, and ideas for action. Everyone is expected to talk, and an egg timer, passed around the room, limits the time each can speak, preventing anyone from monopolizing the conversation.

The discussion often moves from the personal to the political. "People begin to talk about what institutional changes need to happen so they can find community and stop wasting money and resources," Andrews says. They talk about open space, parks for their kids, improved public transit, longer library hours, more effective local government. "Voluntary simplicity is not just a personal-change thing. Study circles can save the world," Andrews adds with a wink.

SIMPLICITY AS SUBVERSION

Since 1992, Cecile Andrews has helped start hundreds of voluntary simplicity study circles. Seeds of Simplicity, a national organization she codirects, has started many more. Her book, *Circle of Simplicity*, explains how anyone can start them. Most important, says Andrews, is that participants not see voluntary simplicity as a sacrifice.

"One person I know calls what we're doing the 'self-deprivation movement,' but it's not," she argues. "The way to fill up emptiness is not by denying ourselves something. It's by putting positive things in place of the negative things, by finding out what we really need, and that's community, creativity, passion in our lives, connection with nature. People help each other figure that out. They learn to meet their real needs instead of the false needs that advertisers create. They learn to live in ways that are high fulfillment, but low environmental impact."

In the good sense of the word, Andrews sees herself as a subversive (imagine Emma Goldman as Grandma Moses). "The thing about the voluntary simplicity movement is that it looks so benign," she suggests. "Like, 'Isn't that sweet? They're trying to cut back, to live more simply.' So people don't understand how radical it is. It's the Trojan horse of social change. It's really getting people to live in a totally different way."

STUDY GROUPS IN CHURCHES

The voluntary simplicity discussion groups that began with Cecile Andrews can be found in a variety of forms throughout the United States. One place where they're especially popular is in churches, many of whose leaders recognize that if we are indeed our brothers' keepers, Americans must "live simply so that others can simply live."

The United Methodist Church has produced a six-part video series called *Curing Affluenza*, featuring progressive evangelical theologian Tony Campolo, who was a spiritual adviser to President Clinton. (Campolo probably wishes his ministrations had been more effective, but that's another issue.) Churches use the videos to promote a continuing discussion of consumption issues.

Also popular are the discussion groups that begin with a book called *Simpler Living, Compassionate Life*, a collection of excellent essays edited and compiled by Michael Schut, a staff member of the Earth Ministry organization in Seattle. Churches use the book to conduct twelve-week courses in voluntary simplicity. Weekly topics include Time as Sacred, Your Money or Your Life, How Much Is Enough?, Everyday Food Choices, the Politics of Simplicity, Theology, History, and Widening the Community.

THE ROYS OF DOWNSHIFTING

Churches seem a natural arena to question ideologies built on greed, but Dick and Jeanne Roy's study groups take the battle against affluenza into unexpected places. Until he reached the age of fifty-three, Dick Roy had been a leader in the most traditional fashion: president of his class at Oregon State University, an officer in the Navy, and finally, a high-priced corporate attorney in one of America's most prestigious law firms, with a thirty-second-floor office overlooking all of Portland. But he was also married to Jeanne, a strong environmentalist and a believer in frugality.

So despite their six-figure income, the Roys lived simply and often had to weather teasing from their friends about their old clothes and used bicycles. They went backpacking on their vacations. Once they took their children to Disneyland—by bus, walking with backpacks through the streets of Anaheim, California, from the bus station to their motel.

Jeanne, in particular, found many ways to reduce consumption: using a clothesline instead of a dryer; sending junk mail back until it stopped coming; carefully saving paper; buying food in bulk, and using her own packaging. Eventually, to the amazement of all her neighbors, she reduced the amount of landfill-bound trash the Roys produced to one regular-size garbage can a year! She says it wasn't a sacrifice. "If you ask people what kinds of activities bring them pleasure, it's usually contact with nature, things that are creative, and relationships with people. And the things we do to live simply bring us all of those satisfactions."[3]

Eventually, Jeanne took a leadership role in Portland's recycling program, conducting group workshops in people's homes to teach them how to save energy and water and use resources to maximum effectiveness.

Meanwhile, Dick raised a few eyebrows at work by putting in the fewest billable hours of anyone in the firm so that he could spend more time with his family. Such behavior almost brands you as a heretic in the legal profession, but Dick was a darned good lawyer and he got along well with his colleagues, so they overlooked his transgressions. Yet eventually he grew tired of corporate law. His children were grown and he wanted to do something that more directly expressed his values, especially his concern for the environment. In 1993, Dick Roy left his job to live on his savings and devote his time to saving the earth.

WIDENING THE CIRCLES

He founded the Northwest Earth Institute in Portland (www.nwei.org), an organization that promotes simple living and environmental awareness by running discussion groups in existing institutions. Dick Roy's corporate connections helped him bring workshops—"Voluntary Simplicity," "Choices for Sustainable Living," and "Discovering a Sense of Place"—into many of Portland's largest corporations. Interested employees were encouraged to meet during lunch hours, in groups of a dozen or so, and conduct structured conversations that, Dick hoped, would lead to personal, social, and political action.

A decade later, the Northwest Earth Institute can look back at a surprising track record of success:

- hundreds of discussion courses conducted in private businesses (including such giants as Nike and Hewlett-Packard), government agencies, schools, and nonprofits throughout the Pacific Northwest

- dozens of church discussion groups in the Northwest

- establishment of outreach courses and sister Earth Institutes in all fifty states

- involvement of more than twenty-five thousand people in its courses

While the Earth Institutes have a large and growing staff, Dick and Jeanne still work (full time) as volunteers. The institutes conduct annual training programs for their organizers, always with a big dose of humor, music, and fun.

FINDING EACH OTHER

All of the study programs mentioned in this chapter start with aspirin and chicken soup: the premise that simplifying one's life (curing affluenza, if you will), is easier when we have the support and encouragement of others.

In the late seventies, Duane Elgin conducted a study of people who were choosing simpler, less consumptive lives for the Stanford Research Institute. He found they were "eating lower on the food chain," tending to vegetarian diets, wearing simple, utilitarian clothing, buying smaller, fuel-efficient cars, and cultivating their "inner" lives—living "consciously, deliberately, intentionally," mindful of the impacts of their activities.[4]

Elgin published his findings in the book *Voluntary Simplicity*. His timing was off by a bit. The book came out in 1981, just as Ronald Reagan was encouraging a return to excess and trend watchers were discovering the yuppies. Today Elgin, a gentle man with a gray beard and twinkling eyes, is an acknowledged leader in the new voluntary simplicity movement. Elgin believes that the embarrassment of riches that has marked the last few years of American history, and "the power of commercial mass media to distract us from real ecological crises and focus our attention on shampoo," are "creating a mind-set for catastrophe right now."

But he sees hopeful signs that weren't there during the '70s emphasis on simplicity. Elgin points to the rapidly expanding study-circle movement and the countless ways that seekers of a cure for affluenza can now connect with one another: a plethora of new magazines, some real, some merely opportunistic; the Simple Living Network, a valuable Internet resource; Web sites for dozens of simple-living organizations; list serves and chat groups; radio programs; new books filled with practical tips and inspiration. Ten percent of the population, Elgin says, is making changes. "For a long time they felt alone, but now they're beginning to find each other."

The change will take a generation, he feels, and he fears that's about all the time we have before we run into an ecological wall. "The leading edge of those people choosing a simple life," Elgin says, "have been relatively affluent. They've had a taste of the good life and have found it wanting, and now they're looking for a different kind of life." In that sense, the movement might be seen by some people as elitist. Yet, says Elgin, "it's only when such people begin moderating their consumption that there is going to be more available for people that now don't have enough."

Elgin likes to talk about Arnold Toynbee's "law of progressive simplification." He points out that the great British historian studied the rise and fall of twenty-two civilizations and "summarized everything he knew about the growth of human civilizations in one law: *The measure of a civilization's growth is its ability to shift energy and attention from the material side to the spiritual and aesthetic and cultural and artistic side.*"

Thousands of Americans are coming together in small groups all across the country, trying to bring about that shift.

CHAPTER 24

Fresh air

*It's difficult to imagine being busy and enchanted
at the same time. Enchantment invites us to pause
and be arrested by whatever is before us. Instead
of doing something, something is done to us....
We stumble across a roaring, resplendent water-
fall in the middle of a quiet forest, and we
become profoundly entranced.*

—THOMAS MOORE,
The Re-enchantment of Everyday Life

*A ditch somewhere—or a creek, meadow,
woodlot, or marsh .... These are places
of initiation, where the borders between
ourselves and other creatures break down,
where the earth gets under our nails
and a sense of place gets under our skin.*

—ROBERT MICHAEL PYLE,
The Thunder Tree

In the Age of Affluenza, American culture came indoors, in quest of
ever-greater convenience. Imagine Janet Jones talking to her neighbor.
"We don't ever have to be hot again," she confides as the air conditioning installer pulls into the driveway. Right behind him is a vanload of junipers, vin-
cas, and a birdbath, to fill the space where the vegetable garden used to be. As she
pads slipper-footed across a carpet of Kentucky bluegrass, Janet looks over her
shoulder and adds, "Since we don't cook much anymore, why have a garden?"

In the last decade, the aphorism "Stop and smell the roses" sank to a more cynical "Wake up and smell the coffee." We didn't have time for nature anymore. We
learned to just ignore the damn roses—let the landscaper take care of them.

NATURE GETS EVEN...

©1997 SEATTLE POST-INTELLIGENCER-NORTH AMERICA SYNDICATE

This chapter challenges a widespread, if unconscious, belief that if you make enough money, you don't need to know anything about nature or have contact with it. Conversely, we suggest that the stronger your bond with nature, the less money you'll need, or want, to make. If kicking affluenza is your goal, proven natural remedies may be the way to go.

JUST SAY KNOW

Thirty-four percent of Americans polled in 2003 ranked shopping as their favorite activity, while only 17 percent preferred being in nature. The Las Vegas Strip is ranked the number-one "scenic drive" in the country. One fourth grader, asked if he preferred to play indoors or outdoors, replies, "Indoors, 'cause that's where the electrical outlets are." Another child pokes a stick at a dead beetle, commenting to her friend that the insect's batteries must have run out. On a field trip to trace the source of their drinking water, inner-city New York middle-school kids are spooked by the cool, starry darkness and crescendo of silence in the Catskills.

"I thought potatoes grew on trees," one college student confided as Dave recently helped her plant a garden in her backyard. "I guess I need to know more about where my food comes from." Naturalists urge us to reintroduce ourselves to the real world by becoming familiar with our own backyards and county open spaces. This will help answer a question that lingers in the back of our minds: *Where exactly are we?*

Can you identify a few key species that live in your region and the natural events that take place there?

BIOREGION QUIZ

1. Trace the water you drink from precipitation to tap.

2. Describe the soil around your home.

3. What were the primary subsistence techniques of the cultures that lived in your area before you?

4. Name five native edible plants in your bioregion and their seasons of availability.

5. Where does your garbage go?

6. Name five resident and any migratory birds in your area.

7. What animal species have become extinct in your area?

8. What spring wildflower is consistently among the first to bloom where you live?

9. What kinds of rocks and minerals are found in your bioregion?

10. What is the largest wilderness area in your bioregion?

(adapted from *Deep Ecology*, by Bill Devall and George Sessions)

A CIVILIZATION ON LIFE SUPPORT?

One after another, services that used to be provided free by nature have been packaged and put on the market. Take bottled water, home-delivered in five-gallon bottles, or tanning salons, where creatures of the great indoors bask in simulated sunlight. Human contact with nature has become a *contract* with nature. Even oxygen is for sale. But many educators and thinkers refer to an "extinction of experience" that accompanies our pullback from nature. Like a washed-out sprig of parsley on a dinner plate, the community park is often biologically bland—and sometimes not secure from crime. The only way some know nature is by mentally crunching images of it on TV, like popcorn.

But television can't communicate a multidimensional, sensuous, interactive reality. It shows only the visual realm—and that through the tunnel of a lens. We're not actually *there* to smell nature, and touch it, and feel the breeze. Besides, television nature is often scripted nature—as fake as a paper ficus. Spliced together from hundreds of nonsequential hours of tape, a typical nature program filmed in Africa zooms in on a majestic lion, relentlessly on the prowl for wildebeests, jackals, and gazelles. The reality is, lions are as lazy as your housecat, sometimes sleeping twenty hours a day. Even so, footage of two lions mating is predictably followed by "cubs, tumbling out after a two- or three-minute gestation, full of play. The timeless predatory cycle repeats. . . ."[1]

In *The Age of Missing Information*, quoted above, Bill McKibben compares and contrasts the information contained in a daylong hike in upstate New York with the information content of a hundred cable TV stations, on the same day. He took a few months to watch every single taped program and observed a vast virtual wasteland that hawked a commercial mind-set. Writes McKibben, "We believe that we live in the 'age of information,' that there has been an information 'revolution.' . . . Yet vital knowledge that humans have always possessed about who we are and where we live seems beyond our reach." In one hundred hours of programming, he found very little to enrich his life.

On McKibben's daylong hike, however, all kinds of things were happening. Seven vultures leisurely circled directly above—so close he could count their feathers. "It was nearly unbearable—almost erotic—this feeling of being watched," he writes. "At moments I felt small and vulnerable, like prey." Still, he knew the day's encounters with vultures, water striders, and thrushes would never be Spielberg material. "I had not been gored, chased, or even roared at. I had failed to tranquilize anything with a dart; no creature had inflated stupendous air sacs in a curious and ancient mating ritual."[2] Yet his real-world experiences made him feel actively, rather than passively, alive.

In the closing sentences of *The Age of Missing Information*, McKibben reminds us of the virtual canyon we've put between ourselves and the natural world:

> On *Now You're Cooking,* a lady is making pigs-in-a-blanket with a Super Snacker. "We have a pact in our house—the first one up plugs in the Super Snacker."

> And on the pond, the duck is just swimming back and forth, his chest pushing out a wedge of ripples that catch the early rays of the sun.

OVERCOMING ECOPHOBIA

As McKibben and many others point out, when we lose touch with the origins, habits, and needs of our earthly housemates, we lose our biological sense of balance. As psychologist Chellis Glendinning writes, "We become homeless, alienated from the only home we will ever have."[3]

In an evolutionary sense, we risk losing the living scaffold that supports our biological sack of tricks. (For instance, without a healthy universe of decomposers, we'd all be knee-deep in dinosaur bodies.) And we lose a way of knowing what's *right*. Ecologist Aldo Leopold believed that "a thing is right when it tends to preserve the integrity, stability and beauty of the biotic community. It is wrong when it tends otherwise."[4] But let's face it: most of our daily activities and standard operating procedures walk all over Leopold's law. We don't have a clue about the biotic community, or what it needs.

Educator David Sobel terms our separation from nature "ecophobia"—a symptom characterized by an inability to smell, plant, or even acknowledge the roses. "Ecophobia is a fear of oil spills, rain forest destruction, whale hunting, and Lyme disease. In fact it's a fear of just being outside," Sobel explains. A fear of microbes, lightning, spiders, and dirt. Sobel's first aid for ecophobia emphasizes hands-on contact with nature. "Wet sneakers and muddy clothes are prerequisites for understanding the water cycle," he says.[5] In the book *Beyond Ecophobia*, he describes the magic of overcoming "timesickness" and regaining a more natural pace.

> I went canoeing with my six-year-old son Eli and his friend Julian. The plan was to canoe a two-mile stretch of the Ashuelot River, an hour's paddle in adult time. Instead, we dawdled along for four or five hours. We netted golf balls off the bottom of the river from the upstream golf course. We watched fish and bugs in both the shallows and depths of the river. We stopped at the mouth of a tributary stream for a picnic and went for a long adventure through a maze of marshy streams. Following beaver trails led to balance-walking on fallen trees to get across marshy spots without getting our feet wet. We looked at spring flowers, tried to catch a snake, got lost and found. How fine it was to move at a meandery, child's pace![6]

NATURE: NOUN OR VERB?

One summer night, twenty years ago, Dave's family was abruptly wrenched from sleep by an eerie, piercing sound that cut through the night like a Bowie knife. All four family members jerked upright in their beds, as lights went on in cabins throughout the little rural valley. At 4 a.m., Dave's kids stood shaky-legged on the couch, peering out into the darkness. They hoped to catch a glimpse of the mountain lions that had just faced off in the front yard. This was a primordial experience, connecting them with the fear and the wonder that humans have known throughout our evolution. They felt lucky to have the experience—though none of them slept for the rest of that night. Now, fast-forward twelve years or so to a rocky ledge overlooking Colorado's Sangre de Cristo mountain range. Dave's son, Colin, calls attention to the skeletal remains of an animal feast. As they study an antelope skeleton lying on the ledge, Colin imagines out loud, "A mountain lion dragged the antelope up here to eat it." He likes the idea of a real-world museum exhibit, and he likes the detective work, too.

But Dave was in a different place in his life cycle. Reaching down to the antelope skeleton, he cracked the skull away from the neck, to have a trophy from the hike. The sound of neck vertebrae cracking was one of the most abrupt, jarring sounds he'd ever heard—right up there with the front yard face-off of years before. In fact, Dave was so alarmed he replaced the skull near its rightful place. Although Colin soon forgave the impulsive action, the two spent a few hours that afternoon debating the acquired trait of *having* nature versus the more unconditional *being* in nature.

Spoiled by the pace and panorama of TV nature, we're usually looking for the big event, the spectacle. But more often than adults, kids become absorbed in the small details of nature. "Where did you go?" asks the parent. "Out." "What did you do?" "Oh, nothing," answers the kid, but he's got a vivid image in his head that says otherwise: perhaps a nearly intact robin's eggshell, partially hidden under a bright red maple leaf.

NATURE'S MAGIC

Wilderness leader Robert Greenway has spent many years on the trail and has allowed the child in himself to remain active. He tries to bring out that trait in others, too, with tangible results. Comments from more than a thousand wilder-ness-trip participants (both adult and child) indicate that nature is indeed working its magic:

90 percent described an increased sense of aliveness, well-being, and energy;

77 percent described a major life change upon return (in personal relationships, employment, housing, or life-style);

60 percent of the men and 20 percent of the women stated that a major goal of the trip was to conquer fear, challenge themselves, and expand limits;

90 percent broke an addiction such as nicotine, chocolate, and pop;

57 percent of the women and 27 percent of the men stated that a major goal
of the trip was to "come home" to nature;

76 percent of all respondents reported dramatic changes in quantity, vividness,
and context of dreams after seventy-two hours in the wilderness.[7]

We know intuitively that nature is beneficial, even if we become estranged from
it. Patients recover more quickly when they have beautiful green views to look at.
At the Way Station in Maryland, the suicide rate of emotionally and mentally challenged residents dropped dramatically when a sunny new brick and natural-wood
building became their new home. Natural light and plants provided by windows and
skylights seemed to calm and reassure them.

People like Greenway urge us to "come to our senses." By literally smelling,
touching, and tasting nature, we begin to clear out some of the rubble in our heads.
Says Greenway, "On a wilderness trip, it seems to take about four days for people to
start dreaming nature dreams rather than 'busy' or 'urban' dreams. This recurring
pattern suggests to me that our culture is only four days deep."[8] In contrast, John
McPhee has called the history of life on earth "deep time." For example, without
the ferns, algae, and protozoa of sixty-five million years ago (only yesterday as measured in deep time), we wouldn't be so preoccupied with petroleum.

COMING TO OUR SENSES

When we experience nature with our own noses, skin, lungs, and reptilian brains,
we feel silly about the stress of obsessive projects and timelines. Self-importance
begins to melt into something larger. We see that we're integral members of the
Biosphere Club, and it feels great! Rather than perceiving ourselves as simply
human-paycheck-house-car, we finally understand who and where we are. We see
that in reality, we're human-soil-grains-fruits-microbes-trees-oxygen-herbivores-fish-
salt marshes, and on and on and on! We begin to question the logic and the ethic of
parting out nature like a used-up car.

A few years ago, Lana Porter began to come to her senses. The garden she works
in Golden, Colorado, is far more than a lush, reclaimed vacant lot—it's a biological
extension of her self, and a way of life. "I eat very well out of this garden, just about
all year round," she says, "and the organic produce gives me energy to grow more
produce and get *more* energy. It's a cycle of health that has cut my expenses in half.
My grocery bills are lower, my health bills are lower, I don't need to pay for exercise, and my transportation costs are lower because I don't have to travel so much to
amuse myself."[9]

Asked what she likes best about her personal Garden of Eden, Porter replies, "I like what it does for my head. Sometimes, when I'm watering a healthy crop, or planting seeds, or cultivating between rows, I'm not thinking anything at all—a radical switch from my previous life as an overworked computer programmer. People tell me I should take care of my crops more efficiently—with irrigation systems on timers, designer fertilizers, and pesticides—so I could spend less time out here. But that way of growing disconnects the grower from the garden. The whole point is to spend *more* time with the plants, taking care of things, and less time trying to reshape myself to fit the changing whims of the world."

Like Porter, many other Americans perceive the difference between natural complexity and oversimplified science. Between a juicy, tasty peach that confers health and a pulpy, worthless peach grown in poor soil. Suddenly attuned to the frequency of natural law, they see with new eyes that many of our civilization's customs are counterproductive because they're not grounded in biological reality. Just as laying land fallow is a tenet of the Old Testament, optimizing solar income to prevent global warming should be one of the tenets of the Age of Ecology. But it seems that we won't protect backyard, bioregion, or planet unless we feel connected.

Nature is not "out there"; it's everywhere. Finding out how well the timber was grown that went into your backyard fence is nature. Knowing if the ingredients in a cake mix are biologically compatible with human nutrition is nature. Walking to the store and stopping to ask your neighbor what kind of perennial flowers he's planting— that's nature, too.

AS HAPPY AS A RED-WINGED BLACKBIRD

For aquatic biologist and University of Wisconsin professor Calvin DeWitt, the Garden of Eden is a freshwater marsh that's just beyond his backyard. He knows the marsh so well that he can identify its birds by their calls alone. Standing knee-deep in it, in waders, DeWitt traces the marsh's many cycles and life events. "When the stalk of the cattail here drops down to the marsh, it's converted again into soil, and in the structure of that soil grow all sorts of organisms which these geese feed on and the great herons that live here feed on," he exclaims. "It's things like this that really excite me, because they instill such a sense of awe and wonder. And I think that awe and wonder are really the things we're missing today." DeWitt examines a dragonfly preening on a cattail stalk, then reflects, "This aquatic ecosystem is eleven thousand years old. It's been doing all this for eleven millennia— without any human intervention."[10]

"As you stand for a while, things begin to unfold if you are quiet enough to watch and listen. After a full day, you're still not fulfilled—there's so much to learn here. You're not tired either—you tend to be exhilarated from the experience." DeWitt steps up on the bank of the marsh, water dripping from his waders. "Perhaps most curiously—in our consumptive society—you come home with your wallet just as full as when you left, and you've gotten all this pleasure, education, understanding, peace—for not a single penny."

CHAPTER 25

The right medicine

If you think your actions are too small to make a difference, you've never been in bed with a mosquito.

—ANONYMOUS

If we can harness the ingenuity that has made North America the richest, most successful society in history, our environment can start making a comeback in a single generation.

—ALAN DURNING

We need technologies that more efficiently digest a given resource, not technologies of larger jaws and a bigger digestive tract.

—HERMAN DALY

What if fifty sinful things could save the earth? Wouldn't that be great? What if, for example, we Americans could deploy our favorite sin, greed, as a vaccine against itself, intentionally extending our spending spree at least a few more decades? Even environmentalists could put down their protest signs and join the fun. Instead of "Doing all I can to save the earth," they could consume all they wanted to save the earth.

What if cigarettes increased lung capacity and prevented cancer; SUVs filtered the pollution out of urban air; and luxury beach vacations enhanced the health of habitats like coral reefs and once-abundant fisheries? The problem is, they don't.

OK then, what if fifty *simple* things could save the earth? We're talking about individual choices and actions taken by millions of Americans, without substantial changes in lifestyle. If each of us kept a reusable grocery sack in the car, planted a tree, and screwed in some compact fluorescent light bulbs, maybe we could collectively reverse the decline of the planet's health. That, too, would be fantastic, but nothing on earth is quite that simple. Our economy and the majority of its products are not *designed* to save the planet. They're designed to make money.

We can voluntarily cut back and do simple things by the boatload, but we'll still be paddling against a flash flood, no-conscience economy that's not designed to make sense. For example, we're willing to recycle a few sacks of aluminum cans, but we may have to drive twenty miles to do it. We'll pay a little more for nontoxic paints and cleaners, but we use them in houses glued together with toxic adhesives. We choose to buy natural fibers like cotton, unaware that conventionally grown cotton is drenched with pesticides (about a third of all pesticides used in the United States are applied to cotton crops).

As the author and corporate futurist Paul Hawken points out, 90 percent of the waste we generate never even makes it into products or services but remains at the point of extraction or manufacture, in slash and slag piles and on-site waste impoundments. Of the materials that do become products, 80 percent are thrown away after a single use. In a way, it's a Catch-22. To save the world, we need strong individual action, yet for effective individual action, we need to redesign the world. (Even a task that huge is achievable—we've totally redesigned the world in the last hundred years, haven't we?) Hawken believes we need to see a wider picture than we're used to seeing: "We've spent the last century working our tails off to make fewer people more productive using more resources. Yet we are doing this at a time when we have more people and *fewer* resources."[1] Hawken envisions an economy in which resources are many times more productive per molecule, electron, and photon; natural capital (lakes, trees, grassland) is valued as an indispensable, living support system; and people bring their brains, their hearts, and their hands back into the workplace.

NOT ONLY SUFFICIENT BUT ALSO EFFICIENT

Simple environmental fixes can be designed into our economy and political structure so that they become as natural as breathing. By substituting efficient products like low-flow showerheads, compact fluorescent bulbs, and high-efficiency windows and refrigerators, we've already prevented millions of tons of pollution and environmental impacts in the last decade—and saved billions of dollars. Because they are "smarter" and designed for efficiency, newly available products like front-load washing machines can deliver better performance using fewer resources. A typical family spends about $200 per year on energy, water, and detergent for doing laundry. A state-of-the-art model will cut that expense by about $75 a year.

Buying devices that score high on Energy Star and other rating systems not only lowers fuel bills but also reduces the threat of global warming, reduces our reliance on unstable sources of energy like Middle Eastern oil, and reduces our guilt, too.

Howard Geller of the American Council for an Energy-Efficient Economy does not believe that simple, individual actions will save the planet by themselves, because many of the challenges we face are extremely complex. We need more earth-friendly economic incentives, more green-product certifications and efficiency ratings, and a revamping of codes and specifications—all designed specifically to make saving the earth a cakewalk.

As an example, Geller cited regulations that mandate efficiency. "The nice thing is, regulations don't require consumer education or analysis." Refrigerator standards are one such regulation. "When your old refrigerator gives out, you need to replace it, ASAP. You usually don't have time to read *Consumer Reports*. You just make a beeline to the department store and get something with enough cabinet space to keep your teenagers alive."[2]

But much of the work to produce better refrigerators has already been done behind the scenes, by lobbyists, legislators, engineers, and managers. As Geller explains, a series of progressive state laws were passed first, but each had different requirements. To reduce confusion and a need for many models of the same product, industry actually supported a standardized federal law that required higher efficiency. That law has produced models that use two-thirds less energy than a 1970s unit but have more space, more features, and better performance. More for less, by design. Appliance standards in general that went into effect in 1990 have already saved more energy than is generated by thirty-one regional power plants. To keep our beer and forgotten leftovers cold, we don't have to cut back on anything, ponder anything, or become Greenpeace activists; we just need to harvest the fruits of environment-friendly laws. Now that's simplicity.

"If affluenza compels us to buy something," Geller says, "why don't we buy a state-of-the-art refrigerator or front-loading clothes washer—something that improves our quality of life and makes sense environmentally, too?"

Among the many "hidden benefits" of giving the earth a little TLC are steady savings. Sometimes the life-cycle savings from high-efficiency devices like set-back thermostats and "low-E" windows are as good as returns on stock or bond investments, and you don't have to fret over the market. However, monetary savings are only one of the hidden benefits for the earth.

The changes that take place in our minds are perhaps the most important individual actions of all. We're discovering that it's not just how much or how little we consume as individuals that matters, but how well our purchases were *produced*.

It's not just the quantity of our consumption—although that is important—but also the quality of our designs and choices.

In a super-efficient economy, we'll all save money because we're not spending extra to clean up, recover our health, mine new materials, work in jobs we hate—requiring expensive vacations in compensation—and so on. Efficiency is especially beneficial for low-income consumers, who spend higher proportions of their income for utilities. When we learn to "ride the earth in the direction it's going," by knowing how nature works and designing appropriately, everyone wins.

DRIVING AN SUV TO THE STEAKHOUSE

Meanwhile, we rejoin our regularly scheduled present-in-progress, where news stories about globally scaled environmental problems sometimes overwhelm us. They seem too big to be solved by informed consumer choices, let alone ignorant ones. But Michael Brower and Warren Leon, authors of *The Consumer's Guide to Effective Environmental Choices: Practical Advice from the Union of Concerned Scientists,* are here to help. Their mission is to exorcise mental clutter and guilt by setting priorities in our consumer choices.[3] Rather than stress over which forty things to do, the researchers suggest we address the worst problems first, to get the biggest bang for our collective buck. By their calculations, driving an SUV to the steakhouse is one of the worst consumer actions possible, because automobiles and meat are two primary pathways affluenza takes to infect the earth.

Brower and Leon used a decade's worth of risk analysis from various agencies and experts to determine that air pollution, global warming, habitat alteration, and water pollution are the most critical consumption-related impacts. Big-pattern flaws in design and production often cause the worst impacts: the way our cities and suburbs are designed, the way we purify wastewater, the way agriculture is practiced, the way energy is generated, and the way industry designs and manufactures chemicals, computers, and cars. While consumer choices don't *directly* affect these production systems, informed choices do result in substantial hidden benefits that can speed the earth's recovery. When we buy organic produce, for example, we are also buying farming techniques—such as crop rotation—that prevent erosion, insect damage, and other impacts. When we buy a fuel-efficient hybrid vehicle, we become rolling advertisements for a cool climate and clean air.

When we reduce our consumption of meat, we also dramatically reduce our impact on land, water, air, and atmosphere. Compared with a nutritionally equivalent intake of whole grains, red meat is responsible for twenty times the land use (because of cattle grazing), seventeen times the common water pollution (because of animal wastes), five times the toxic water pollution and water use (from chemicals applied to feed grains and water for irrigation and livestock), and three times the greenhouse gas emissions (from greater energy use), Brower and Leon contend.

Is the quantity of meat we consume a vestige from frontier days, or is it really more a visual habit? Maybe we apportion servings by the way they should look on a plate. Dinner plate aesthetics—and meat consumption—have changed since 1970, but if we stop and think about it, wouldn't our plates look just as appetizing and far more colorful with larger proportions of fresh fruits, grains, and vegetables? That might mean reducing our meat intake from four pounds a week to two pounds, and at the same time reducing our risk of heart disease and stroke.

Brower and Leon praise consumer efforts to reduce waste and promote efficiency, but they also urge us to go easy on ourselves. "The demonization of disposable cups, for example, has caused some individuals and groups to spend too much time

---

PRIORITY ACTIONS FOR AMERICAN CONSUMERS

Transportation

1. Choose a place to live that reduces the need to drive.

2. Think twice before purchasing a second or third car.

3. Choose a fuel-efficient, low-polluting car.

4. Set concrete goals for reducing your travel.

5. Whenever practical, walk, bicycle, or take public transportation.

Food

6. Eat less meat.

7. Buy certified organic produce.

Household operations

8. Choose your home carefully.

9. Reduce the environmental costs of heating and hot water.

10. Install efficient lighting and appliances.

11. Choose an electricity supplier offering renewable energy.

Adapted from Brower and Leon, *The Consumer's Guide to Effective Environmental Choices*

worrying about them. One minister told us that his congregants wanted to purchase ceramic coffee mugs and install a dishwasher in their social hall, so they could avoid using plastic cups at meetings. When we discovered that their total cup use was only about forty a week, we urged them to spend their budgeted $450 on other measures, such as weather-stripping for their old drafty building."[4]

Some actions and activities are high impact even though relatively few people do them, like power boating, and off-road joyriding in ATVs and snowmobiles. An hour of Jet Ski riding, for example, can create as much smog as a car trip from Washington, D.C., to Orlando, Florida, because Jet Ski engines don't have emission controls. (These small engines are prime candidates for redesign.) The engines of gas-powered lawn mowers, in addition to ruining many an afternoon nap, also create red-advisory pollution right in our neighborhoods. In addition, homeowners apply ten times as much pesticide per acre as farmers, because reading labels is a bother, and isn't more better?

But some have opted to take the lawn into their own hands. "Xeriscaping" with water-conservative flowers and shrubs is popular in the arid West and elsewhere, and "lawn busting" with edible landscapes may also become fashionable, as interest in organic produce continues to expand. Instead of spending hours a week to produce a bag of grass clippings, we'll go out and pick a bowl of cherry tomatoes.

An underlying cause of many environmental problems is "high-impact thinking" such as the compulsive need for spotlessness and tidiness. It seems that the more flawlessly green our lawns, the browner our streams, from all the nutrients and pesticides that run off. The cleaner our houses, the more toxic our environment, from runaway chemicals used to overpolish, oversterilize, and overdeodorize our homes.

Simple things to save the earth? Sure, let's do as many as we can, because they reduce impacts, stimulate better design, and save money. In a sense, we're substituting information and awareness for overconsumption, a painless path to take, because not much change is required. But while we're at it, let's not forget a few other details that need to be taken care of by the week after next: redesigning the economy and many of its products, and recycling the American mindset.

SAVING THE EARTH BY DESIGN

When a toaster is designed well, it makes our day go better, because the toast comes out golden brown, and the appliance itself is so stylish! If the toaster is designed to be repairable, that's also a good thing, and if we could recycle it into another toaster, that too would be a good thing. We would have a smart product that created a minimum of impacts, by design. Most countries in Western Europe now mandate "extended producer responsibility" that includes taking back products at the end of their lives. In the future, your toaster might "swim upstream" to be recycled at the very factory where it was manufactured.

What kind of green design features do we want in other consumer products? The highly successful hybrid vehicle combines qualities such as efficiency, low levels of pollution, and low maintenance. And far more efficient vehicles are possible—even inevitable. Envisioned years ago by energy guru Amory Lovins, the "hypercar" is now being manufactured in prototype by Ford, GM, Honda, Toyota, and others. A Rocky Mountain Institute colleague of Lovins recently attended Detroit's annual Auto Show, where dinosaurs like the ten-mile-per-gallon Ford Excursion were on exhibit next to the high-tech sixty-mile-per-gallon Prius and the eighty-mpg GM Precept.

By reducing wind drag, mechanical friction, tire resistance, and weight, the designers of these high-IQ cars set the stage for a new kind of car engine—a flameless, pollutionless fuel cell that will ultimately consume hydrogen as a fuel source and emit water vapor as exhaust.[5] By design, we may soon see the world's air pollution take a dramatic turn for the better—though of course, hypercars can't decongest the highways of a hyper society.

The new-millennium wind generator, an offspring of aerospace and computer technologies, is another great example of how design can deliver a service much more elegantly than its old-millennium counterpart. Much cleaner and faster to

---

DESIGN Rx FOR AFFLUENZA

Nontoxic, nonpolluting

Renewable energy and material sources

Socially equitable and affordable

Flexible, reversible

Durable, repairable

Diverse, unique

Efficient, precise

Easy to understand

Light "extraction footprint"

Low maintenance

Life sensitive, biocompatible

Culture-sensitive, people-friendly

build than coal-fired or nuclear power generators, state-of-the-art wind farms are already supplying enough electricity to power millions of homes. In fact, wind-generated electricity worldwide increased eightfold between 1995 and 2003, growing at over 30 percent per year. Windfarms with Statue of Liberty–size wind generators could meet the electrical needs of the whole country, say experts at the Department of Energy, and in the process wind-rich states like Texas, Kansas, and North Dakota would see their economies boom.[6] The American Wind Energy Association says that if wind supplied just 10 percent of the world's energy, close to two million jobs could be created. One in four electricity customers in the United States now has the option of buying "green power" from renewable sources like wind. (One great example is Colorado's Wind Source program, in which Dave has invested.)

Geller, of the American Council for an Energy-Efficient Economy, emphasized, "Efficiency is critical because the more wasteful we are, the more difficult it will be to make a transition to an economy powered by wind, biomass, and sun. With efficient products and processes, the transition can be relatively easy. Historically, the transitions from wood to coal and from coal to oil took place in a few decades."[7]

The potential for "smart stuff" to provide greater value with fewer impacts is nearly endless. Until now, industry has pursued other design goals, such as cost per unit and ease of manufacture. "There's no reason why we shouldn't be able to manufacture footwear that lasts as long as the foot in this age of high technology," states Alan Durning of Northwest Environment Watch. "We can move from a hydrocarbon economy, based on nonrenewable petrochemicals, to a carbohydrate economy, based on plant materials," says David Morris of the Institute for Local Self-Reliance.[8]

Even everyday products like newspaper ink and toothpaste have been redesigned to meet needs precisely, without unwanted side effects. Tom Chappell of Tom's of Maine wondered, "Why were toothpastes filled with complex abrasives, dyes, artificial flavors, preservatives, binders, fluoride, and worst of all saccharin, long suspected as a cause of cancer? . . . Why were Americans spending more than a billion dollars a year to fill their mouths with chemicals?"[9] Chappell's innovative baking-soda toothpaste attracted millions of customers and prompted companies like Colgate and Procter & Gamble to market similar products.

CHANGING FOR GOOD

Why do people change behavior to become more environmentally friendly? Behaviorists report that the most effective stimulants for change emphasize a perception both of large benefits and of limited barriers. People need to know basic facts about global warming, water pollution, and so on, and understand how their actions can make a difference—without requiring Mission Impossible efforts.

Ecopsychologist Terrance O'Connor thinks environmental responsibility is really about enlightened self-interest. He asks, "If this is not my planet, whose is it? I am the cause, and I am the cure. When I act out of this realization, I act not out of guilt but out of self-love. I break through my denial and see that humankind is facing an absolutely unprecedented crisis. I act not out of obligation or idealism, but because I live in a straw house and I smell smoke."[10]

CHAPTER 26

Back to work

> Markets flatter our solitary egos but leave our yearnings for community unsatisfied. They advance individualistic, not social, goals, and they encourage us to speak the language of "I want" not the language of "we need."
>
> —BENJAMIN BARBER,
> *A Place for Us*

> If you don't go to somebody's funeral, they won't come to yours.
>
> —YOGI BERRA

Is there any better feeling than being back in the world after an extended illness? Good-bye, daytime TV, and Hello, energy! The challenge is to channel the energy productively. Gandhi said, "there's more to life than increasing its speed." We might add that there's more to life than increasing its greed. And despite the million-dollar ads to the contrary, there's more to life than "me." Buy the luxury car, the ads suggest (over and over!) and the pristine, deserted country roads roll out obediently, like endless swaths of Persian carpet. On these mythical, mist-covered highways, exotic women adorn the passenger seats, wearing short black dresses and pearl-white smiles of delight. Speeding is mandatory, wet surfaces be damned! The ads are all about "me," chasing an illusion of personal grandeur.

But political scientist Benjamin Barber is skeptical that those roads can take us where we want to go. In *A Place for Us,* Barber explains his gripe with an economy based solely on profit. "Markets are as likely to undermine as to sustain full employment, environmental safety, public health, social safety nets, education, cultural diversity, and real competition," he writes.[1] He believes these qualities need to be championed by *us*, the people—a slumbering yet historically potent third force in American society.

He urges us to rise up from our couches and collectively reenergize the third place, between big government and big business, where "citizens breathe freely and behave democratically without regarding themselves as passive complainers, grasping consumers, or isolated victims."[2] This third place, treasured throughout American history, is where civic life thrives. Barn raisings and Habitat for Humanity raisings; church philanthropic projects; holiday festivals and block parties; demonstrations and protests; volunteer activities like PTA and Red Cross; neighborhood watches, community gardens, and lively discussion groups—all these activities remind us that we belong to an extended family that needs and values our participation.

Barber's beef with big government is its inability, or refusal, to awaken and empower civic life. In the early 2000s, a mighty chorus of snores can be heard from coast to coast, which filmmaker Michael Moore praises facetiously in an open e-mail to the country's nonvoters. "Way to go!" he writes, "In 1996, you helped set the all-time American record for lowest turnout ever at a presidential election. And during the 2000 primaries, nearly eighty percent staged a sit-in on their living room couches."[3] (We did better in November 2000, but no doubt there are many silent Floridians who still wish they'd made time to vote.)

In ancient Greece, the word *idiot* meant someone not involved in public life, but let's face it, since national politics became a corporate-funded media show in the '60s, we sometimes have to wonder if we're *all* idiots.

At the local level, where voices can be heard and politicians held accountable, we aren't doing much better. The living-room sit-ins continue during city council meetings, free concerts in the park, and public hearings—especially when their time slots compete with *CSI Miami* or *Desperate Housewives.* (Is that idiots, or "vidiots"?)

Barber argues that there's much more to citizenship than voting and jury duty. The potentials are limitless for bringing civic energy back to the workplace, the health care industry, or the public review of new technologies—all sorely in need of new direction. He even proposes that public meeting spaces become mandated features in malls. How might malls be designed to make space for neighborhood health clinics, speaker's corners, child care centers, and public art galleries?

EMERGING FROM LUXURY COCOONS

What do we want "people power" to accomplish? Social theorist Jean Elshtain believes that "the essential task of civil society, the families, neighborhood life, and community, and the web of religious, civic associations . . . is to foster competence and character in individuals, provide the foundations for social trust, and turn children into citizens."[4] But affluenza is often an obstacle to those lofty goals, because time-famine and chronic self-absorption limit our participation. We may wish we could look outside ourselves, but we're just too busy, too uncertain where to start, or too tired. What's more, we feel guilty about the time, money, and energy we've already invested to make things worse! But this painful awakening can be a first step on the road to recovery.

THE POWER OF TEN

Of course, humans have always been a social species, guided by the shared wisdom of the tribe or clan. Gatherings around the fire weren't called "citizenship," but that's what they really were. They played an important role in formulating and expressing shared values and goals.

They still do, even if the fires are now artificial living room fireplaces. Portland resident Dick Roy, director of the Northwest Earth Institute (see chapter 23), organizes discussion circles, often in people's homes, with the goal of "detaching participants from commercial messages and encouraging them to think for themselves."

The mission—self-discovery and personal motivation—is lofty, but the institute's approach is low-key. "We don't claim to be teachers or preachers," says Roy. "We're simply a resource that enables people to express their highest values to others, *and then align their actions with those values.*"[5]

Why do people take the time to come to nine sessions per course? Maybe because the classes offer easy access to citizenship and social expression they can't find in their communities or workplaces. Roy has found that groups of about ten encourage the sharing of opinions, stories, and convictions that stimulate personal change. "We see participants move from awareness and consciousness of an issue—let's say the impacts of the automobile—through motivation/inspiration, and intent to change, to action."

"One woman, Rosemary Cordello, was a successful labor lawyer," he recalls. "After taking our courses, she made basic changes in her life. She got rid of her car and her professional wardrobe and started a nonprofit foundation to build low-cost, 'green' housing. She says she's never been happier."

Roy also sees change happening right on his block. "We formed a group that's organized around a physical feature, a ravine that's in back of twenty-five households in the neighborhood. We put together a neighborhood directory, organized a drop point where a local farmer delivers produce by subscription, and began meeting every Friday night for poker. We also have neighborhood work groups to clean up and restore the ravine, and we work on each other's home projects when help is needed."

It's an appealing notion—to have help when we need it. "I call our work 'gathering with a sense of purpose,'" says Roy. "I really believe that if we could get everyone in the country to go through our discussion courses, we could change the culture overnight."

Roy's beliefs are right on target with research about how, and why, behavior change happens. Commitment, trust, and intent are all key factors. In one classic study, conducted thirty years ago, a researcher posed as a sunbather, spreading a blanket near another sunbather. After a few minutes, he asked, "Excuse me, I'm here alone and have no matches—do you have a light?" The researcher then got up and walked down the beach, leaving his blanket and radio behind. When a second researcher ran by and "stole" the radio, the thief was pursued four times out of twenty. However, when the first researcher asked the person beside him to "watch his things," in nineteen out of twenty cases the thief was pursued.[6] We take action when we've made a commitment to others.

Similar research shows that written commitments are even more binding than verbal ones. Three different methods were used experimentally, urging households to recycle newspapers. One group of households received a pamphlet stressing the importance of recycling. The second group made verbal commitments, and the third group was persuaded to sign written commitments. Although verbal commitments yielded a higher recycling rate than receiving pamphlets, a follow-up survey a year later revealed that only those who had signed written commitments were still recycling.[7]

CHANGING THE WORLD, ONE NEIGHBORHOOD AT A TIME

About eleven years ago, Dave made a written commitment, in the form of a membership check, to a group of people interested in designing a neighborhood from scratch. The group took the formula for "co-housing," a design concept imported from Denmark, and applied it to a chunk of land in Colorado. They found a scenic, ten-acre property west of Denver, and, with help from an architect and a developer, they designed and contracted twenty-seven private homes, a workshop, a garden/orchard and a "common house." (The common house is used for group meals a few times a week, meetings, parties, and late-night soul sessions.)

Co-housing emphasizes design for community: high density and lots of common space when possible. Many visioning sessions made even a slow-moving process exciting. In one brainstorming session, architect Matt Worswick (who's now a resident) led the group through a process of imagining what activities would be done, where. The group imagined the pedestrian walkways, the community garden, the kids' playgrounds, and various rooms in the common house. Since the architecture is southwestern, they pictured a mission bell in a bell tower. And ten years later, that imaginary bell has a very real clang; kids love to be asked to pull the rope that rings it. Salvaged from an old farm where one of the members grew up, the massive bell calls everyone in the community (called Harmony Village) for meals, meetings, and celebrations.

By clustering homes in blocks of two and four, Harmony residents preserved both land and energy, since heat is "borrowed" from the walls of neighboring homes. And by mandating that cars be parked in garages and parking spaces at the edge of the neighborhood, the group preserved the sanity of its members. There's a sense of calmness in the center of the neighborhood, kind of like a courtyard in a college campus. The design also helps the neighborhood's security, because there's usually activity in the common area, and there's also a good chance of having "eyes on the green" as people make dinner or do the dishes.

When Dave began to incrementally invest in the future of that neighborhood, he was also investing in his new neighbors. Instead of now wondering who lives six houses down, neighbors all got to know each other very well before moving in, because they had met regularly with each other for two and a half years before a single foundation was dug. In the process of building the physical community, they also laid social foundations. They became citizens by necessity, because once the neighborhood was built, it had to be governed. Each resident serves on a team, and once a month, a large gathering is held to take care of community business, work collectively on maintenance or building projects, or just have a big party or dance.

The neighborhood that emerged is a diverse band of individuals, ranging in age from one year to eighty-three. Just about everybody has been profiled in the neighborhood newsletter, also an open forum for ideas, creative writing, and true confessions. Rich Grange is an entrepreneur whose telecommunications business provides local jobs for many of his neighbors. The company is committed to social activism, offering time off with pay for employees who volunteer. Edee Gail is a musician and community activist who helped "Save the Mesa"—a landmark seen from the community green. Recently, she was singing a song in an assisted-living center. An elderly woman walked away from the group and, according to a nurse who was there, died singing the song.

The community lost a good neighbor and role model when Ginny Mackey, a retired minister, died. Throughout her later years, the topic of "restorative justice" was a passion; this approach seeks genuine healing by creating a one-to-one dialogue between criminal and victim.

Virginia Moran is an expert on environmentally and socially responsible investing. Her expertise developed as she researched corporate involvement during the Vietnam war. "It was to their benefit to keep the war going," she says, recalling her initial research. "I decided to teach myself so I could help people align their investments with their values. Then I happened to be in San Francisco and attended some of the early meetings of the Social Investment Forum. After Desmond Tutu came to the United States asking investors to withdraw financial support for South African apartheid, we began canvassing specific sectors, asking them to participate in that cause. Churches were especially effective in getting the word out. Five years later, the [South African] economy started to falter, partly as a result of our efforts."[8]

Moran has personal investments in diversified hardwood tree plantations in Costa Rica, and in small loans to micro-enterprises, which she calls "bootstraps banking." You can see her excitement as she explains how well some of the funds she works with are performing. "There are now more than fifty mutual funds that apply social and environmental criteria to their portfolios, and many receive higher ratings than their unscreened counterparts. Not one of the SR funds has been involved in the trading scandals that have tarnished the reputations of many of the better-known funds," she says.

"Some of the reasons the SR funds provide superior financial returns is that the companies they represent don't experience the problems associated with waste and pollution. They don't pay huge EPA fines," she explains. "They are good citizens of the communities where their plants are located, and they provide a safe, healthy environment for their workers. Their fair hiring practices attract quality employees resulting in high productivity. Their CEOs don't receive excessive compensation. Eventually all of this shows up on the bottom line."

These are just a few of the residents of Harmony Village, and most of the others are also involved with activities that stretch the conventional meaning of the word *value*. The way they spend their time makes money less critical. Save enough for retirement? Sure. But do they need a new car, to keep up with the Joneses? Not really, because the Joneses drive a well-maintained Saab old enough to wear plates that label the car an antique.

The neighborhood's mission statement is *To create a cooperative neighborhood of diverse individuals sharing human resources within an ecologically responsible community setting.* To make good on that mouthful of intentions, the group recycles, composts, cultivates a community garden, and works on local issues like battling the last leg of a metro beltway. Like the rest of the country, Harmony residents are victims of an economy that doesn't always "get it." Recently, they caught employees of the recycling company red-handed—mixing carefully sorted materials together with trash bound for the landfill.

The group also experiments with more innovative activities, like community-supported agriculture. Since their own garden is still evolving, many in the neighborhood subscribe to a produce service from a local farmer who delivers eight or ten bushel baskets of produce to the neighborhood every week. This enables J. P., the farmer, to know at the beginning of the growing season how much to plant. ("So who's got a great coleslaw recipe?")

Another concept being actively discussed is an effective, businesslike car-sharing cooperative. As Worldwatch Institute writer Gary Gardner phrases it, "Cars spend most of their lives (an average of 95%) parked, taking up space, not taking people where they want to go—*not* doing what they were built to do."[9] In an era with high percentages of at-home workers and retired people, and a desperate need for the reemergence of public transportation, some Harmony residents wonder why we can't get around in fewer cars, which would use less land for parking spaces and roads and gobble smaller bites of income for car insurance.

The neighborhood already has an informal network of car lending, and a very supportive approach to transportation. "When you need to pick your car up from the shop, just walk around the neighborhood and see who's around," says Laura Herrera, a renter in the community. One Sunday morning at 4:20 a.m., Dave got a frantic call from a neighbor who was trying to board a plane to go on vacation, but whose ID had expired. "Do you think you could go into my house, get my work ID, and be out here at the airport in less than forty-seven minutes, when the plane leaves?" he asked, hopefully. Since there was no traffic, Dave made it in thirty-six minutes.

Though the residents don't call their neighborhood utopia, they're learning trial-by-fire citizenship—an exciting and challenging, if sometimes frustrating, proposition. Co-housing is only one of many ways to create vital, people-friendly neighborhoods, and it doesn't have to take place in newly constructed buildings. (The Nomad community in Boulder, Colorado, for example, shares public space with an existing theater, while the On-Going Community in Portland, Oregon, rehabilitated old neighborhood houses that members were able to purchase cheaply.) Whenever developers, city leaders, and active citizens successfully create a place that optimizes social opportunities and minimizes wasted effort (including resources, time, and money), they are taking a swipe at affluenza.

RESPONSIBLE WEALTH

As we've seen throughout this section of the book, many Americans' economic values may be changing—perhaps just in time. Another indication comes from a seemingly unlikely place—the ranks of the rich and famous. The phrase "a roomful of millionaires" may bring to mind high-powered, aggressive deals struck behind closed doors, but if it's a meeting of an organization known as Responsible Wealth, the millionaires may be plotting to give money *away*.

More than four hundred of its members have already redistributed millions in profits they could have reaped from a recent law cutting capital gains taxes. They also opposed recent efforts to abolish the estate tax, a tax that affects only people like them. Says one of the group's founders, Mike Lapham, "It's not in society's long-term interest to have people at the top living in gated communities while people at the bottom are behind bars or living in poverty." Among the members of Responsible Wealth are the singer Cher and the actress Christine Lahti.

Another member, software millionaire Michele McGeoy, says, "If I'm earning money watching my stocks grow and someone else is working hard as a teacher, why should I pay a lower tax rate? That may be good for me economically, but it doesn't build a healthy society."[10]

What's up with these people? Why don't they get over it, rake in the money, and get back to the mergers and takeovers? Apparently because they've reached a point of having "enough." Now, greater satisfaction comes from acting for the common good. In a sense, they *are* reinvesting the money—not just for profit, but for people.

CHAPTER 27

Vaccinations and vitamins

People who for years have been fighting the pollution of the physical environment suddenly realize that we have a perhaps even bigger problem that has to be solved first, and that is cleaning up the toxic areas of our mental environment.

—KALLE LASN,
Adbusters

An ounce of prevention is worth a pound of cure, or so the old saying goes. Many of us take that suggestion seriously each fall when we line up dutifully for flu shots. When we feel a virus coming on, we pop vitamin C tablets into our mouths, hoping Linus Pauling knew what he was talking about. Of course, there are no real shots or pills that can prevent or soften the impact of affluenza (with one exception: for the small percentage of Americans who are truly addicted, the compulsive shoppers, psychiatrists sometimes prescribe anticompulsion drugs and antidepressants, with promising results). But in a metaphorical sense, some powerful antiviruses are floating around that can help vaccinate us against affluenza, and so are some equally effective vitamins that can help keep us from harm's way.

ADBUSTERS

During the 2004–05 flu season, when the United States discovered it was desperately short of influenza vaccine, thousands of Americans traveled north of the border to get their shots. The Victoria Clipper, a ferry offering service between Seattle and Victoria, British Columbia, even offered package deals whereby people could buy a round-trip on the boat and get vaccinated upon landing in Canada. Hundreds of senior citizens braved stormy weather and seasickness for the privilege. It was a little egg on the face for those American politicians who mocked the Canadian health care system, eh?

But the Canadians are also leading the way in vaccinating for affluenza. Vancouver, British Columbia, might be called the headquarters of anti-affluenza vaccine research. It's the home of Kalle Lasn, the author of *Culture Jam* and director of the Media Foundation, publishers of a magazine called *Adbusters*. The magazine (which seems to have lost its sense of humor lately and has become grim, shrill, and rhetorical) became popular with its clever "uncommercials," anti-ads that often mock real ads. For example, a parody of Calvin Klein's "Obsession" ads shows men staring into their underwear, while another mocking Absolut Vodka shows a partially melted plastic vodka bottle, with the caption "Absolute Impotence" and a warning in small print that "drink increases the desire but lessens the performance."

John's favorite ad mocks no real product but shows a handsome young businessman who says he's one of many who are turning to "Mammon," because "I want a religion that doesn't complicate my life with unreasonable ethical demands." It's an obvious play on Christ's declaration that "you cannot serve both God and Mammon." "We're not the biggest player in the spiritual arena, but we're the fastest growing," the Mammon anti-ad declares. It's a subtle but powerful reminder of the decline of true spirituality in the Age of Affluenza.

Perhaps the most successful of *Adbusters'* parodies were its anti-smoking ads. In one of them, two Marlboro Man–type cowboys ride side by side in the sunset. "I miss my lung, Bob," reads the caption. A series of anti-ads mocks Joe Camel, a cartoon character devised to sell cigarettes to kids, according to anti-smoking critics. Joe Camel becomes "Joe Chemo," a camel dying of cancer, lying in a hospital bed hooked to an array of life-support equipment, or already dead from cancer and lying in his coffin. In Seattle, the city's public health department paid to put Joe Chemo on outdoor billboards.

TURNING ADVERTISING AGAINST ITSELF

The anti-ads work like vaccines because they use the virus itself to build up resistance. "We discovered early on in the publication of *Adbusters* that if we come up with an ad that looks like a Chevron ad or a Calvin Klein ad and fool people for a couple of seconds before they realize it's saying exactly the opposite, then we have created a kind of moment of truth that forces them to think about what they've seen," says Lasn.[1]

Born during World War II in Estonia, Lasn spent the early years of his life in a refugee camp. He remembers that period as tough in a material sense, "but it was a time when our family was very together, when the community in which we lived was very together, and I recall it with fondness." Lasn moved around a lot, from Germany to Australia to Japan, where he worked for ten years in marketing until he had a sudden change of heart. He emigrated to Vancouver and became a documentary filmmaker. In 1989 Lasn produced his first television "uncommercial," a parody of British Columbia Tourist Commission ads that showcased the province's stunning natural beauty. Lasn's spoof showed what was happening to that beauty as logging companies clear-cut B.C.'s ancient forests. Not surprisingly, television stations refused to air the uncommercial even though Lasn was willing to pay for the airtime.

Lasn still hopes to get uncommercials on commercial television, which he calls "the command center of our consumer culture." Lasn and his co-workers, most of whom are less than half his age, have produced dozens of TV uncommercials. One trumpets "the end of the age of the automobile," as a metal dinosaur constructed from model cars topples to the ground. Others promote "TV Turnoff Week," challenge the "beauty" industry for promoting anorexia and bulimia, and depict a bull running through a china shop while criticizing the gross national product as a measure of economic health.

Many of the uncommercials are produced by people who actually work in the advertising industry. "They have qualms about the ethics of their business," says Lasn, "so clandestinely they come and help us to come up with our messages, which are trying to use television to change the world for the better."

NO ROOM IN THE BOX

But Lasn admits he's still had virtually no success in getting those messages on television. He says, "All the major networks in North America have rejected just about all of our television uncommercials." He describes a discussion with an executive at CNN. It came when Lasn wanted to buy time for one of his anti-beauty industry ads during a CNN fashion show.

"Listen, personally I like your campaign," the executive told Lasn. "I think it says something very important about our society. We should be airing spots like this, but on an official level I can tell you right now, we will never air that spot because we would have Revlon and Maybelline and Calvin Klein coming down our throats the very next day, and that's where our bread and butter is."

Lasn continues to challenge the rejections in court, but the courts nearly always rule that his ads are political commercials and the only political commercials networks must accept are those for candidates in election campaigns. So much for free speech and First Amendment protections. "We need a free marketplace of ideas instead of a closed shop where only consumption messages are allowed," Lasn says with a touch of anger. "This is really a battle for the right to communicate. I think it's one of the really great human rights battles of our information age."

BUY NOTHING DAY

CNN did agree (alone among the networks) to air one of Lasn's uncommercials, a spot showing a pig protruding from a map of North America. After a short narration: "The average North American consumes five times more than a Mexican, ten times more than a Chinese person, and thirty times more than a person from India. We are the most voracious consumers in the world," the pig burps loudly. "Give it a rest," the narrator continues. The spot promotes an annual event called "Buy

Nothing Day," held on the Friday after Thanksgiving, which, in the United States, kicks off the Christmas shopping season.

Begun in Vancouver in 1992, Buy Nothing Day is now celebrated in many other countries. Participants agree not to purchase anything that day, cut up their credit cards, and demonstrate to encourage others to follow suit. In Vancouver, just before Buy Nothing Day, teams of young adbusters race through the streets ahead of the police, slapping hard-to-remove Buy Nothing Day posters on store windows.

"Buy Nothing Day has exploded," says Lasn. "It's becoming a truly international celebration of frugality and living lightly on the planet, and of voluntary simplicity." Lasn believes the spirit of Buy Nothing Day must catch on as an effective vaccine

against affluenza, because the North American lifestyle is simply unsustainable. "Overconsumption is the mother of all of our environmental problems," he says.

CREDIT CARD CONDOMS

When the producers of *Affluenza* included several of Lasn's uncommercials in the program, viewers got to see them on PBS. Many found them to be one of the highlights of that program. But when John and his co-producers tried to create an uncommercial of their own—a fake public service announcement (PSA)—to include in the follow-up program, *Escape from Affluenza,* they were required to remove it. Otherwise, PBS wouldn't show the program in prime time.

The fake PSA—"a public service announcement from your heirs"—promoted a little protection device against affluenza called a credit card prophylactic. It's a little envelope to store your credit card in with a warning on the outside. "Before you buy, ask yourself: Do I really need it? Can I borrow it from someone else? Are the materials in it reusable or recyclable? How much time will I need to work to afford it?" An older woman tells a young friend to "practice safe shopping" using the prophylactic. "And remember," she says with a smile, spoofing American Express, "don't leave home without it."

PBS refused to allow the PSA in *Escape from Affluenza* because programmers would have to alert local stations to the reference to credit card prophylactics. The programmers were convinced that fifty or more local PBS affiliates in conservative rural areas wouldn't air the program because in their markets, condoms are taboo. PBS knows its audience. But call it what you want, we think the credit card condom is a great idea that can help people think twice before spending.

VACCINATING KIDS

To be truly effective, vaccination programs for affluenza will have to start with children, especially now, when marketers have them squarely in their crosshairs. At least three Web sites provide valuable advice in this area—Don't Buy It (www.pbskids.org/dontbuyit), a site created by PBS to help kids understand how advertising manipulates them; Consumer Jungle (www.consumerjungle.org), a Wenatchee, Washington, site that offers activities for teachers, parents, and high school age kids to help them become savvy consumers; and ShareSaveSpend (www.sharesavespend.com), created by Nathan Dungan, the Minneapolis author of the excellent book *Prodigal Sons and Material Girls: How Not to Be Your Child's ATM.*

The first two are cleverly produced, interactive sites, while Dungan's promotes what we think is a healthy philosophy. It starts with teaching children the value of giving, then shows them how to save money and, finally, how to spend it wisely when they need to. We recommend all three sites, and you can probably find other good ones with a little searching.

MEDIA LITERACY

In many schools around the country, teachers help their students protect themselves from affluenza-carrying commercials by teaching them to analyze how media messages manipulate them. The concept is called "media literacy," and in the Age of Affluenza it may be as important as learning to read. Students dissect television ads to discover the psychological techniques the ads use to persuade them to buy. They analyze what needs each advertisement suggests the product might fill, then ask if there are better, less-costly ways to meet the same needs. Increasingly, enlightened school districts require media literacy courses.

Often, the most successful combine ad analysis with video production workshops so that students learn directly the techniques that make television effective. When Malory Graham taught media literacy in Seattle, she received support from the county's solid-waste division to teach video techniques to high school students and then have them produce their own PSAs promoting recycling and sustainable consumption. Even though Seattle has one of the best recycling rates in the United States, increased consumption means that landfills are still growing—recycling can't keep pace with the accelerating rate of waste.

Graham's media literacy and production classes combined the opportunity for hands-on production, which is very exciting for the students, with a greater understanding of the impact of their consumption. "I think it's harder for advertisers to manipulate students who've gone through a program like this," says Graham.[2]

Around the country, many students who have been exposed to media literacy are also learning about the deplorable wages and working conditions in factories that make some of the products and brands teenagers have been taught to desire. They demonstrate against child labor and sweatshops in other countries where their products are made, and they refuse to be walking billboards for global corporations.

"Today's teens and preteens are going to be tomorrow's revolutionaries," predicted trend watcher Gerald Celente a decade ago. "They're going to be very antimaterialistic."[3] Unfortunately, his prediction hasn't come true yet. But it still might if the kids get vaccinated against affluenza.

CHAPTER 28

Political prescriptions

Our country is set up structurally to oppose voluntary simplicity.

—MICHAEL JACOBSON,
Marketing Madness

We are today paying the debt for the material growth that characterized the postwar "Golden Age": disfigured landscapes, polluted air and water, erosion of the ozone layer, the greenhouse effect. Since the Third World also needs significant growth of its material production, only a reorientation of the overdeveloped countries towards a model of development centered on the immaterial growth of free time is capable of guaranteeing our common future.

—ALAIN LIPIETZ,
French Green Party economist

Sit down and pour yourself a cold one. This chapter is a little longer than most.

In the previous chapters we've been exploring voluntary personal, community, and workplace strategies for beating the affluenza bug. All are necessary and will help keep the disease in check for millions of people. But sometimes an epidemic reaches such proportions that political action is called for, usually in the form of a quarantine. We believe that point has been reached in the case of affluenza.

Thomas even wants the quarantine to begin around his state, Vermont. He's been leading a campaign called the Second Vermont Republic, which actually calls for that state to secede from the United States, to protect its unique quality of life. Vermont may be less infected by affluenza than any other state. It's almost Wal-Mart-free, and few other big-box stores or tacky mini-malls mar its quiet beauty. Vermont towns still have the feel of permanence and livability; citizens still participate regularly in public forums; everybody in the state has a guaranteed right to health insurance. Shopping locally and buying wholesome food is encouraged. Many Vermonters, like Thomas, who moved there because of Vermont's quality of life, want to prevent their good life from being overtaken by affluenza.

But we can't all live in Vermont, so we've got to figure out policies to turn back affluenza in every part of the country.

Despite twenty-five years of bad-mouthing that has left the American public deeply cynical about whether government can ever do anything right, we believe it can play an important role in helping create a society that is affluenza unfriendly, or, to put it in more positive terms, simplicity friendly. We line up squarely on the side of those who say our social ills won't be cured by personal action alone.

Just as the symptoms of affluenza are many and interconnected, so must be public efforts to quarantine it. There is no silver bullet that by itself will do the trick. It will take a comprehensive strategy, at all levels of government from local to federal, built, we believe, around several key areas of action:

- reducing annual working hours—trading money and stuff for time

- restructuring the tax and earnings systems

- instituting corporate reform, including establishing responsibility for entire product cycles

- investing in a sustainable infrastructure

- redirecting government subsidies

- formulating a new concept of child protection

- instituting campaign-finance reform

and finally,

- generating new ideas about economic growth

BACK TO THE ROAD NOT TAKEN

First of all, if we want to put a lid on the further spread of affluenza, we should restore a social project that topped organized labor's agenda for half a century, then suddenly fell from grace.

In 1912, when thousands of women walked out of the textile mills of Lawrence, Massachusetts, in a famous strike, they carried banners that read *We Want Bread, and Roses Too*. Bread and roses—symbols for the material and nonmaterial sides of life. The Lawrence strikers needed bread—higher wages. They could barely afford to feed themselves at the time. But they also knew they needed roses—shorter hours of work, allowing time for families, art, love, beauty, spirit: time to "smell the roses." Until World War II American labor always fought for both higher wages and shorter hours, for both bread and roses. But somehow, after the war, we got what was called "bread-and-butter unionism." Notice the difference. Suddenly, the unions were only about wages; the roses were left to wilt. But now, Americans need roses more than ever.

Since the Second World War, Americans have been offered what economist Juliet Schor calls "a remarkable choice." As our productivity more than doubled, we *could* have chosen to work half as much—or even less—and still produce the same material lifestyle we found "affluent" in the '50s. We could have split the difference, letting our material aspirations rise somewhat but also taking an important portion of our productivity gains in the form of more free time. Instead, we put all our apples into making and consuming more.

Our friends in Europe made a different choice. They took a big part of their gains in labor productivity in the form of time. In his book *Happiness*, British economist and House of Lords member Richard Layard shows that, as a result, general happiness in Europe continues to increase while in the United States it stagnated after the 1950s. At the same time, general health in every European country is better than that in the United States.

Established as law in 1938, the forty-hour workweek is still our standard (though most full-time American workers average closer to 45 hours a week). By law, we could set a different standard, and we should. It need not be a one-size-fits-all standard, like a thirty-hour week of six-hour days as proposed in the 1930s (and more recently in a 1993 congressional bill written by Democratic representative Lucien Blackwell of Pennsylvania) or a thirty-two-hour week composed of four eight-hour days, though for many working Americans either of those choices would be ideal.

More important, perhaps, is to get annual working hours—now averaging about 1,850 per year[1] and exceeding those even of the workaholic Japanese—under control.

Were the average workday to be six hours, we'd be putting in only about 1,500 hours a year, about the norm in western Europe. That's an additional 350 hours—nine working weeks!—of free time. So here's a suggestion: Set a standard working year of 1,500 hours for full time employees, keeping the forty-hour a week maximum. Then allow workers to find flexible ways to fill the 1,500 hours.

FLEXIBLE WORK REDUCTION

Some excellent international ideas for shortening working hours can be found in Anders Hayden's little-known but important book, *Sharing the Work, Sparing the Planet*.

Any of these scenarios could be voluntarily agreed upon between worker and employer, but shorter-hours legislation would include stiff employer penalties for work required beyond the 1,500-hour maximum per year.

Polls have shown that half of all American workers would accept a commensurate cut in pay in return for shorter working hours.[2] But the cut needn't be based on a one-to-one ratio. Workers are more productive per hour when they work fewer hours. Absenteeism is reduced and health improves. Therefore, as W. K. Kellogg recognized in the 1930s, their thirty-hour weeks should be worth at least thirty-five hours' pay and perhaps more. In fact, in the 1990s, Ron Healey, a business consultant in Indianapolis, persuaded several local industries to adopt what he calls the "30-40 now" plan. They offer prospective employees a normal forty-hour salary for a thirty-hour week. Increased employee productivity has made the experiment successful for most.

THE 'TAKE BACK YOUR TIME' CAMPAIGN

But to combat affluenza, we ought not fear trading income for free time. Beyond the reduction to 1,500 hours per year, legislation could ensure the right of workers to choose further reductions in working hours—instead of increased pay—when productivity rises, or further reductions in working hours at reduced pay, when productivity is stagnant.

In the short run, we need immediate legislation to provide time protections for American workers that resemble those that virtually every other industrial nation takes for granted. The Simplicity Forum, of which John is a Steering Committee member, has launched a national initiative called Take Back Your Time (www.timeday.org). The Simplicity Forum has joined other organizations, including Mothers Ought to Have Equal Rights (www.mothersoughttohaveequalrights.org/) and Work to Live (www.worktolive.info/index.cfm), to propose a six-point Time to Care legislative agenda:

- Guarantee paid childbirth leave for all parents. Today, only 40 percent of Americans are able to take advantage of the twelve weeks of unpaid leave provided by the Family and Medical Leave Act of 1993.

- Guarantee at least one week of paid sick leave for all workers. Many Americans work while sick, lowering productivity and endangering other workers.

- Guarantee at least three weeks of paid annual vacation leave for all workers. Studies show that 28 percent of all female employees and 37 percent of women earning less than $40,000 a year receive no paid vacation at all.[3]

- Place a limit on the amount of compulsory overtime work that an employer can impose, with the goal being to give employees the right to accept or refuse overtime work. Hundreds of thousands of workers hardly ever see their families, and several recent industrial strikes have centered on eliminating this employer prerogative.

- Make Election Day a holiday, with the understanding that Americans need time for civic and political participation.

- Make it easier for Americans to choose part-time work. Provide hourly wage parity and protection of promotions and pro-rated benefits for part-time workers.

FALLING BEHIND THE REST OF THE WORLD

Asked about the longer-vacations idea, a staff person for presidential candidate George W. Bush, said, "That sounds great. We need that here." But of the candidates themselves, only Ralph Nader actually endorsed the idea.

On July 2, 2004, during an appearance on PBS's *Now with Bill Moyers*, Republican pollster and strategist Frank Luntz observed that a majority of "swing" voters were working women with young children. Luntz said his focus groups revealed that "lack of free time" is the number-one issue with these voters. "The issue of time matters to them more than anything else in life," Luntz declared.

Yet President Bush paid only lip service to the issue, commenting on it in his speeches but offering no real solutions. And John Kerry, the Democratic candidate, failed to address it at all. "Shut up and work overtime" seems to be the message from American politicians of both major parties.

American public policies protecting our family and personal time fall far short of those in other countries. A recent study released by the Harvard School of Public Health, covering 168 of the world's nations (www.globalworkingfamilies.org), concluded that "the United States lags dramatically behind all high-income countries, as well as many middle- and low-income countries, when it comes to public policies designed to guarantee adequate working conditions for families." The study found that

- 163 of 168 countries guarantee paid leave for mothers in connection with childbirth, and 45 countries offer such leave to fathers. The United States does neither.

- 139 countries guarantee paid sick leave. The United States does not.

- 96 countries guarantee paid annual (vacation) leave. The United States does not.

- 84 countries have laws that fix a maximum limit on the workweek. The United States does not.

- 37 countries guarantee parents paid time off when children are sick. The United States does not.

The Take Back Your Time campaign believes that:

> America can do better. We believe there is no compelling reason for the world's richest country to lag so far behind in so many areas when it comes to work/life balance. It is time for the United States to join all other industrial nations in guaranteeing that our nation's tremendous productivity be used to allow Americans freedom from overwork, stress and burnout. Such stress relief will make Americans happier and healthier, and reduce the pressures on our health care system, lowering costs for all. It will also make us more productive. Studies show that job performance goes up after breaks and vacations. A healthier workplace will save money for American business, too, which loses $300 billion a year in job stress-related costs.[4]

WORK SHARING WHEN RECESSIONS COME

Plans for spreading work around by shortening hours should begin now for another reason: When the next recession does come, will we simply say, "Sayonara, tough luck" to those whose jobs are lost? There is a better way. Say a company needs to reduce production by 20 percent and believes it must lay off one-fifth of its workforce. What if, instead, it cut everybody's workweek by one day?

Sure, all workers would have to learn to live with less—not a bad idea anyway—but no one would be tossed to the wolves. And we predict that everyone would soon *love* the time off. On the other hand, if we don't make such plans and millions suddenly face unemployment, then all other negative social indicators—crime, family breakdowns, suicide, depression, and so forth—can be expected to skyrocket again. Remember, you read it here.

RETIRING STEP BY STEP

There are other ways of exchanging money for time. Many academics receive sabbaticals, anything from three months to a year off every several years, usually accepting a reduced salary during the period. Why not a system of sabbaticals every seven to ten years for all workers who desire them and are willing to take moderate salary reductions when they are on sabbatical? We all need to recharge our batteries every so often.

Or how about a system of graduated retirement? For many of us, self-esteem takes a hit and boredom a bounce when we suddenly go from forty-hour weeks to zero upon retiring. Instead, we could design a pension and social security system that would allow us to retire gradually. Let's say that at fifty we cut 300 hours from our work year—nearly eight workweeks. Then at fifty-five we cut 300 more. At sixty, 300 more. And at sixty-five, 300 more. Now, we're down to 800 (given no change in the present annual pattern). We might then have the option to stop paid labor entirely, or to keep working 800 hours for as long as we are capable.

What this would do is allow us to begin learning to appreciate leisure, volunteer more, and broaden our minds long before final retirement. It would allow more young workers to find positions and allow older workers to stay on longer to mentor them. It would allow older workers to both stay involved with their careers and also find time for more balance in their lives.

A variation on this idea that also has merit is to allow workers to take some of their "early retirement" at different stages of their careers, perhaps when they need more parenting time, for example. The ultimate idea, promoted in some European countries, is that a certain number of hours would constitute a total *paid work life,* with considerable flexibility around when the hours are worked.

REMOVING THE BIG OBSTACLE TO WORK SHARING

Of course, one additional public policy change would help make work sharing possible. It is *single-payer health care,* which would relieve the cost of health care provision for American employers. Because health care is so expensive, businesses find it more cost-effective to hire fewer workers and work them longer than pay benefits for more employees. The cost of employer-financed health care is the single most important factor in reducing the international competitiveness of American firms.

With a single-payer system, Canada manages to cover all its citizens at a total cost per person that is far less than what we spend in the United States. And despite criticisms of the Canadian system by American politicians, Canadians are healthier and live longer than Americans. And Canadians are so fond of their health care system that a nationwide poll to determine "the greatest Canadian of all time," done by the Canadian Broadcasting Company, ended up bestowing the honor on Tommy Douglas. Douglas, the late Socialist premier of Saskatchewan, was chosen, according to those who voted for him, because he was the father of the Canadian health care system (he was also the grandfather of American actor Kiefer Sutherland, but that probably didn't affect the polling a whole lot).

In any case, many Americans now work much longer than is healthy just to keep their health benefits, a problem that a public single-payer system would solve.

TAXES

In one sense, the 2000 and 2004 elections were about taxes. Gore and Kerry wanted to tax Americans less, and Bush wanted to tax them even less than Gore and Kerry did. What was missing was a discussion about the kinds of taxes and what they might do.

But a change in the tax system, similar to one already under way in parts of Europe, could considerably help contain affluenza. The first step toward a change could come through an idea called the progressive consumption tax. Proposed by economist Robert Frank in his book *Luxury Fever,* the tax would replace the personal income tax. Instead, people would be taxed on what they consumed, at a rate rising from 20 percent (on annual spending under $40,000) to 70 percent (on annual spending over $500,000). Basically the idea is to tax those with the most serious cases of "luxury fever" (which seems to be Frank's synonym for affluenza) at the highest rates, thus encouraging saving instead of spending.

At the same time, we must make it possible for lower-income Americans to meet their basic needs without working several jobs. The old Catholic idea of a family, or living wage, championed by Pope Leo XIII in his 1891 encyclical *Rerum Novarum,* could be accomplished by a negative income tax or tax credits that guarantee all citizens a simple but sufficient standard of living above the poverty line.

Equally promising are so-called green taxes. Their proponents would replace a portion of taxes on "goods" such as income—and payroll taxes, which discourage increased employment—with taxes on "bads" such as pollution or waste of nonrenewable resources. The point would be to make the market reflect the true costs of our purchases. We'd pay much more to drive a gas guzzler, for example, and a little more for this book (to cover the true costs of paper), but no more for a music lesson or theater ticket.

Additional *carbon taxes* would discourage the burning of fossil fuels. *Pollution taxes* would discourage the contamination of water and air. The costs of cleaning up pollution would be added as a tax on goods whose production causes it. Such a tax could make organic foods as cheap as pesticide-laced produce. *Depletion taxes* would increase the price of nonrenewable resources and lower the comparative price of goods made to last.

While such a green tax system would be complicated, it could go a long way toward discouraging environmentally or socially harmful consumption, while encouraging benign alternatives. As things stand, we more often subsidize what we should be taxing—extractive industries like mining ($2.6 billion in subsidies a year), and air and auto travel. We could, and should, turn that around, subsidizing clean technologies and activities (see chapter 25) like wind and solar power or organic family farms instead of oil and agribusiness. One excellent idea for doing so is the New Apollo Initiative (see www.apolloalliance.org).

CORPORATE RESPONSIBILITY

Another way to reduce the impact of consumption is to require that corporations take full responsibility for the entire life cycle of their products, an idea gaining widespread acceptance in Europe. The concept is simple and well explained in the book *Natural Capitalism*, by Paul Hawken and Amory and Hunter Lovins. In effect, companies would no longer sell us products but lease them. Then, when the products reach the end of their useful lives, the same companies would take them back to reuse and recycle them, saving precious resources.

This cradle-to-grave idea is winning considerable corporate support already, with leadership from Ray Anderson, CEO of Interface Corporation, an industrial carpet company, and from businesses that have joined the Natural Step movement, agreeing to full life-cycle responsibility for their products. The Natural Step movement seems to be spreading rapidly in Europe and is also gaining adherents, including the governors of several states, in the United States. If companies take such full responsibility, they will have to include the attendant costs in the price of their goods.

GOING DUTCH

Such responsibility will be made law by 2006 in the European Union, for automobile companies at least. But with so many companies and so many products traveling all over the world, a Dutch law may provide a more effective solution. In the Netherlands, car buyers pay an additional "disassembly tax" when they buy their vehicle. When the car reaches the end of its useful life, they take it to an auto disassembly plant, where it is carefully stripped of anything that can still be used. Then only the metal shell is crushed and recycled (in the United States everything—wires, plastic, and so forth—just gets crushed, and a large percentage is simply lost as waste). By 2001, the Dutch plants were taking 90 percent of all end-of-life vehicles and recyling 86 percent of the materials from them.

The plants, which are cheap and low-tech, employ many workers and take any cars. The disassembly tax is part of the Dutch National Environmental Policy Plan (or "Green Plan") and is being extended to include many other consumer goods.[5]

STOPPING CHILD ABUSE

Consumer advocate Ralph Nader has called the recent upsurge in marketing targeting children a form of "corporate child abuse." It's as if marketers have set out knowingly to infect our children with affluenza by spreading the virus everywhere kids congregate. It's time to protect our kids. At a minimum, we can keep commercialism out of our schools, starting with Channel One. The fight against Channel One unites Left and Right—Nader and Phyllis Schlafly both testified in Congress against it—and offers a place to begin building bridges in a country increasingly torn apart by ideology.

Second, we can begin to restrict television advertising targeted to children. Already, places such as Sweden and the Canadian province of Quebec don't allow it. If you're a parent, you probably long for relief from TV advertising's manipulation of your kids. Moreover, a stiff tax on all advertising would send a strong message to corporate America that curbing the spread of affluenza is serious business.

CAMPAIGN-FINANCE REFORM

There are, of course, dozens of other good anti-affluenza legislative ideas, but none will come to fruition as long as those who profit most from affluenza pull the strings in our political system. The sheer cost of elections—a single New Jersey Senate race in 2000 resulted in $100 million in spending—leaves candidates beholden to those who pay, and those who pay are those that have and want to keep.

So the first anti-affluenza legislation has to be campaign-finance reform, taking the PACs out of politics and offering competing candidates equal media time to present their ideas, but no time for clever, yet meaningless thirty-second commercials. Former Texas agriculture commissioner Jim Hightower has it right. "The water won't clear up," he says, "until you get the hogs out of the creek."[6]

THE POLITICS OF WELL-BEING

An exciting development along the lines we'll be taking is now happening in the United Kingdom, where Labour Party economists and ordinary citizens of different political persuasions are working to create a "Politics of Well-Being." Based in part on the ideas of eighteenth-century philosopher Jeremy Bentham, who argued that the goal of government was to seek the greatest happiness for the greatest number of people, the new politics is centered on creating tax and other policies that give people more time and support for important nonmaterial sources of happiness, such as friendships, family, and good health. These ideas are well explored in the books *Happiness,* by Richard Layard, and *Willing Slaves: How the Overwork Culture Is Ruling Our Lives,* by Madeleine Bunting. Many of the examples in the books are British, but wholly appropriate to the situation in the United States. The new movement in the UK also has an excellent Web site (www.neweconomics.org) and a stirring manifesto.

BUT WON'T OUR ECONOMY COLLAPSE?

What if Americans started buying smaller, more fuel-efficient cars, driving them less and keeping them longer? What if we took fewer long-distance vacations? What if we simplified our lives, spent less money, bought less stuff, worked less, and enjoyed more leisure time? What if government began to reward thrift and punish waste, legislated shorter work hours, and taxed advertisers? What if we made consumers and corporations pay the real costs of their products? What would happen to our economy? Would it collapse, as some economists suggest?

Truthfully, we don't know exactly, since no major industrial nation has yet embarked on such a journey. But there's plenty of reason to suspect that the road will be passable, if bumpy, at first, and smoother later. If we continue on the current freeway, however, we'll find out that it ends like Oakland's Interstate 880 during the 1989 earthquake—impassable and in ruins.

Surely we can't deny that if every American took up voluntary simplicity tomorrow, massive economic disruption would result. But that won't happen. A shift away from affluenza, if we're lucky enough to witness one, will come gradually, over a generation perhaps. Economic growth, as measured by the gross domestic product, will slow down and might even become negative.

But as Juliet Schor points out, there are many European countries (including Holland, Denmark, Sweden, and Norway) whose economies have grown far more slowly than ours, yet whose quality of life—measured by many of the indicators we say we want, including free time, citizen participation, lower crime, greater job security, income equality, health, and overall life contentment—is higher than our own. Such economies show no sign of collapse. Indeed, their savings rates are high, their deficits are low, and their currencies, especially the euro, are increasing in value while the dollar plummets. Their emphasis on balancing growth with sustainability is widely accepted across the political spectrum. As former Dutch prime minister Ruud Lubbers, a conservative, put it:

It is true that the Dutch are not aiming to maximize gross national product per capita. Rather, we are seeking to attain a high quality of life, a just, participatory and sustainable society. While the Dutch economy is very efficient per working hour, the number of working hours per citizen are rather limited. We like it that way. Needless to say, there is more room for all those important aspects of our lives that are not part of our jobs, for which we are not paid and for which there is never enough time.[7]

TIME FOR AN ATTITUDE ADJUSTMENT

If anti-affluenza legislation leads to slower rates of economic growth or a "steady state" economy that does not grow at all, so be it. (As we argue in the next chapter, growth of GDP is a poor measure of social health anyway.) Beating the affluenza bug will also lead to less stress, more leisure time, better health, and longer lives. It will offer more time for family, friends, and community. And it will lead to less traffic, less road rage, less noise, less pollution, and a kinder, gentler, more meaningful way of life.

In a '60s TV commercial, an actor claims that Kool cigarettes are "as cool and clean as a breath of fresh air." We watch that commercial today and can't keep a straight face, but when it first aired, nobody laughed. Since that time, we've come to understand that cigarettes are silent killers. We've banned TV ads for them. We tax them severely, limit smoking areas, and seek to make tobacco companies pay the full costs of the damage cigarettes cause. We once thought them sexy, but today most of us think they're gross.

Where smoking is concerned, our attitudes have certainly changed. Now, with growing evidence that affluenza is also hazardous, it's surely time for another attitude adjustment.

CHAPTER 29

Annual check-ups

The gross national product includes air pollution and advertising for cigarettes, and ambulances to clear our highways of carnage. It counts special locks for our doors, and jails for the people who break them. . . . It does not allow for the health of our families, the quality of their education, or the joy of their play.

—ROBERT KENNEDY, 1968

A patient in remission from cancer requires routine check-ups to evaluate how things are going. It's the same with affluenza. Once we're on the road to recovery, annual check-ups help prevent costly, energy-sapping relapses. Lingering germs like debt, susceptibility to advertising, and possession obsession can cause recurrences not only in individuals, but communities and national economies as well. Check-ups help track these germs down where they hide, and wipe 'em out!

We argue here that quantitative indicators such as return on investment, tax revenues, and GDP can't tell us everything we need to know about our health. We present alternative indicators that give a more holistic picture: personal consumption audits, community indicators, the Genuine Progress Indicator (GPI), and even a Fever Index, to be tracked by the authors and publisher of this book and reported annually to the press.

IS OUR TEMPERATURE RISING?

The Fever Index includes ten key variables that indicate whether affluenza is getting better or worse in the United States each year:

1. The *Guzzle Gauge* measures fossil-fuel consumption per capita.

2. *Wiggle Room* measures the average size of new homes.

3. The *Bull Sheet* tracks expenditures per capita for advertising.

4. The *Fat Cat Factor* reveals the amount of income earned by the top 10 percent and bottom 10 percent of the population.

5. The *Waste Line* measures the volume of obsolete electronic products that are thrown away (not recycled).

6. The *Clock Market* reports on the average amount of vacation time, sick leave, and family or maternity leave provided by employers.

7. The *Waist Line* divulges the average amount of obesity.

8. *Wing Nut Weight* is the number of miles traveled in airplanes every year.

9. The *Debit Sheet* tallies the amount of consumer debt per capita.

10. The *Care Share* measures per capita contributions to charity and other tax-deductible giving.

In 2005, our national temperature is hovering at 101 degrees, the level at which students are requested to stay home from school. Each year, if one of the ten factors above gets worse, the temperature will rise 0.2 degrees. But if improvement is shown for a factor, the temperature will fall by 0.2 degrees.

Recovery from affluenza is not a simple matter, but it CAN be beaten!

ENOUGH?

Too often, life's complexities get boiled down to a single, nagging question: "Do we have enough money?" Vicki Robin, the coauthor of *Your Money or Your Life*, believes this question is far too narrow. Pointing out that money is really what we trade our life energy for, she asks,

- Do we receive fulfillment, satisfaction, and value in proportion to life energy spent?

- Is this expenditure of life energy in alignment with our values and life purpose?

You don't expect weight alone to measure whether a person is sick or well. Nor would blood pressure, by itself, tell you if a person is healthy. Similarly, a grand total of expenditures (like GDP) blindly measures quantity but not quality. It can't distinguish thriving from surviving.

MAKING PERSONAL HISTORY

A very simple measurement of well-being, or gladness to be alive, is whether you're anxious to get out of bed in the morning. But the cold, hard truth is, you may jump energetically out of bed one morning only to be laid off by midafternoon (so much for gladness to be alive). Or worse, you could suddenly find out you have an illness even more critical than affluenza and have only a year to live. Are you really doing what's most important, such as making connections with people, ideas, and nature? What have you always wanted to do that you haven't done yet, because you've been too busy making and spending money? How can you do more of what you're most proud of accomplishing?

These are the kinds of questions that enable us to take stock, and take control, of our lives. Honest answers strip away illusions and worn-out patterns. They help get to the heart of what really matters. As Irvin Yalom observed, "Not to take possession of your life plan is to let your existence be an accident."[1]

A good first step in repossessing your life is to identify what you value most. Record the most significant events of your life in a notebook, including personal relationships, births and deaths, achievements, adventures, enlightenments, and disappointments. Recall the first house of your adult life, the first time you fell in love. Note the relative importance of material possessions. Have they satisfied as fully as the connections, emotions, and actions of your life?

Now, jot down a list of principles that are most important to you—things like fairness, trust, unconditional love, taking care of nature, financial security, fearlessness, maintenance of health. These are the principles to base your life decisions on, because they are your greatest, highest values. Apply these principles in your relationships, your career, and your plans for the future, and ask yourself if the constant pursuit of wealth and stuff isn't more effort than it's worth.

When you perform your annual check-up, get out your notebook and review the memoir in progress. Do any events of the past year deserve inclusion in life's "greatest hits"? With another year behind you, are there events that now seem less important? Which people from the past year of your life do you most admire? Have you followed your personal code of ethics, with maybe a few forgivable exceptions?

WHAT REALLY MATTERS

Now comes the knockout punch—good night, affluenza! By cross-referencing your personal history and values with your annual expenditures, you can determine if you're living life on your terms. Every year when you file your taxes, also file your self-audit—but don't give yourself a deadline. (After all, the idea here is to give yourself a *life*line.) Are your consumption expenditures consistent with what really matters? Have you spent too much on housing, entertainment, or electronic gadgets? Did your expenditures cause you to work overtime, in turn reducing family time? Are you happy with the charitable contributions you made? Are you getting anything back from the money you spent?

COMMUNITY CHECK-UP: INDICATORS OF SUSTAINABILITY

A recent issue of the *Denver Post* reported various surveys in which the mile-high city ranked high, nationally, in terms of "livability." But the same issue reported that Denver's growing traffic problem also ranked near the top. Sure, you take some bad with the good, but how much bad do you take?

That's essentially the question community activists asked themselves a decade ago in Seattle, when they pulled together a cross-section of business leaders, elected officials, doctors, environmentalists, and others to create a checklist of sustainability indicators for the metropolitan area. (By "sustainability," they mean "long-term health and vitality—cultural, economic, environmental, and social.") Keeping track of forty indicators is no small feat, but project coordinator Lee Hatcher is convinced the indicators provide more comprehensive feedback on the health of people, places, and the economy of Seattle than conventional gauges like property values and housing starts. Already, hundreds of Seattle citizens have put in thousands of hours of volunteer time to create and maintain the indicators.

In 2005, Sustainable Seattle began a process of analyzing its indicators and creating new ones where needed. Hatcher points out how linkages among indicators help foster holistic thinking in a community. "Take the indicator for the number of wild salmon returning to spawn," he says. "That one is linked to the economy—tourism, recreation, and fishing—as well as the environment—logging and runoff from streets that pollute streams. If we begin to see larger populations of salmon, it probably means we're taking better care of the habitat we share with them."[2]

If a community has excellent *arts education* for children, the *juvenile crime rate* may fall, *high school graduation rates* may increase, and overall *employment* may also improve. However, if the number of *children in poverty* increases, both crime and sickness may increase, resulting in long-term scars in the community.

SEATTLE'S FORTY SUSTAINABILITY INDICATORS (2000)

- Wild Salmon
- Wetlands
- Biodiversity
- Soil Erosion
- Air Quality
- Pedestrian-Friendly Streets
- Open Space in Urban Villages
- Impervious Surfaces
- Population
- Residential Water Consumption
- Solid Waste Generated and Recycled
- Pollution Prevention and Renewable Resource Use
- Farm Acreage
- Vehicle Miles Traveled and Fuel Consumption

- Renewable and Non-renewable Energy Use
- Employment Concentration
- Real Unemployment
- Distribution of Personal Income
- Health Care Expenditures
- Work Time Required for Basic Needs
- Housing Affordability Ratio
- Children Living in Poverty
- Emergency Room Use
- Community Capital
- Adult Literacy
- High School Graduation Rates

- Ethnic Diversity of Teachers
- Arts Instruction
- Volunteer Involvement in Schools
- Juvenile Crime
- Youth Involvement in Community Service
- Equity in Justice
- Low Birthrate Infants
- Asthma Hospitalization Rate for Children
- Voter Participation
- Library and Community Center Usage
- Public Participation in the Arts
- Gardening Activity
- Neighborliness
- Perceived Quality of Life

For Linda Storm, a Seattle resident for eighteen years, the indicators provide important feedback about specific qualities that she values. "What Sustainable Seattle means to me is being able to find places close to home where I can walk and see my neighbors (*Pedestrian-Friendly Streets, Open Space in Urban Villages, Neighborliness*), breathe fresh, clean air (*Air Quality*), and see native plants (*Biodiversity, Wetlands*)."[3] Yet many of these qualities are declining in proportion to the decline in indicators such as *Impervious Surfaces* (59 percent of Seattle's land area has now been paved over).

The news isn't always what we want to hear, but having relevant feedback about community health can at least stimulate intensive care. Says Hatcher, "Indicators are like the gauges and dials of an aircraft's instrument panel. By designing them carefully and watching them closely, we know the status of our flight and can make good decisions about where to go. Without indicators, we're just flying by the seat of our pants."

NATIONAL CHECK-UP: THE GENUINE PROGRESS INDICATOR (GPI)

Newscasters, investment brokers, and lenders are among those who rely on the gross domestic product (GDP) as an indicator of national prosperity. But does GDP really tell us if our economy is healthy? Economists with an organization called Redefining Progress don't think so. In a report titled "Why Bigger Isn't Better" they write,

> Imagine receiving an annual holiday letter from distant friends, report-
> ing their best year, because more money was spent than ever before. It

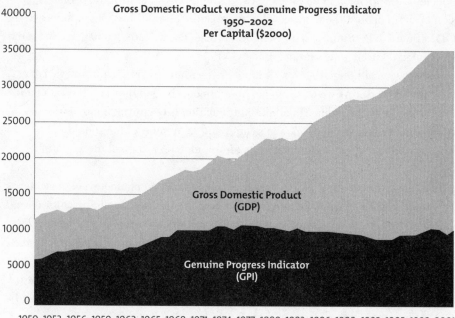

Source: Redefining Progress, *Why Bigger Isn't Better: The Genuine Progress Indicator—2002 Update* (San Francisco: Redefining Progress)

began during the rainy season when the roof sprang leaks and their yard in the East Bay hills started to slide. The many layers of roofing had to be stripped to the rafters before the roof could be reconstructed, and engineers were required to keep the yard from eroding away. Shortly after, Jane broke her leg in a car accident. A hospital stay, surgery, physical therapy, replacing the car, and hiring help at home took a bite out of their savings. Then they were robbed, and replaced a computer, two TVs, a VCR, and a video camera. They also bought a home security system, to keep these new purchases safe.[4]

These people spent more money than ever and contributed slightly to a rise in GDP, but were they happier? Not likely, in that year from hell. And what about a nation in which GDP continues to grow? Are its citizens happier? Clearly, that depends on *how the money is being spent*.

A central mission of Redefining Progress is to spotlight the "bads" that are hiding out in the gross domestic product, a yardstick that has for the last half century been a drug of choice for conventional economists. As long as the GDP goes higher, everything's cool. Politicians point to a swelling GDP as proof that their economic policies are working, and investors reassure themselves that with the overall expansion of the economy, their stocks will also expand. Yet even the chief architect of the GDP (then GNP), Simon Kuznets, believed that "the welfare of a nation can scarcely be inferred from a measurement like GNP."[5]

Here's why: although the overall numbers continue to rise, many key variables have grown worse. As we have already mentioned, the gap between the rich and everyone else is expanding. In addition, the nation is borrowing more and more from abroad, a symptom of anemic savings and mountains of household debt. The economic and environmental costs of our addiction to fossil fuels continue to mount.

When a city cuts down shade trees to widen a street and homeowners have to buy air conditioning, the GDP goes up. It also goes up when families pay for day care and divorce, when new prisons are built, and when doctors prescribe antidepressants. Pollution is a big hitter, too, as Redefining Progress's Michel Gelobter explains. "The GDP counts pollution at least four times—when it's produced, when it's cleaned up, when there are health care costs, and when there are legal fees to settle lawsuits."[6] In fact, careful analysis reveals much of the economy as tracked by GDP is based on crime, waste, and environmental destruction!

In contrast to GDP—which lumps all monetary transactions together—GPI *evaluates* the expenses, adding in "invisible" assets such as housework, parenting, and volunteer work, but subtracting the following "bads" from the national economy:

GPI EXPENSES

- cost of crime
- cost of family breakdown
- loss of leisure time
- cost of under-employment
- cost of consumer durables
- cost of commuting

- cost of household pollution abatement
- cost of automobile accidents
- cost of water pollution
- cost of air pollution
- cost of noise pollution
- loss of wetlands

- loss of farmland
- depletion of non-renewable resources
- cost of long-term environmental damage
- cost of ozone depletion
- loss of old-growth forests

As a tool for an annual check-up of the nation, a growing legion of top-level economists propose that the Genuine Progress Indicator be reported right alongside the annual GDP, to show the well-being of the economy.

And additional measures are needed to track our use of natural resources—what we have versus what we use. Measures like RP's Ecological Footprint help us to see how our consumptive lifestyles are annually eating up resources faster than nature can regenerate them. Like the spendthrift who goes on a shopping spree with a savings account, we won't have the steady supply of interest coming to us from nature in future years if we keep this up.

Swiss economist Mathis Wackernagel says, "The ecological footprint is gaining a foothold in the market analysis. Some banks have hired us to analyze the security of government bonds. They want to know, Do countries have ecological deficits? Are they overspending their natural wealth?"[7]

The Genuine Progress Indicator and the Ecological Footprint are really common sense with an analytical, pragmatic edge. National vitality, like personal health and community health, is not really about PowerPoint graphs and mindless business-as-usual, but about real things like the health of people, places, natural capital, and future generations. At all levels of our society, it's time to schedule a holistic annual check-up.

CHAPTER 30

Healthy again

One word to you and your children:
stay together, learn the flowers, go light.

—GARY SNYDER,
Turtle Island

veryone knows the feeling of waking up after a long illness and suddenly, miraculously, feeling full of life again! Being anxious to dive back
into things that have been neglected and to try new things, too. Not
feeling isolated, powerless, or estranged anymore. That's what happens when we
beat affluenza. Imagine a dial on your wristwatch with only two readings—Life and
Death. (Wouldn't that simplify things?) When you shift priorities to pursue what
really matters, the needle on that dial buoyantly wobbles back toward Life.

In the course of writing this book, we've talked with many people whose ideas
became part of our own thought processes. One early reader of the manuscript saw
similarities between victims of affluenza and prisoners of war. "Except we're prisoners of an economy that destroys our environment, our communities, and our peace
of mind," he said. "Imagine what it must feel like when the war is over and we're

liberated. Or when affluenza is purged from our lives. We'll feel such a sense of freedom and such a sense of lightness."

After reading about historically low savings rates in the United States, another reviewer imagined fifty million people retiring all at once with virtually no savings and rapidly gearing down their lifestyles. "There's gonna be one huge garage sale," he said, shaking his head. "I can see the signs now: Ford Excursion, near-new, $300. Big-screen TV (56-inch), free. Hot tub, free."

A third reader commented that each of our homes seems to have an elephant in the living room that we try desperately to ignore: it represents our preoccupation with an excessive and often obsessive lifestyle. "We can't figure out how to chase it out, so we learn to just live with it," he said.

But maybe we don't have to. There are thousands of actions we can take to beat the Bug—and oust the elephant. Though largely out of sight of the mainstream media, much is already being done, in classic grassroots style. There are major changes in the workplace, from dress codes to employee ownership. There's a resurgence of faith and spirituality, and a growing commitment to better health, including high-quality food, alternative medicine, and personal-care products "green" enough to eat (skin cream made of oatmeal, shampoo made from rice and ginger). A recent poll conducted by professional homebuilders found that energy efficiency has in recent years become one of the top considerations for homebuyers. Connections are being made between what we consume and what's happening to the environment. Clearly, our economy is in transition.

We hope this book equips readers with remedies for affluenza that have already worked for millions of people. A common thread in the recovery process is being able to admit we have a problem—which is equally true at the scale of the individual, the community, the bioregion, and the nation.

COMING BACK TO LIFE

Systems thinker Joanna Macy urges our civilization to take a deep breath, admit we have a major problem, and collectively go cold turkey. She's working to create a new world ethic based on the way nature—and human nature—actually work (lifestyles based on reality—what a concept). In the past, as she discusses in the book *Coming Back to Life*, we've looked at the world as a collection of parts and pieces, but now we're ready for a Great Turning, a new way of understanding.[1]

The idea that life is interdependent and self-organizing has always been perceived on a spiritual level, and now that perception is manifesting itself in biology and physics. Faith, says Macy, is becoming fact, as scientists compile evidence that the world's living systems "are not heaps of disjunct parts, but are dynamically organized and intricately balanced—interdependent in every movement, every function, every exchange of energy and information."[2]

Macy points out that the earth's systems use feedback just as a thermostat does, to stay healthy. But she believes human feedback is being squelched by an economy with a one-track mind. "It's natural for us to be distressed over the state of the world," she believes. "We are integral components of it, like cells in a larger body. When that body is traumatized, we feel it. . . . However, our culture conditions us to view pain as dysfunction. A successful person, as we conclude from commercials and electoral campaigns, brims with optimism. . . . 'Be sociable,' 'Keep smiling,' 'If you can't say something nice, don't say anything at all.'"

But until we acknowledge that our environment and many aspects of our culture are sick, how can we take focused action to heal them? "The problem lies not with our pain for the world, but in our repression of it," she concludes. "Our efforts to dodge or dull it block effective response." Similarly, our voluntary separation from political and social participation diminishes the collective power of citizens. When we operate strictly as "me" rather than "we," we've essentially been divided and conquered.

We live our lives in the shadow of delirious assumptions such as "We own the earth," and "Faster is better." (To this latter belief, Gandhi responded, "Speed is irrelevant if you're traveling in the wrong direction.") A vintage Doritos commercial typifies our flu-contaminated worldview: "Crunch all you want, we'll make more." But Macy and many others present new ways of seeing the world that strengthen our immune systems against this conveyor-belt mind-set. They see beyond the glitter and glitz to a more grounded, abundant reality. Instead of window-shopping (or e-shopping) to *buy* life, they urge us to more passionately *live it*.

DREAMING A NEW DREAM

Betsy Taylor, director of the Center for a New American Dream, consciously operates in the "we" mode. She has the courage to see the damage we're doing and work actively to counter it. "Our house is on fire," she says with conviction, "and there are children inside."[3] (Like many of her colleagues, she believes the smoke alarm went off when the Industrial Revolution began.) "Global warming now threatens the very fabric of life," she says. "Yet humanity remains in denial."

"Individuals acting alone can't solve the problem," Taylor says, though she acknowledges the critical role that each of us plays. She envisions a positive future—a new dream—shaped by a combination of technological innovation, policy reform, and a

significant shift in consciousness. "In twenty-five years, we will have new government policies that provide incentives for us to use materials and energy differently,"
she predicts. "New policies for transportation, waste management, recycling, and taxes
will help individuals and institutions consume wisely. . . . Prices of goods will reflect
the true environmental costs of natural resource use and waste. Government will use
its purchasing power to create markets for environmentally friendly products."

In effect, Taylor sees strong evidence that our sleepwalking culture is right on
the verge of waking up! "Go into any bookstore and you'll see hundreds of books
about values, balance, meditation, and simplicity," she says, adding, "Our Web site
is another example. This year we'll have eight to ten million hits on it, as people
learn more about sustainable living." The overall goals of the center are not just to
reduce consumption, but also to *redirect* it with smarter choices about how to purchase sustainable products. In other words, if we're smart, we'll increasingly substitute better design and more complete information for consumption. For example,
we'll support sustainable farming in which natural pest control—a biologically rich
bank of information—substitutes for pesticide applications. We'll support better
design of walkable communities, reducing the need to spend hours lost in wasteful
gridlock.

"People assume that a so-called sustainable economy means we have to make sacrifices and give up 'the good life,'" says Taylor. "But look what we're already giving
up in our current dream: we're losing cultural traditions, indigenous wisdom,
species, languages, relationships, trust, community, and health—all things that are
precious beyond money." In Taylor's new dream, the word *simplicity* means far
more than cutting back on consumption. It means cutting back on unwanted
thoughts, waste, and stress—scrapping the artificial and superficial in favor of the
authentic. It's not just simplicity of stuff, but also simplicity of purpose, and clarity
of mind. It's about being content and connected, rather than confused.

The emerging dream she describes is not meager and sparse, but precise, elegant, and full of quality. When we wake up from our troubled sleep, we won't be
wearing burlap bags—we'll be meeting needs *well*, without having to lug extrane-
ous, expensive baggage. We'll still have the same or better value, but it will be redistributed to more productive ends. Taylor cites the emerging generation of cleaner,
leaner vehicles; "green power" like space-age wind turbines; clothing made without
petroleum fibers; organic food, grown locally; and buildings that don't make us sick
(especially when we open the utility bills). "Look what's happening in the corporate
culture, as companies promote green product lines, like Philips' more efficient computer chips, which may eliminate the need for a half-dozen huge power plants. Or
look at a city like Santa Monica, California, which has solar-heated public buildings
and organic salad bars in public schools.

"Much of what is being marketed is not tied to quality of life, but status and image. We can change that, with the help of better role models," Taylor says. "When growing numbers of people act on their convictions, and those convictions are based on positive values, we'll be dreaming a new dream."

MOVING AT THE SPEED OF QUALITY

The people we interviewed agree that our current repertoire of assumptions is out of date. One of the most time-worn slogans is "the show must go on." But those who have successfully kicked affluenza ask, "Why?" If the buyer must always beware, and if our economy seems to resemble a pyramid scheme in which risks are pushed onto the poor and the environment, why don't we change the script? they ask. Why don't we announce a new mission, much bigger than going to the moon, or even stopping the Nazis? Why don't we move (quickly!) toward a new Renaissance, in which quality, ecology, equity, diversity, flexibility, and democracy blend together in a sustainable economy? It's clear that by redistributing the unprecedented wealth of this generation, we can make historic improvements in our own lives as well as those of our great-great-grandchildren. Why settle for junk when we can have quality?

In a way, quality is to affluenza what garlic is to vampires. Durability, appropriate materials, and good design eliminate the need for mountains of stuff, without reducing overall value. It's a different kind of math, which asks not how *much*, but rather how *well*.

Throughout this book, we've talked about hidden costs in an economy that tolerates waste, the loss of natural capital, and a decline in social participation. On the other hand, there are many hidden *benefits* in an economy designed for sustainability. For example, eating organic produce has the hidden benefits of preventing soil erosion from farmland and protecting algal blooms in lakes from wasted, runaway nutrients. Healthy food generally comes from healthy farms. Similarly, buying recycled paper has the hidden benefit of helping to create a viable recycling industry, complete with products made solely from recycled material. We're talking about very productive yet relatively effortless changes in the way we live our lives. Though it sometimes seems overwhelming to think about changing something as huge as a "worldview," Macy's Great Turning and Taylor's New Dream are really just part of our everyday lives, as Paul Hawken sees it:

> Join a diverse group of people in a room—different genders, races, ages, occupations, and levels of education—and ask them to describe a world they want to live in 50 years from now. Do we want to drive two hours to work? No. Do we want to be healthy? Yes. Do we want to live in places that are safe? Do we want our children to grow up in a world where they

are hopeful? Do we want to be able to worship without fear of persecution? Do we want to live in a world where nature is rebounding and not receding? No one disagrees; our vision is the same. What we need to do is identify, together, the design criteria for how we get there.[4]

With inspired design, we can have architecture that lasts a thousand years (instead of eight, like many Wal-Mart buildings). With maturing knowledge about ecology, we can have waste treatment that mimics nature, like John Todd's "living machines," which use diverse, efficient biosystems to purify water, aesthetically. We can have energy that comes directly from income (the sun) rather than savings (fossil fuels). We can support local banks that in turn support local needs. We can have less stressful lifestyles and more time with family and friends, as advocated by members of the "slow food" movement, for whom fast food is synonymous with anxiety. Chances are we can have what we want, if we recycle our worn-out paradigm into a new one, in which our decisions and our policies are driven more by our hopes than by our fears. We know what a dysfunctional future would feel like: an endless string of bad-news days that deplete our energy and strip away our sense of balance. If we continue on the same path, our economy will ultimately crash like the Titanic, and the waters will be icy.

"It can't happen," we tell each other, "our economy is now unsinkable." But it can—and will—happen, unless we get busy. We need to convert convictions into public policy, and ideas about sustainability into reality.

THE LAST PICTURE SHOW

As individuals, we don't need to be millionaires to eat well, sleep soundly, or get to know our neighbors. Without any doubt, we *do* need to consume less, because we're running out of affordable resources as well as tolerable places to dump our wastes. But the core issue of this book goes beyond consuming less to *wanting* less and *needing* less. From Lifestyles of the Rich and Famous we can progress to the more rewarding Lifestyles of the Content and Healthy.

Think about all the money we spend to fight various diseases, many of which (like allergies, cancer, diabetes, and stroke) are caused or aggravated by affluent lifestyles. Then remember that affluenza is one disease that we can cure by spending *less* money, not more.

The bottom line is this: When your time comes and your whole life flashes before you, will it hold your interest? How much of the story will be about moments of clarity and grace, kindness and caring? Will the main character—you—appear as large and noble as life itself, or as tiny and absurd as a cartoon figure, darting frantically among mountains of stuff? It's up to you, and indeed, it's up to all of us!

NOTES

INTRODUCTION

1. Al Gore, *Earth in the Balance: Ecology and the Human Spirit* (Boston: Houghton Mifflin, 1992), 221.

2. Richard Harwood in discussion with John de Graaf, April 1996.

3. Gerald Celente in discussion with John de Graaf, October 1996.

CHAPTER 1

1. U.S. Census Bureau, *Statistical Abstract of the United States* (Washington, DC: U.S. Government Printing Office, 2004–5).

2. *All-Consuming Passion: Waking Up from the American Dream,* a pamphlet produced by the New Road Map Foundation and Northwest Environment Watch (Seattle, 1998), 6.

3. Pamela Rands interview with Don Buckloh of the American Farmlands Trust, May 3, 2005.

4. KCTS Television interviews, October 1995.

5. *All-Consuming Passion,* 7.

6. Michael Jacobson, in discussion with John de Graaf, April 1996.

7. *All-Consuming Passion,* 6.

8. Bob Walker, "Mall Mania," *The Sacramento Bee,* October 19, 1998.

9. Ibid.

10. David Sharp, "Online Sales Fail to Slow Onslaught of Catalog Mailings," Associated Press, December 25, 2004, http://www.signonsandiego.com/uniontrib/20041225/news_1b25catalogs.html.

11. IT Facts, http://www.itfacts.biz/index.php?id=P2118.

12. IT Facts, http://www.itfacts.biz/index.php?id=P779.

13. Kevin Maney, "The Economy According to eBay," *USA Today,* December 29, 2003. http://www.usatoday.com/money/industries/retail/2003-12-29-ebay-cover_x.htm.

CHAPTER 2

1. Marielle Oetjen, in discussion with John de Graaf, May 1996.

2. "Card Questions," cardweb.com/cardlearn/faqs/2001/nov/20.amp. Accessed December 6, 2004.

3. Robert Frank, *Luxury Fever* (New York: Free Press, 1999), 46.

4. U.S. Census Bureau, *Usage of General Purpose Credit Cards by Families, 1992–2001,* www.census.gov/prod/2004pubs/04statab/banking.pdf.

5. U.S. Census Bureau, *Statistical Abstract* (Washington, D.C.: U.S. Government Printing Office), 2004–5.

6. Keaton Adams in discussion with John de Graaf, May 1996.

7. Leslie Earnest, "Household Debt Grows Precarious as Rates Increase," *Los Angeles Times,* May 13, 2000.

8. Elizabeth Warren in an interview with Bill Moyers, February 6, 2004, "Now with Bill Moyers," Public Broadcasting Service, http://www.pbs.org/now/transcript/transcript306_full.html.

9. Elizabeth Warren, "Bankruptcy Borne of Misfortune, Not Excess," *The New York Times,* September 3, 2000.

10. Earnest, "Household Debt Grows Precarious."

11. Michael Mantel, "Commentary: What Bush vs. Gore Means for Empty Piggy Banks," *Business Week,* September 11, 2000, http://www.businessweek.com/archives/2000/b3698106.arc.htm.

12. Steve Lohr, "Maybe It's Not All Your Fault," *New York Times,* December 5, 2004, http://www.nytimes.com/2004/12/05/weekinreview/05lohr .html?ex=1114488000&en=fb64db7b97922844&ei=5070.

13. *USA Weekend* magazine, May 12–14, 2000.

14. *All-Consuming Passion,* 11.

CHAPTER 3

1. David Myers, *The American Paradox* (New Haven, Conn.: Yale University Press, 2000),136.

2. Paul Wachtel in discussion with John de Graaf, April 1996.

3. LaNita Wacker in discussion with John de Graaf, September 1996.

4. Mike Sillivan in discussion with John de Graaf, September 1996.

5. Keith Bradshear, "GM Has High Hopes for Road Warriors," *New York Times,* August 6, 2000.

6. *All Things Considered,* National Public Radio, April 30, 2002.

7. *Day to Day,* National Public Radio, June 21, 2004.

8. See the wealth of information on changing expectations in Richard McKenzie, *The Paradox of Progress: Can Americans Regain Their Confidence in a Prosperous Future?* (New York: Oxford University Press, 1997).

9. U.S. Census Bureau, *Statistical Abstract,* 2004–5.

10. Paul Andrews, "Compaq's New iPaq May Be the PC for Your Pocket," *Seattle Times,* November 5, 2000.

11. *All-Consuming Passion,* 4.

12. Patch Adams in discussion with John de Graaf, October 1987.

13. Juliet Schor in discussion with John de Graaf, May 1997.

14. James Lardner, "The Urge to Splurge," *U.S. News and World Report,* May 24, 1998.

CHAPTER 4

1. Michael Kidd, white paper on self-storage (Springfield, Va.: Self-Storage Association, March 2000).

2. Beth Johnson in discussion with David Wann, January 2000.

3. John Fetto, "Time for the Traffic," *American Demographics,* January 2000, http://www.findarticles.com/p/articles/mi_m4021/is_2000_Jan/ai_59172246.

4. Steven Ashley, "Smart Cars and Automated Highways," *Mechanical Engineering* online, May 1998, http://www.memagazine.org/backissues/may98/features/smarter/smarter.html.

5. Stephanie Simon, "Scientists Inspect Humdrum American Lives," *Los Angeles Times,* October 28, 1999.

6. Ellen Goodman, as quoted in *All-Consuming Passion.*

7. Erich Fromm, *To Have or to Be?* (New York: Harper & Row, 1975), 5.

8. Quoted in Stephanie Simon, "A Life More Ordinary, All the Better, for These Anthropologists," *Los Angeles Times,* A-5, http://www-personal.umich.edu/%7Ebhoey/Press/Publications/press_article_latimes1.html.

9. William Rathje in discussion with David Wann, September 2000.

10. John Naisbitt, *High Tech/High Touch: Technology and Our Accelerated Search for Meaning* (London: Nicholas Brealey Publishing, 2001), 102.

CHAPTER 5

1. Richard Swenson in discussion with John de Graaf, September 1996.

2. Barbara Neely in discussion with John de Graaf, October 1992.

3. From the film *Running Out of Time,* 1994.

4. Staffan Linder, *The Harried Leisure Class* (New York: Columbia University Press, 1970), 4.

5. Linder, *The Harried Leisure Class,* 40.

6. Rodney Clapp, "Why the Devil Takes Plastic," *The Lutheran,* March 1999.

7. Linder, *The Harried Leisure Class,* 71.

8. Juliet Schor in discussion with John de Graaf, October 1992.

9. Karen Nussbaum in discussion with John de Graaf, September 1993.

10. Juliet Schor in discussion with John de Graaf, October 1992.

11. Author's tabulations based on data from the International Labour Organization, the *Economist,* and other sources.

12. Dr. Stephen Bezruchka, University of Washington School of Public Health, in discussion with John de Graaf, October 2004.

13. John Robinson in discussion with John de Graaf, May 1993.

14. See for instance, Martin Moore-Ede, *The Twenty-Four Hour Society: Understanding Human Limits in a World That Never Stops* (Reading, Mass.: Addison-Wesley, 1993).

15. From the film *Running Out of Time,* 1994.

16. Bart Sparagon in discussion with John de Graaf, October 1993.

17. Meyer Friedman in discussion with John de Graaf, October 1993.

CHAPTER 6

1. From the documentary *Running Out of Time,* 1994.

2. William Bennett, *The Index of Leading Cultural Indicators* (New York: Touchstone, 1994), 68.

3. Keaton Adams in discussion with John de Graaf, May 1996.

4. Mike Pauly in discussion with John de Graaf, May 1996.

5. Terri Pauly in discussion with John de Graaf, May 1996.

6. Ted Haggard in discussion with John de Graaf, May 1996.

7. Arlie Russell Hochschild, *The Time Bind* (New York: Metropolitan, 1997), back cover.

8. Glenn Stanton in discussion with John de Graaf, May 1996.

9. Edward Luttwak in discussion with John de Graaf , October 1996.

CHAPTER 7

1. John de Graaf, "Childhood Affluenza." In *About Children,* by Arthur Cosby et al. (Washington D.C.: American Academy of Pediatrics Press, 2005), 10-13.

2. Joan Chiaramonte in discussion with Vivian Boe, April 1996.

3. See, for example, James McNeal, *Kids as Customers: A Handbook of Marketing to Children* (New York: Lexington Books, 1992).

4. Susan Linn, *Consuming Kids: The Hostile Takeover of Childhood* (New York: New Press, 2004).

5. *Yearning for Balance: Views of Americans on Consumption, Materialism, and the Environment,* a report prepared by the Harwood Group for the Merck Family Fund (Bethesda, Md., 1995), quoted in "CNAD Asks America: 'How Much Is Enough?'" Center for a New American Dream, September 1, 2004, http://www.newdream.org/newsletter/kickoff.php.

6. David Walsh in discussion with John de Graaf, October 1999.

7. Geoffrey Cowley and Sharon Begley, "Fat for Life," *Newsweek,* July 3, 2000: 40-47.

8. As seen in the TV program *Affluenza,* 1997.

9. Caroline Sawe in discussion with John de Graaf, October 1999.

10. Laurie Mazur in discussion with John de Graaf, April 1996.

11. Kenneth Burnley in discussion with John de Graaf, May 1996.

12. Alex Molnar in discussion with John de Graaf, April 1996.

13. Interview with psychologist David Elkind, October 1993.

14. David Korten, *The Post-Corporate World: Life after Capitalism* (San Francisco: Kumarian/Berrett-Koehler, 2000), 33.

15. Jennifer Gailus in discussion with John de Graaf, May 1996.

CHAPTER 8

1. Ray Oldenburg, *The Great Good Place: Cafes, Coffee Shops, Bookstores, Bars, Hair Salons, and Other Hangouts at the Heart of a Community* (New York: Paragon House, 1989), xv.

2. James Kuntsler in discussion with David Wann, March 1997.

3. Robert Putnam, *Bowling Alone: The Collapse and Revival of American Community* (New York: Simon & Schuster, 2000), 49.

4. Eileen Daspin, "Volunteering on the Run," *Wall Street Journal,* November 15, 1999, W1.

5. "Our Separate Ways," *People,* September 25, 1995, 125.

6. Dan Cullen, "Independents Hold Market Share for 2001; Market Share by Dollar Grows," *Bookselling This Week,* April 18, 2002.

7. "2003 Market Measure," *Do-It-Yourself Retailing,* November 2002.

8. Todd Dankmyer, communications director, National Community Pharmacists Association, July 2001, quoted in Stacy Mitchell, Institute for Local Self-Reliance, *10 Reasons Why Vermont's Homegrown Economy Matters and 50 Proven Ways to Revive It* (Burlington, Vt.: Preservation Trust of Vermont, 2003). http://www.ptvermont.org/publications/HomegrownEconomy/sprawl_book.htm.

9. "Video Stores Seek Class Action in Suit against Blockbuster," *The Home Town Advantage Bulletin,* Institute for Local Self-Reliance, November 2000.

10. Mary Hendrickson, et al., "Consolidation in Food Retailing and Dairy: Implications for Farmers and Consumers in a Global Food System," National Farmers Union, January 8, 2001.

11. "Top 100," *Nation's Restaurant News,* June 24, 2002.

12. *Irish Independent,* September 26, 2003, as quoted in Richard Freeman and Arthur Ticknor, "Wal-Mart Is Not a Business, It's an Economic Disease," *Executive Intelligence Review,* November 14, 2003.

13. Stacy Mitchell, Institute for Local Self-Reliance, in discussion with David Wann, February 2000.

14. Jeff Milchen, Boulder Independent Business Alliance, in discussion with David Wann, February 2000.

15. Al Norman in discussion with David Wann, February 2000.

16. Peter Calthorpe in discussion with David Wann, October 1998.

17. Edward J. Blakely and Mary Gail Snyder, *Fortress America: Gated Communities in the United States* (Washington, D.C.: Brookings Institution Press, 1997).

18. Dyan Machan, in an interview with Daniel Yankelovich, *Forbes,* November 16, 1998, 194.

19. Putnam, *Bowling Alone.*

20. Marc Miringoff in discussion with David Wann, May 2000.

CHAPTER 9

1. Harry Boyte in discussion with John de Graaf, October 1999.

2. John Beal in discussion with John de Graaf, April 1999.

3. Robert Seiple in discussion with John de Graaf, September 1996.

4. Lee Atwater and T. Brewster, "Lee Atwater's Last Campaign," *Life* magazine, February 1991, 67.

5. Michael Lerner, *The Politics of Meaning* (Reading, Mass.: Addison-Wesley, 1996), 5–8.

6. Myers, *The American Paradox*, 6–7.

7. U.S. Department of Health and Human Services, "Substance Abuse News," December 15, 2004.

8. Tim Kasser and Richard Ryan, "A Dark Side of the American Dream," *Journal of Personality and Social Psychology* 65, no. 2 (1993): 410–422.

9. Tom Hayden, *Reunion* (New York: Random House, 1988), 82.

10. Studs Terkel in discussion with John de Graaf, May 1998.

11. William Willimon and Thomas Naylor, *The Abandoned Generation: Rethinking Higher Education* (Grand Rapids, Mich.: Eerdmans, 1995), 7–8.

12. Wilhelm Ropke, *A Humane Economy: The Social Framework of the Free Market* (Indianapolis, Ind.: Liberty Fund, 1971), 102.

13. Ibid., 113.

14. Ibid., 114.

15. Ernest van den Haag, "Of Happiness and of Despair We Have No Measure," in, Eric Josephson and Mary Josephson, eds., *Man Alone* (New York: Dell, 1970), 184.

16. Ibid., 197.

CHAPTER 10

1. Worldwatch Institute, *Vital Signs 2003* (New York: W. W. Norton, 2003), 88–89.

2. From the film *Affluenza*, 1997.

3. Personal interview, November, 1996.

4. Sylvia Nasar, "Even among the Well-Off, the Richest get Richer," *New York Times*, May 24, 1992.

5. Felicity Berringer, "Giving by the Rich Declines," *New York Times*, May 24, 1992.

6. Isaac Shapiro and Robert Greenstein, The Widening Income Gulf (Washington, D.C.: Center on Budget and Policy Priorities, September 4,1999), http://www.cbpp.org/9-4-99tax-rep.htm.

7. "Millions Still Going Hungry in U.S., Report Finds," Reuters, September 9, 2000.

8. Associated Press, August 17, 2004.

9. Ken Silverstein, "Trillion-Dollar Hideaway," *Mother Jones,* November-December 2000, http://www.motherjones.com/news/feature/2000/11/offshore.html.

10. "Study: Bush Tax Cuts Favor the Wealthy," CBSNews.com, August 16, 2004, http://www.cbsnews.com/stories/2004/08/16/politics/main636398.shtml.

11. Jennifer Reingold and Ronald Grover, "Special Report: Executive Pay," *Business Week,* April 19, 1999, http://www.businessweek.com/datedtoc/1999/9916.htm.

12. David Broder, "To Those Who Toil Invisibly amid Billionaires," *Seattle Times,* April 16, 2000.

13. Barbara Ehrenreich, "Maid to Order," *Harper's,* April 2000: 59–70.

14. Ibid.

15. Gerald Celente in discussion with John de Graaf, October 1996.

16. Ibid.

17. Barry Yeoman, "Steel Town Lockdown," *Mother Jones,* May/June, 2000, http://www.motherjones.com/news/feature/2000/05/steeltown.html. See also Drew Leder, "It's Criminal the Way We've Put 2 Million in Cages, *San Francisco Examiner,* February 10, 2000.

18. David Korten in discussion with John de Graaf, October 1996.

CHAPTER 11

1. Paul Hawken with Amory and Hunter Lovins, *Natural Capitalism* (Boston: Little, Brown, 1999), 51–52.

2. Sandra Postel, *Dividing the Waters: Food, Security, Ecosystem Health, and the New Politics of Security,* Worldwatch paper 132 (Washington, D.C.: Worldwatch Institute, 1996).

3. Energy Information Administration, *Annual Energy Review 1997,* DOE/EIA-0384(97) (Washington, D.C.: U.S. Government Printing Office, July 1998), Tables 1.5 and 5.1.

4. John C. Ryan and Alan Thein Durning, *Stuff: The Secret Lives of Everyday Things* (Seattle: Northwest Environment Watch, 1997), 43.

5. Donella Meadows, "How's a Green Group to Survive without Junk Mail?" *Global Citizen,* June 2000.

6. Ryan and Durning, *Stuff,* 55.

7. Gary Gardner and Payal Sampat, "Forging a Sustainable Materials Economy," in Worldwatch Institute, *State of the World 1999* (New York: W. W. Norton, 1999), 47.

8. Hawken, Lovins, and Lovins, *Natural Capitalism;* Consumers Union, "How Green Is Your Pleasure Machine," April 20, 2000, http://www.grist.org/advice/possessions/2000/04/20/possessions-cars/; Clifford Cobb, W. "Roads Aren't Free: The Estimated Full Social Cost of Driving and the Effects of Accurate Pricing," *Working Paper Number 3.* San Francisco: Redefining Progress, July 1998.

9. Ryan and Durning, *Stuff,* 8.

10. Alan Durning in discussion with David Wann, July 1999.

11. Mathis Wackernagel in discussion with David Wann, August 2000.

12. A. Ricciardi and J.B. Rasmussen, "Extinction Rates of North American Freshwater Fauna," *Conservation Biology* 13 (1999): 1220-22.

13. Ibid.

14. For more information, see the World Conservation Union's list of threatened species at http://www.iucn.org/redlist/2000/animals.html.

CHAPTER 12

1. Theo Colburn, Diane Dumanoski, and John Peterson Myers, *Our Stolen Future: Are We Threatening Our Fertility, Intelligence, and Survival? A Scientific Detective Story* (New York: Dutton, 1996), 137.

2. Suzanne Wuerthele in discussion with David Wann, March 2000.

3. U.S. Environmental Protection Agency, Chemical Information and Data Development Web site, http://www.epa.gov/opptintr/chemtest/index.htm.

4. Sandra Steingraber, *Living Downstream: An Ecologist Looks at Cancer and the Environment* (Reading, Mass.: Addison-Wesley, 1997), 99.

5. Ibid., 6-7.

6. Worldwatch Institute, "Phasing Out Persistent Organic Pollutants," *State of the World 2000* (New York: W. W. Norton), 85.

7. Ruth Rosen, "Polluted Bodies," *San Francisco Chronicle*, February 3, 2003.

8. Dan Fagin, Marianne Lavelle, and the Center for Public Integrity, *Toxic Deception: How the Chemical Industry Manipulates Science, Bends the Law, and Endangers Your Health* (Monroe, Maine: Common Courage Press, 1999), 43.

9. Trish Riley, "How Healthy Is Your Home?" *South Florida Parenting*, 2004, http://www.southflorida.com/sfparenting/sfe-sfp-healthy-home,0,851127.story.

10. Chris Bowman, "Medicines, Chemicals Taint Water: Contaminants Pass through Sewage Plants," *Sacramento Bee,* March 28, 2000, http://www.wallofhope.org/articles_032800.htm.

11. Quoted in Bowman, "Medicines, Chemicals Taint Water."

12. Douglas Frantz, "E.P.A. Asked to Crack Down on Discharges of Cruise Ships," *Ameriscan* online, March 20, 2000.

13. Colburn et al., *Our Stolen Future*, 24.

14. Ibid., 236.

15. Webster Donovan, "The Stink about Pork," *George,* April 1999: 94.

CHAPTER 13

1. National Institute on Drug Abuse, Bethesda, Md., http://www.nida.nih.gov/.

2. Scott Cohen, "Shopaholics Anonymous," *Elle* magazine, May 1996:120.

3. "News and Trends," *Psychology Today,* January/February 1995: 8.

4. David Myers, "Wealth, Well-Being, and the New American Dream," Center for a New American Dream Web site, July 4, 2000, http://www.newdream.org/ live/column/2.php.

5. Herman Daly in discussion with David Wann, August 1997.

6. "Money Changes Everything," *American Behavioral Scientist,* July/August 1992: 809.

7. Ibid.

8. Alex Prud'Homme, "Taking the Gospel to the Rich," *New York Times,* February 14, 1999: BU 13.

CHAPTER 14

1. Richard Ryan in discussion with David Wann, June 2000.

2. Donella H. Meadows, Dennis Meadows, and Jorgen Randers, *Beyond the Limits* (Post Mills, Vt.: Chelsea Green, 1992), 216.

3. Taichi Sakaiya, *The Knowledge-Value Revolution; or, A History of the Future* (Tokyo and New York: Kodansha International, 1991), 43.

4. Edward Hoffman, *The Right to Be Human: A Biography of Abraham Maslow* (Wellingborough, UK: Crucible Press, 1989), 122, 128.

5. Andrew Weil, *Eating Well for Optimum Health* (New York: Alfred A. Knopf, 2000), 21.

6. Eric Fromm, *To Have or to Be?* (New York: Bantam, 1982), 155.

7. Jane Brody, "Cybersex Gives Birth to a Psychological Disorder," *New York Times,* May 16, 2000: D7.

8. Jerry Mander, *Four Arguments for the Elimination of Television* (New York: William Morrow, 1978), 118.

9. Eric Schlosser, "Fast Food Nation: The True Costs of America's Diet," *Rolling Stone* magazine, September 3, 1998: 3.

10. D. J. Forman in discussion with David Wann, December 2000.

11. Lester Brown, "China Replacing the United States as World's Leading Consumer," Earth Policy Institute, February 16, 2005, http://www.earth-policy.org/Updates/Update45.htm.

12. American Society of Plastic Surgeons, "2003 Cosmetic Surgery Trends," Arlington Heights, Ill.: 2004, as found at www.plasticsurgery.org/; Sandra G. Boodman, "For More Teenage Girls, Adult Plastic Surgery," *Washington Post,* October 26, 2004.

13. *Rocky Mountain News* editorials, June 20, 2000: 31.

CHAPTER 15

1. Marshall Sahlins, "The Original Affluent Society," in *The Consumer Society,* ed. Neva Goodwin, Frank Ackerman, and David Kiron (Washington, D.C.: Island Press, 1997), 18–20.

2. Allen Johnson in discussion with John de Graaf, May 1993.

3. Cited in James Childs Jr., *Greed: Economics and Ethics in Conflict* (Minneapolis: Fortress Press, 2000), 1.

4. Jerome Segal, *Graceful Simplicity* (New York: Henry Holt, 1999), 167.

5. Daniel Schwarz in discussion with John de Graaf, April 1996.

6. In Segal, *Graceful Simplicity,* 6.

7. Ibid., 189.

8. Ibid.

9. Matthew 19:22.

10. Richard Swenson in discussion with John de Graaf, October 1996.

11. Calvin DeWitt in discussion with John de Graaf, April 1996.

12. T. C. McLuhan, *Touch the Earth: A Self-Portrait of Indian Existence* (New York: Touchstone, 1976), 90.

CHAPTER 16

1. David Shi in discussion with John de Graaf, April 1996.

2. Segal, *Graceful Simplicity,* 13.

3. Ibid.

4. Ibid., 14.

5. From the documentary *Running Out of Time,* 1994.

6. Juliet Schor, *The Overworked American* (New York: Basic Books, 1992).

7. Rodney Clapp, ed., *The Consuming Passion* (Downer's Grove, Ill.: Intervarsity, 1998), 173.

8. Karl Marx and Friedrich Engels, "The Communist Manifesto," in *Basic Writings on Politics and Philosophy,* ed. Lewis Feuer (Garden City, N.Y.: Anchor, 1959), 1–41.

9. Karl Marx, "The Economic and Philosophical Manuscripts of 1844," *Marx's Concept of Man,* by Erich Fromm (New York: Frederick Ungar, 1971), 55.

10. Ibid., 107.

11. Ibid., 37.

12. Karl Marx and Friedrich Engels, *Capital III* (New York: Modern Library, 1906), 954.

13. Perry Miller, ed., *The American Transcendalists* (Garden City, N.Y.: Anchor, 1957), 313.

14. Ibid., 309–310.

15. Ibid., 310.

CHAPTER 17

1. Jeremy Rifkin in discussion with John de Graaf, April 1996.

2. Paul Lafargue, *The Right to Be Lazy* (Chicago: Charles Kerr, 1989), 40.

3. William Morris, in *Political Writings of William Morris,* ed., A. L. Morton (New York: International Publishers, 1973), 112.

4. Susan Strasser in discussion with John de Graaf, April 1996.

5. David Shi in discussion with John de Graaf, October 1996.

6. Quoted in Benjamin Hunnicutt, *Work without End* (Philadelphia: Temple University Press, 1988), 82.

7. Ibid., 75.

8. Ibid., 88–97.

9. Ibid., 99.

10. Ibid., 53.

11. James Twitchell, "Two Cheers for Materialism," *Utne Reader,* November/December 2000.

12. Benjamin Hunnicutt in discussion with John de Graaf, October 1993.

13. Quoted in the documentary *Running Out of Time,* by John de Graaf and Vivia Boe.

14. Ibid.

CHAPTER 18

1. From the documentary *Affluenza,* 1997.

2. Ibid.

3. Susan Strasser in discussion with John de Graaf, April 1996.

4. Ibid.

5. From *Affluenza,* the film.

6. From *Affluenza,* the film.

7. From *Affluenza,* the film.

8. Gary Cross, *An All-Consuming Century* (New York: Columbia University Press, 2000), 169.

9. From the documentary *Escape from Affluenza,* 1998.

10. Ropke, *A Humane Economy,* 109.

11. John Kenneth Galbraith, *The Affluent Society* (Boston: Houghton Mifflin, 1998), 258.

12. Ibid., 266.

13. Mario Savio, "Stop the Machine" address to the Free Speech Movement demonstration, Berkeley, California, 1964.

14. Quoted in Hayden, *Reunion,* 264.

15. Cross, *All-Consuming Century,* 261.

16. David Shi in discussion with John de Graaf, October 1996.

CHAPTER 19

1. Pierre Martineau, *Motivation in Advertising* (New York: McGraw-Hill, 1971), 190.

2. *All-Consuming Passion,* 6.

3. Kim Chapman, "Americans to Spend More on Media than Food in 2003," *Rocky Mountain News,* December 17, 1999.

4. Quoted in Michael Jacobson and Laurie Ann Mazur, *Marketing Madness* (Boulder, Colo.: Westview, 1995), 131.

5. Laurie Mazur in discussion with John de Graaf, April 1996.

6. Ibid.

7. Michael Jacobson in discussion with John de Graaf, April 1996.

8. Pat Kearney, "Driving for Dollars, the *Stranger,* May 4, 2000.

9. Jacobson in discussion with John de Graaf, April 1996.

10. Mazur in discussion with John de Graaf, April 1996.

11. Susan Faludi, *Stiffed* (New York: Morrow, 1999), 35.

12. Ropke, *A Humane Economy*, 128-9.

CHAPTER 20

1. Kalle Lasn, *Culture Jam* (New York: Eagle Brook, 1999), 27.

2. John Stauber in discussion with David Wann, April 2000.

3. Joel Makower, *The Green Business Letter*, March 1994: 1, 6–7.

4. Rob Walker, "The Hidden (in Plain Sight) Persuaders," *New York Times Magazine*, December 5, 2004, http://query.nytimes.com/gst/abstract .html?res=F20912FC3A5A0C768CDDAB0994DC404482&incamp=archive:search.

5. Walker, "Hidden (in Plain Sight) Persuaders"; Linda Tischler, "What's the Buzz?" *Fast Company* 82 (May 2004): 76.

6. Sharon Beder, *Global Spin: The Corporate Assault on Environmentalism* (White River Junction, Vt.: Chelsea Green, 1997), 28–29.

7. John Stauber in discussion with David Wann, April 2000.

8. Mark Dowie, introduction to John C. Stauber and Sheldon Rampton, *Toxic Sludge Is Good for You: Lies, Damn Lies, and the Public Relations Industry* (Common Courage Press, Monroe, Me., 1995), 1.

9. Stauber and Rampton, *Toxic Sludge Is Good for You*, 28.

10. Beder, *Global Spin*, 32.

11. Jamie Lincoln Kitman, "The Secret History of Lead," the *Nation*, March 20, 2000: 6.

12. Joyce Nelson, "Great Global Greenwash: Barston-Marsteller, Pax Trilateral and the Brundtland Gang vs. the Environment," *CovertAction* 44: 26–33, 57–58.

13. George Orwell, *1984* (New York: Signet Books, 1981), 312.

14. Stauber and Rampton, *Toxic Sludge*, 28.

15. Beder, *Global Spin*, 112–113.

16. Meadows, Meadows, and Randers, *Beyond the Limits*, 1.

CHAPTER 22

1. Fred Brown in discussion with John de Graaf, October 1997.

2. Evy McDonald in discussion with John de Graaf, November 1996.

3. Joe Dominguez in discussion with John de Graaf, November 1996.

4. Vicki Robin in discussion with John de Graaf, November 1996.

5. See also the book *Getting a Life* (New York: Viking, 1997), by Jacqueline Blix and David Heitmiller.

6. *Yearning for Balance* (see chap. 7, n. 5).

CHAPTER 23

1. Gerald Celente in discussion with John de Graaf, October 1996.
2. Cecile Andrews in discussion with John de Graaf, November 1996.
3. Jeanne Roy in discussion with John de Graaf, September 1996.
4. Duane Elgin in discussion with John de Graaf, July 1996.

CHAPTER 24

1. Bill McKibben, *The Age of Missing Information* (New York: Random House, 1992), 70.
2. Ibid., 71.
3. Chellis Glendinning, "Recovery from Western Civilization," in *Deep Ecology for the 21st Century,* ed. George Sessions (Boston: Shambala Press, 1995), 37.
4. Aldo Leopold, *A Sand County Almanac* (New York: Ballantine Books, 1986), 24.
5. David Sobel in discussion with David Wann, October 2000.
6. David Sobel, *Beyond Ecophobia: Reclaiming the Heart in Nature Education* (Great Barrington, Mass.: Orion Society, 1996), 34.
7. Robert Greenway, "The Wilderness Effect and Ecopsychology," in *Ecopsychology,* ed. Theodore Roszak, Mary E. Gomes, and Allen D. Kanner (San Francisco: Sierra Club Books, 1995), 128–9.
8. Ibid.
9. Lana Porter in discussion with David Wann, March 2000.
10. Calvin DeWitt in discussion with David Wann, April 1996.

CHAPTER 25

1. Paul Hawken in discussion with David Wann, March 1997.
2. Howard Geller in discussion with David Wann, June 2000.
3. Warren Leon in discussion with David Wann, July 2000.
4. Michael Brower and Warren Leon, *The Consumer's Guide to Effective Environmental Choices* (New York: Three Rivers Press, 1999), 134.
5. Michael Brylawski, "Car Watch: Move Over, Dinosaurs," *RMI Solutions Newsletter,* Rocky Mountain Institute, Spring 2000: 12.
6. Lester R. Brown, "Europe Leading World into Age of Wind Energy," Earth Policy Institute Web site, April 8, 2004, http://www.earth-policy.org/Updates/Update37.htm.
7. Howard Geller in discussion with David Wann, June 2000.
8. David Morris in discussion with David Wann, September 2000.
9. Tom Chappell, *The Soul of a Business: Managing for Profit and the Common Good* (New York: Bantam, 1993), 12.
10. Terrance O'Connor, "Therapy for a Dying Earth," in *Ecopsychology,* ed. Roszak, Gomes, and Kanner, 153.

CHAPTER 26

1. Benjamin R. Barber, *A Place for Us* (New York: Hill & Wang, 1998), 73.
2. Ibid., 10.
3. Michael Moore, "Bush and Gore Make Me Wanna Ralph," Michael Moore Web site, July 19, 2000, http://www.michaelmoore.com/words/message/index .php?messageDate=2000-07-19.
4. Quoted in Harry C. Boyte, "Off the Playground of Civil Society," Duke University Press, October 1998, 5.
5. Dick Roy in discussion with David Wann, August 2000.
6. Doug McKenzie-Mohr and William Smith, *Fostering Sustainable Behavior* (Gabriola Island, B.C.: New Society Publishers, 1999), 49.
7. Ibid., 53.
8. Personal interview, October, 2000.
9. Gary Gardner, "Why Share?" *World Watch* magazine, July–August 1999: 10.
10. Leah Brumer, "Capital Idea," *Hope* magazine, Fall 1999: 43–45.

CHAPTER 27

1. Kalle Lasn in discussion with John de Graaf, November 1996.
2. Malory Graham in discussion with John de Graaf, April 2000.
3. Gerald Celente in discussion with John de Graaf, October 1996.

CHAPTER 28

1. Jon Messenger, senior research officer, International Labour Organization, Geneva, in discussion with John de Graaf, August 2004.
2. *All-Consuming Passion,* 16 (see chap. 1, n. 2).
3. AFL-CIO, "Ask a Working Woman" report, 2004, available at http://www.aflcio.org/ yourjobeconomy/women/index.cfm.
4. De Graaf, *Take Back Your Time,* 78.
5. From the documentary *Green Plans,* by Jack Hamann, David Davis, and John de Graaf (Seattle: KCTS Television), 1995.
6. Speech by Jim Hightower at Santa Barbara, California, May 13, 2000.
7. Hayden, *Sharing the Work,* 36.

CHAPTER 29

1. Irvin D. Yalom, *Existential Psychotherapy* (New York: Basic Books, 1980), 12.
2. Lee Hatcher in discussion with David Wann, October 1998.
3. Linda Storm in discussion with David Wann, October 1998.

4. Redefining Progress, *Why Bigger Isn't Better: The Genuine Progress Indicator—1999 Update* (San Francisco: Redefining Progress), http://www.rprogress.org/projects/gpi/updates/gpi1999.html.

5. Ibid.

6. Michel Gelobter in discussion with David Wann, February, 2005.

7. Mathis Wackernagel in discussion with David Wann, November 1999.

CHAPTER 30

1. Joanna Macy and Molly Young Brown, *Coming Back to Life: Practices to Reconnect Our Lives, Our World* (Gabriola Island, B.C.: New Society Publishers, 1998), 27.

2. Ibid., 40.

3. Betsy Taylor in discussion with David Wann, October 2000.

4. Paul Hawken, "Natural Capitalism," interview with Allan Hunt Badiner, *Yoga Journal,* September/October 1994: 68, 70.

BIBLIOGRAPHY AND SOURCES

Abdullah, Sharif. *Creating a World That Works for All*. San Francisco: Berrett-Koehler, 1999.

Ableman, Michael. *From the Good Earth*. New York: Abrams, 1993.

————. *On Good Land*. San Francisco: Chronicle Books, 1998.

Acuff, Dan. *What Kids Buy and Why*. New York: Free Press, 1997.

Affluenza. A documentary produced by John de Graaf and Vivia Boe for the Public Broadcasting Service, 1997.

American Society of Plastic Surgeons, "2003 Cosmetic Surgery Trends," Arlington Heights, Ill.: 2004, as found at www.plasticsurgery.org.

Andrews, Cecile. *The Circle of Simplicity*. New York: HarperCollins, 1997.

Andrews, Paul. "Compaq's New iPaq May Be the PC for Your Pocket," *Seattle Times*, November 5, 2000.

Aronowitz, Stanley, and William DiFazio. *The Jobless Future*. Minneapolis: University of Minnesota Press, 1994.

Ashley, Steven. "Smart Cars and Automated Highways," *Mechanical Engineering* online, May 1998. http://www.memagazine.org/backissues/may98/features/ smarter/smarter.html.

AtKisson, Alan. *Believing Cassandra*. White River Junction, Vt.: Chelsea Green, 1999.

Atwater, Lee, and T. Brewster. "Lee Atwater's Last Campaign," *Life* magazine, February 1991, 67.

Ayres, Ed. *God's Last Offer: Negotiating for a Sustainable Future*. New York: Four Walls Eight Windows, 1999.

Barber, Benjamin R. *A Place for Us*. New York: Hill & Wang, 1998.

Bartlett, Donald, and James Steele. *America: What Went Wrong?* Kansas City, Mo.: Andrews & McNeal, 1992.

————. *America:Who Really Pays the Taxes?* New York: Touchstone, 1994.

Beder, Sharon. *Global Spin: The Corporate Assault on Environmentalism*. White River Junction, Vt: Chelsea Green, 1997.

Bellah, Robert, et al. *Habits of the Heart*. Berkeley and Los Angeles: University of California Press, 1985.

————. *The Good Society*. New York: Knopf, 1991.

Bennett, William. *The Index of Leading Cultural Indicators*. New York: Touchstone, 1994.

Berringer, Felicity. "Giving by the Rich Declines," *New York Times*, May 24, 1992.

Blakely, Edward J., and Mary Gail Snyder. *Fortress America: Gated Communities in the United States*. Washington, D.C.: Brookings Institution Press, 1997.

Blix, Jacqueline, and David Heitmiller. *Getting a Life*. New York: Viking, 1997.

Bodnar, Janet. *Mom, Can I Have That?* Washington, D.C.: Kiplinger, 1996.

————. *Dr. Tightwad's Money-Smart Kids*. Washington, D.C.: Kiplinger, 1997.

Boodman, Sandra G. "For More Teenage Girls, Adult Plastic Surgery," *Washington Post*, October 26, 2004.

Bowman, Chris. "Medicines, Chemicals Taint Water: Contaminants Pass through Sewage Plants," *Sacramento Bee*, March 28, 2000.

Boyte, Harry, and Nancy Kari. *Building America*. Philadelphia: Temple University Press, 1996.

Bradshear, Keith. "GM Has High Hopes for Road Warriors," *New York Times*, August 6, 2000.

Brandt, Barbara. *Whole Life Economics*. Philadelphia: New Society, 1995.

Brockway, Sandy, ed. *Macrocosm USA: Possibilities for a New Progressive Era*. Cambria, Calif.: Macrocosm USA, 1992.

Brody, Jane. "Cybersex Gives Birth to a Psychological Disorder," *New York Times*, May 16, 2000: D7.

Brooks, David. *On Paradise Drive*. New York: Simon & Schuster, 2004.

Brower, Michael, and Warren Leon. *The Consumer's Guide to Effective Environmental Choices*. New York: Three Rivers Press, 1999.

Brown, Lester. *Eco-Economy: Building an Economy for the Earth*. New York: W. W. Norton, 2001.

———. "Europe Leading World into Age of Wind Energy," Earth Policy Institute Web site, April 8, 2004. http://www.earth-policy.org/Updates/Update37.htm.

———. "China Replacing the United States as World's Leading Consumer," Earth Policy Institute Web site, February 16, 2005. http://www.earth-policy.org/Updates/Update45.htm.

———. *Outgrowing the Earth: The Food Security Challenge in an Age of Falling Water Tables and Rising Temperatures*. New York: W. W. Norton, 2005.

Brumer, Leah. "Capital Idea," *Hope* magazine, Fall 1999: 43–45.

Brylawski, Michael. "Car Watch: Move Over, Dinosaurs," *RMI Solutions Newsletter*, Rocky Mountain Institute, Spring 2000: 12.

Bunting, Madeleine. *Willing Slaves: How the Overwork Culture Is Ruling Our Lives*. London: HarperCollins, 2004.

Callahan, David. *The Cheating Culture: Why More Americans Are Doing Wrong to Get Ahead*. New York: Harcourt Publishers, 2004.

Callenbach, Ernest. *Living Cheaply with Style*. Berkeley, Calif.: Ronin Publishing, 1993.

Celente, Gerald. *Trends 2000*. New York: Warner, 1997.

Chapman, Kim. "Americans to Spend More on Media than Food in 2003," *Rocky Mountain News*, December 17, 1999.

Chappell, Tom. *The Soul of a Business*. New York: Bantam, 1993.

Childs, James Jr. *Greed: Economics and Ethics in Conflict*. Minneapolis: Fortress Press, 2000.

Chiras, Dan, and David Wann. *Superbia*. Gabriola Island, BC: New Society Publishers, 2003.

Clapp, Rodney, ed. *The Consuming Passion*. Downer's Grove, Ill.: Intervarsity, 1998.

———. "Why the Devil Takes Plastic," *The Lutheran*, March 1999.

Cobb, Clifford W. "Roads Aren't Free: The Estimated Full Social Cost of Driving and the Effects of Accurate Pricing," *Working Paper Number 3*. San Francisco: Redefining Progress, July 1998.

Cobb, Clifford W., Gary Sue Goodman, and Joanne Kliejunas. *Blazing Sun Overhead and Clouds on the Horizon: The Genuine Progress Report for 1999*. San Francisco: Redefining Progress, December 2000.

Cohen, Joel. *How Many People Can the Earth Support?* New York: W. W. Norton, 1995.

Cohen, Scott. "Shopaholics Anonymous," *Elle* magazine, May 1996:120.

Colburn, Theo, Diane Dumanoski, and John Peterson Myers. *Our Stolen Future: Are We Threatening Our Fertility, Intelligence, and Survival? A Scientific Detective Story*. New York: Dutton, 1996.

Consumers Union, "How Green Is Your Pleasure Machine?" April 20, 2000. http://www.grist.org/advice/possessions/2000/04/20/possessions-cars/.

Courtright, Alan. *The 6/12 Plan*. Self-published, 1989.

Cowley, Geoffrey, and Sharon Begley. "Fat for Life," *Newsweek*, July 3, 2000: 40–47.

Cross, Gary. *An All-Consuming Century*. New York: Columbia University Press, 2000.

Cullen, Dan. "Independents Hold Market Share for 2001; Market Share by Dollar Grows," *Bookselling This Week*, April 18, 2002.

Daly, Herman. *Steady-State Economics*. Washington, D.C.: Island Press, 1991.

Daly, Herman with John Cobb. *For the Common Good*. Boston: Beacon, 1994.

Daspin, Eileen. "Volunteering on the Run," *Wall Street Journal*, November 15, 1999, W1.

De Bell, Garrett, ed. *The Environmental Handbook*. New York: Ballantine, 1970.

De Geus, Marius. *The End of Over-consumption*. Utretcht, the Netherlands: International Books, 2003.

De Graaf, John, ed. *Take Back Your Time*. San Francisco: Berrett-Koehler, 2003.

———. "Childhood Affluenza." In *About Children*, by Arthur Cosby et al., 10–13. Washington D.C.: American Academy of Pediatrics Press, 2005.

De Grote-Sorenson, Barbara, and David De Grote-Sorenson. *Six Weeks to a Simpler Lifestyle*. Minneapolis: Augsburg, 1994.

Devall, Bill. *Living Richly in an Age of Limits*. Salt Lake City: Gibbs Smith, 1993.

Devall, Bill, and George Sessions. *Deep Ecology*. Layton, Utah: Gibbs Smith Publishers, 1985.

DeWitt, Calvin. *Earth-wise*. Grand Rapids, Mich.: CRC Publications, 1994.

Dickson, Paul. *Timelines*. Reading, Mass.: Addison-Wesley, 1991.

Dlugozima, Hope, James Scott, and David Sharp. *Six Months Off*. New York: Henry Holt, 1996.

Dominguez, Joe, and Vicki Robin. *Your Money or Your Life: Transforming Your Relationship with Money and Achieving Financial Independence*. New York: Viking, 1992.

Donovan, Webster. "The Stink about Pork," *George*, April 1999: 94.

Doyle, Kenneth. *The Social Meanings of Money and Property*. Thousand Oaks, Calif.: Sage, 1999.

Dungan, Nathan. *Prodigal Sons and Material Girls: How Not to Be Your Child's ATM*. New York: Wiley, 2003.

Durning, Alan. *How Much Is Enough?* New York: W. W. Norton, 1992.

Durning, Alan, and John C. Ryan. *Stuff: The Secret Lives of Everyday Things*. Seattle: Northwest Environment Watch, 1997.

Earnest, Leslie. "Household Debt Grows Precarious as Rates Increase," *Los Angeles Times*, May 13, 2000.

Easterbrook, Gregg. *The Progress Paradox*. New York: Random House, 2003.

Ehrenhalt, Alan. *The Lost City*. New York: Basic Books, 1995.

Ehrenreich, Barbara. "Maid to Order," *Harper's*, April 2000: 59–70.

Elkin, Bruce. *Simplicity and Success*. Victoria, BC: Trafford Publishing, 2003.

Elkind, David. *The Hurried Child*. Reading, Mass.: Addison-Wesley, 1988.

Ellul, Jacques. *The Technological Society*. New York: Vintage, 1964.

Elwood, J. Murray. *Not for Sale*. Notre Dame, Ind.: Sorin, 2000.

Energy Information Administration. *Annual Energy Review 1997*, DOE/EIA- 0384(97). Washington, D.C.: U.S. Government Printing Office, July 1998.

Escape from Affluenza. A documentary produced by John de Graaf and Vivia Boe for the Public Broadcasting Service, 1998.

Etzioni, Amitai. *The Spirit of Community*. New York: Crown, 1993.

Fagin, Dan, Marianne Lavelle, and Center for Public Integrity. *Toxic Deception: How the Chemical Industry Manipulates Science, Bends the Law, and Endangers Your Health*. Monroe, Maine: Common Courage Press, 1999.

Faludi, Susan. *Stiffed*. New York: Morrow, 1999.

Fassel, Diane. *Working Ourselves to Death*. San Francisco: Harper San Francisco, 1990.

Fetto, John. "Time for the Traffic," *American Demographics*, January 2000. http://www.find-articles.com/p/articles/mi_m4021/is_2000_Jan/ai_59172246.

Folbre, Nancy. *The New Field Guide to the U.S. Economy*. New York: New Press, 1995.

Forbes, Peter, ed. *Our Land, Ourselves*. San Francisco: Trust for Public Land, 1999.

Foster, Richard. *Freedom of Simplicity*. San Francisco: Harper & Row, 1981.

Fox, Matthew. *The Reinvention of Work*. San Francisco: Harper San Francisco, 1994.

Frank, Robert. *Luxury Fever*. New York: Free Press, 1999.

Frank, Thomas. *One Market under God*. New York: Doubleday, 2000.

Freeman, Richard, and Arthur Ticknor. "Wal-Mart Is Not a Business, It's an Economic Disease," *Executive Intelligence Review*, November 14, 2003.

Fromm, Erich. *The Sane Society*. New York: Rinehart, 1955.

———. *The Heart of Man*. New York: Harper & Row, 1964.

———. *Marx's Concept of Man*. New York: Frederick Ungar, 1971.

———. *The Anatomy of Human Destructiveness*. Greenwich, Conn.: Fawcett, 1973.

———. *To Have or to Be?* New York: Bantam, 1982.

Fukuyama, Francis. *Trust*. New York: Free Press, 1995.

Galbraith, John Kenneth. *The Affluent Society*. Boston: Houghton Mifflin, 1998.

Galeano, Eduardo. *Upside Down*. New York: Metropolitan, 2000.

Gardner, Gary. "Why Share?" *Worldwatch* magazine, July–August 1999: 10.

Gardner, Gary, and Payal Sampat. "Forging a Sustainable Materials Economy," in Worldwatch Institute, *State of the World 1999*. New York: W. W. Norton, 1999.

Giddens, Anthony. *Beyond Left and Right: The Future of Radical Politics*. Stanford, Calif.: Stanford University Press, 1994.

Gini, Al. *The Importance of Being Lazy*. New York: Routledge, 2003.

Goldberg, M. Hirsh. *The Complete Book of Greed*. New York: William Morrow, 1994.

Goodwin, Neva, Frank Ackerman, and David Kiron, eds. *The Consumer Society*. Washington, D.C.: Island Press, 1997.

Gore, Al. *Earth in the Balance: Ecology and the Human Spirit*. Boston: Houghton Mifflin, 1992.

Grieder, William. *The Soul of Capitalism: Opening Paths to a Moral Economy*. New York: Simon & Schuster, 2003.

Grigsby, Mary. *Buying Time and Getting By*. Albany: SUNY Press, 2004.

Hammond, Jeff, et al. *Tax Waste, Not Work: How Changing What We Tax Can Lead to a Stronger Economy and a Cleaner Environment*. San Francisco: Redefining Progress, April 1997.

Hawken, Paul. *The Ecology of Commerce*. New York: Harper Business, 1993.

Hawken, Paul with Amory and Hunter Lovins. *Natural Capitalism*. Boston: Little, Brown, 1999.

Hayden, Anders. *Sharing the Work, Sparing the Planet*. London: Zed Books, 1999.

Hayden, Tom. *The Love of Possession Is a Disease with Them*. New York: Holt, Rinehart & Winston, 1972.

———. *Reunion*. New York: Random House, 1988.

Heloise. *Hints for a Healthy Planet*. New York: Perigee, 1990.

Hendrickson, Mary, et al. "Consolidation in Food Retailing and Dairy: Implications for Farmers and Consumers in a Global Food System," National Farmers Union, January 8, 2001.

Henwood, Doug. *After the New Economy*. New York: New Press, 2003.

Hertsgaard, Mark. *Earth Odyssey*. New York: Broadway Books, 1998.

Hewlett, Sylvia Ann, and Cornell West. *The War against Parents*. Boston: Houghton Mifflin, 1998.

Hochschild, Arlie Russell. *The Time Bind*. New York: Metropolitan, 1997.

Hoffman, Edward. *The Right to Be Human: A Biography of Abraham Maslow*. Wellingborough, UK: Crucible Press, 1989.

Holy Bible. New International Version.

Honore, Carl. *In Praise of Slowness*. New York: HarperCollins, 2004.

Hunnicutt, Benjamin. *Work without End: Abandoning Shorter Hours for the Right to Work*. Philadelphia: Temple University Press, 1988.

———. *Kellogg's Six-Hour Day*. Philadelphia: Temple University Press, 1996.

Ikuta, Yasutoshi. *Cruise O Matic: Automobile Advertising of the 1950s*. San Francisco: Chronicle Books, 2000.

Illich, Ivan. *Tools for Conviviality*. New York Harper & Row, 1973.

———. *Energy and Equity*. New York: Perennial, 1974.

———. *Shadow Work*. Boston: Marion Boyars, 1981.

Jacobson, Michael, and Laurie Ann Mazur. *Marketing Madness*. Boulder, Colo.: Westview, 1995.

Josephson, Eric, and Mary Josephson, eds. *Man Alone*. New York: Dell, 1970.

Kasser, Tim. *The High Price of Materialism*. Cambridge, Mass.: MIT Press, 2002.

Kasser, Tim, and Allen D. Kanner, eds. *Psychology and Consumer Culture: The Struggle for a Good Life in a Materialistic World*. Washington D.C.: American Psychological Association, 2003.

Kasser, Tim, and Richard Ryan., "A Dark Side of the American Dream," *Journal of Personality and Social Psychology* 65, no. 2 (1993): 410–422.

Kawachi, Ichiro, and Bruce Kennedy. *The Health of Nations*. New York: Free Press, 2002.

Kelley, Linda. *Two Incomes and Still Broke*. New York: Times Books, 1996.

Kelly, Marjorie. *The Divine Right of Capital*. San Francisco: Berrett-Koehler, 2001.

Kidd, Michael. White paper on self-storage. Springfield, Va.: Self-Storage Association, March 2000.

Kitman, Jamie Lincoln. "The Secret History of Lead," the *Nation*, March 20, 2000, 6.

Klein, Naomi. *No Logo*. New York: Harper Collins, 2000.

Korten, David. *When Corporations Rule the World*. San Francisco: Kumarian/Berrett-Koehler, 1995.

———. *The Post-Corporate World*. San Francisco: Kumarian/Berrett-Koehler, 2000.

Lafargue, Paul. *The Right to Be Lazy*. Chicago: Charles Kerr, 1989.

Lane, Robert E. *The Loss of Happiness in Market Democracies*. New Haven, Conn.: Yale University Press, 2000.

Lardner, James. "The Urge to Splurge," *U.S. News and World Report*, May 24, 1998.

Lasch, Christopher. *The Culture of Narcissism: American Life in an Age of Diminishing Expectations*. New York, W. W. Norton, 1978.

———. *The Minimal Self: Psychic Survival in Troubled Times*. New York, W. W. Norton, 1984.

———. *The True and Only Heaven: Progress and Its Critics*. New York, W. W. Norton, 1991.

———. *The Revolt of the Elites: And the Betrayal of Democracy*. New York: W. W. Norton, 1995.

Lasn, Kalle. *Culture Jam*. New York: Eagle Brook, 1999.

Layard, Richard. *Happiness*. New York: Penguin, 2005.

Leder, Drew. "It's Criminal the Way We've Put 2 Million in Cages," *San Francisco Examiner*, February 10, 2000.

Leider, Richard, and David Shapiro. *Repacking Your Bags*. San Francisco: Berrett-Koehler, 1996.

Leopold, Aldo. *A Sand County Almanac*. New York: Ballantine Books, 1986.

Lerner, Michael. *The Politics of Meaning*. Reading, Mass.: Addison-Wesley, 1996.

Levering, Frank, and Wanda Urbanska. *Simple Living*. New York: Viking, 1992.

Lewis, David, and Darren Bridger. *The Soul of the New Consumer*. London: Nicholas Brealey Publishing, 2000.

Lewis, Sara Elizabeth. *Waterfront Property*. New York: Universe, 2003.

Lightman, Alan. *The Diagnosis*. New York: Pantheon, 2000.

Linden, Eugene. *The Future in Plain Sight*. New York: Simon & Schuster, 1998.

Linder, Staffan. *The Harried Leisure Class*. New York: Columbia University Press, 1970.

Linn, Susan. *Consuming Kids: The Hostile Takeover of Childhood*. New York: New Press, 2004.

Loh, Jonathan, ed. *Living Planet Report 2000*. Sponsored by the World Wildlife Fund, the UNEP World Conservation Monitoring Centre, Redefining Progress, and the Centre for Sustainability Studies. Available through Redefining Progress and World Wildlife Fund International, October 2000.

Lohr, Steve. "Maybe It's Not All Your Fault," *New York Times*, December 5, 2004. http://www.nytimes.com/2004/12/05/weekinreview/05lohr.html?ex=1114488000&en=fb64db7b97922844&ei=5070.

Louv, Richard. *Childhood's Future*. New York: Houghton Mifflin, 1990.

———. *The Web of Life*. Berkeley, Calif.: Conari Press, 1996.

Luhrs, Janet. *The Simple Living Guide*. New York: Broadway, 1997.

Luttwak, Edward. *Turbo-Capitalism*. New York: HarperCollins, 1999.

Mack, Burton. *The Lost Gospel*. San Francisco: Harper San Francisco, 1993.

———. *Who Wrote the New Testament?* San Francisco: Harper San Francisco, 1995.

Macy, Joanna, and Molly Young Brown. *Coming Back to Life: Practices to Reconnect Our Lives, Our World*. Gabriola Island, B.C.: New Society Publishers, 1998.

Makower, Joel. *The Green Business Letter*, March 1994.

Mander, Jerry. *Four Arguments for the Elimination of Television*. New York: William Morrow, 1978.

———. *In the Absence of the Sacred*. San Francisco: Sierra Club, 1991.

Maney, Kevin. "The Economy According to eBay," *USA Today*, December 29, 2003. http://www.usatoday.com/money/industries/retail/2003-12-29-ebay-cover_x.htm.

Marchard, Roland. *Advertising the American Dream*. Berkeley and Los Angeles: University of California Press, 1985.

Marcuse, Herbert. *One Dimensional Man*. Boston: Beacon, 1964.

———. *An Essay on Liberation*. Boston: Beacon, 1969.

Martineau, Pierre. *Motivation in Advertising*. New York: McGraw-Hill, 1971.

Marx, Karl. "The Economic and Philosophical Manuscripts of 1844," in *Marx's Concept of Man*, by Erich Fromm. New York: Frederick Ungar, 1971.

Marx, Karl, and Friedrich Engels. *Capital*. New York: Modern Library, 1906.

———. "The Communist Manifesto," in *Basic Writings on Politics and Philosophy*, edited by Lewis Feuer, 1–41. Garden City, N.Y.: Anchor, 1959.

McCarthy, Eugene, and William McGaughey. *Non-Financial Economics*. New York: Praeger, 1989.

McElvaine, Robert. *What's Left?* Holbrook, Mass.: Adams Media, 1996.

McKenzie, Richard. *The Paradox of Progress: Can Americans Regain Their Confidence in a Prosperous Future?* New York: Oxford University Press, 1997.

McKenzie-Mohr, Doug, and William Smith. *Fostering Sustainable Behavior*. Gabriola Island, BC: New Society Publishers, 1999.

McKibben, Bill. *The Age of Missing Information*. New York: Random House, 1992.

———. *The Comforting Whirlwind*. Grand Rapids, Mich.: Eerdmans, 1994.

———. *Hope, Human and Wild*. New York: Little Brown, 1995.

———. *Enough*. New York: Henry Holt, 2003.

McLuhan, T. C. *Touch the Earth: A Self-Portrait of Indian Existence*. New York: Touchstone, 1976.

McNeal, James U. *Kids as Customers: A Handbook of Marketing to Children*. New York: Lexington Books, 1992.

Meadows, Donella. "How's a Green Group to Survive without Junk Mail?" *Global Citizen,* June 2000.

Meadows, Donella, Dennis Meadows, and Jorgen Randers. *Beyond the Limits*. White River Junction, Vt.: Chelsea Green, 1992.

———. *Limits to Growth: The 30-year Update*. White River Junction, Vt: Chelsea Green, 2004.

Merkel, Jim. *Radical Simplicity*. Gabriola, Island, B.C.: New Society Publishers, 2003.

Messenger, Jon, ed. *Working Time and Workers' Preferences in Industrialized Countries*. London: Routledge, 2004.

Miller, Perry, ed. *The American Transcendentalists*. Garden City, N.Y.: Anchor, 1957.

"Millions Still Going Hungry in U.S., Report Finds," Reuters, September 9, 2000.

Mitchell, Stacy. *10 Reasons Why Vermont's Homegrown Economy Matters and 50 Proven Ways to Revive It*. Burlington, Vt.: Preservation Trust of Vermont, 2003.

Molnar, Alex. *Giving Kids the Business*. New York Westview, 1996.

"Money Changes Everything," *American Behavioral Scientist,* July/August 1992: 809.

Moore, Michael. "Bush and Gore Make Me Wanna Ralph," Michael Moore Web site, July 19, 2000, http://www.michaelmoore.com/words/message/index.php?messageDate=2000-07-19.

Moore-Ede, Martin. *The Twenty-four Hour Society: Understanding Human Limits in a World That Never Stops*. Reading, Mass.: Addison-Wesley, 1993.

Morton, A. L., ed. *Political Writings of William Morris*. New York: International Publishers, 1973.

Myers, David. *The American Paradox*. New Haven, Conn.: Yale University Press, 2000.

———. "Wealth, Well-Being, and the New American Dream," Center for a New American Dream Web site, July 4, 2000. http://www.newdream.org/live/ column/2.php.

Myers, Norman, and Julian Simon. *Scarcity or Abundance?* New York: W. W. Norton, 1994.

Nabhan, Gary, and Stephen Trimble. *The Geography of Childhood*. Boston: Beacon, 1994.

Naisbitt, John. *High Tech/High Touch: Technology and Our Accelerated Search for Meaning*. London: Nicholas Brealey Publishing, 2001.

Nasar, Sylvia. "Even among the Well-Off, the Richest Get Richer," *New York Times*, May 24, 1992.

National Conference of Catholic Bishops. *Economic Justice for All*. Washington, D.C.: National Conference of Catholic Bishops, 1986.

Naylor, Thomas, and William Willimon. *Downsizing the USA*. Grand Rapids, Mich.: Eerdmans, 1997.

Naylor, Thomas, William Willimon, and Magdalena Naylor. *The Search for Meaning*. Nashville, Tenn.: Abingdon Press, 1994.

Naylor, Thomas, William Willimon, and Rolf Ostenberg. *The Search for Meaning in the Workplace*. Nashville: Abingdon Press, 1996.

Needleman, Jacob. *Money and the Meaning of Life*. New York: Doubleday Currency, 1991.

Nelson, Joyce. "Great Global Greenwash: Barston-Marsteller, Pax Trilateral and the Brundtland Gang vs. the Environment," *CovertAction* 44: 26–33, 57–58.

Netherlands National Institute of Public Health and Environmental Protection. *Concern for Tomorrow*. Bilthoven, the Netherlands: Netherlands National Institute of Public Health and Environmental Protection, 1989.

New Road Map Foundation and Northwest Environment Watch. *All-Consuming Passion: Waking Up from the American Dream*. Pamphlet. Seattle: New Road Map Foundation and Northwest Environment Watch, 1998.

"News and Trends," *Psychology Today*, January/February 1995: 8.

New York Times. *The Downsizing of America*. New York: Times Books, 1996.

Northwest Earth Institute Discussion Courses. *Deep Ecology, Voluntary Simplicity*. Portland, Ore.: Northwest Earth Institute Discussion Courses, 1998.

O'Connell, Brian. *Civil Society: The Underpinnings of American Democracy*. Medford, Mass.: Tufts University Press, 1999.

O'Hara, Bruce. *Working Harder Isn't Working*. Vancouver, BC: New Star, 1993.

Oldenburg, Ray. *The Great Good Place: Cafes, Coffee Shops, Bookstores, Bars, Hair Salons, and Other Hangouts at the Heart of a Community*. New York: Paragon House, 1989.

O'Neill, Jessie. *The Golden Ghetto*. Center City, Minn.: Hazelden, 1997.

Orwell, George. *1984*. New York: Signet Books, 1981.

Packard, Vance. *The Waste Makers*. New York: McKay, 1960.

———. *The Status Seekers*. New York: Pelican, 1961.

———. *The Hidden Persuaders*. New York: Pocket Books, 1973.

Panati, Charles. *Extraordinary Origins of Everyday Things*. New York: Harper & Row, 1987.

Parker, Thornton. *What If Boomers Can't Retire? How to Build Real Security, Not Phantom Wealth*. San Francisco: Berrett-Koehler, 2000.

Perucci, Robert, and Earl Wysong. *The New Class Society*. Lanham, Md.: Rowman & Littlefield, 1999.

Philipson, Ilene. *Married to the Job*. New York: Free Press, 2002.

Phillips, Kevin. *The Politics of Rich and Poor*. New York: Random House, 1990.

Postel, Sandra. *Dividing the Waters: Food, Security, Ecosystem Health, and the New Politics of Security*. Worldwatch paper 132. Washington, D.C.: Worldwatch Institute, 1996.

Postman, Neil. *Amusing Ourselves to Death*. New York: Viking, 1986.

———. *Conscientious Objections*. New York: Vintage, 1988.

Princen, Thomas, Michael Maniates, and Ken Conca. *Confronting Consumption*. Cambridge, Mass.: MIT Press, 2002.

Prud'Homme, Alex. "Taking the Gospel to the Rich," *New York Times*, February 14, 1999: BU 13.

Putnam, Robert D. *Bowling Alone: The Collapse and Revival of American Community*. New York: Simon & Schuster, 2000.

Rampton, Sheldon, and John Stauber. *Trust Us, We're Experts*. New York: Tarcher/ Putnam, 2001.

Redefining Progress. *Why Bigger Isn't Better: The Genuine Progress Indicator—1999 Update*. San Francisco: Redefining Progress, 1999. http://www.rprogress.org/newpubs/1999/gpi1999.html.

———. *The Genuine Progress Indicator: 2000 Update*. San Francisco: Redefining Progress, 2000.

Reingold, Jennifer, and Ronald Grover. "Special Report: Executive Pay," *Business Week*, April 19, 1999. http://www.businessweek.com/datedtoc/1999/9916.htm.

Ricciardi, A., and J.B. Rasmussen. "Extinction Rates of North American Freshwater Fauna," *Conservation Biology* 13 (1999): 1220–22.

Rifkin, Jeremy. *Time Wars*. New York: Simon & Schuster, 1987.

———. *The End of Work*. New York: Tarcher/Putnam, 1995.

———. *The Age of Access*. New York: Tarcher/Putnam, 2000.

———. *The European Dream*. New York: Tarcher, 2004.

Riley, Trish. "How Healthy Is Your Home?" *South Florida Parenting*, 2004. http://www.south-florida.com/sfparenting/sfe-sfp-healthy-home,0,851127.story.

Robbins, John. *Diet for a New America*. Tiburon, Calif.: H. J. Kramer, 1998.

Robbins, Ocean, and Sol Solomon. *Choices for Our Future: A Generation Rising for Life on Earth*. Summertown, Tenn.: Book, 1994.

Robinson, Joe. *Work to Live*. New York: Perigee, 2003.

Robinson, John, and Geoffrey Godbey. *Time for Life*. University Park, Pa.: Pennsylvania State University Press, 1997.

Ropke, Wilhelm. *A Humane Economy: The Social Framework of the Free Market*. Indianapolis, Ind.: Liberty Fund, 1971.

Rosen, Ruth. "Polluted Bodies," *San Francisco Chronicle*, February 3, 2003.

Rosenblatt, Roger, ed. *Consuming Desires*. Washington, D.C.: Island Press, 1999.

Roszak, Theodore, Mary E. Gomes, and Allen D. Kanner, eds. *Ecopsychology*. San Francisco: Sierra Club Books, 1995.

Roth, Larry, ed. *The Best of the Living Cheap News*. Chicago: Contemporary, 1996.

———. *The Simple Life*. New York: Berkley, 1998.

Rubin, Lilian. *Families on the Fault Line*. New York: Harper Perennial, 1994.

Running Out of Time. A documentary produced by John de Graaf and Vivia Boe for the Public Broadcasting Service, 1994.

Ryan, John. *Seven Wonders*. San Francisco: Sierra Club Books, 1999.

Rybczynski, Withold. *Waiting for the Weekend*. New York: Viking, 1991.

Sahlins, Marshall. "The Original Affluent Society." In *The Consumer Society*, edited by Neva Goodwin, Frank Ackerman, and David Kiron. Washington, D.C.: Island Press, 1997.

Sakaiya, Taichi. *The Knowledge-Value Revolution; or, A History of the Future*. Translated by George Fields and William Marsh. Tokyo and New York: Kodansha International, 1991.

Saltzman, Amy. *Downshifting*. New York: HarperCollins, 1991.

Sanders, Barry. *A Is for Ox*. New York: Pantheon, 1994.

Schleuning, Neala. *Idle Hands and Empty Hearts*. New York: Bergin & Garvey, 1990.

Schlosser, Eric. "Fast Food Nation: The True Costs of America's Diet," *Rolling Stone* magazine, September 3, 1998. http://www.mcspotlight.org/media/press/ rollingstone1.html and http://www.mcspotlight.org/media/press/ rollingstone2.html.

———. *Fast Food Nation*, Boston: Houghton Mifflin, 2001.

Schor, Juliet. *The Overworked American*. New York: Basic Books, 1992.

———. *The Overspent American*. New York: Basic Books, 1998.

———. *Born to Buy*. New York: Charles Scribner, 2004.

Schut, Michael, ed. *Simpler Living, Compassionate Life*. Denver: Living the Good News, 1999.

Schwartz, Barry. *The Paradox of Choice: Why More Is Less*. New York: Ecco Press, 2004.

Schwarz, Walter, and Dorothy Schwarz. *Living Lightly*. Charlbury, UK: Jon Carpenter, 1998.

Segal, Jerome. *Graceful Simplicity*. New York: Henry Holt, 1999.

Seiter, Ellen. *Sold Separately*. New Brunswick, N.J.: Rutgers, 1995.

Sessions, George, ed. *Deep Ecology for the 21st Century*. Boston: Shambala Press, 1995.

Shames, Lawrence. *The Hunger for More*. New York: Times Books, 1989.

Shapiro, Isaac, and Robert Greenstein. *The Widening Income Gulf*. Washington, D.C.: Center on Budget and Policy Priorities, September 4, 1999. http://www.cbpp.org/ 9-4-99tax-rep.htm.

Sharp, David. "Online Sales Fail to Slow Onslaught of Catalog Mailings," Associated Press, December 25, 2004. http://www.signonsandiego.com/uniontrib/20041225/ news_1b25catalogs.html.

Shenk, David. *The End of Patience*. Bloomington, Ind.: Indiana University Press, 1999.

Shi, David. *The Simple Life: Plain Living and High Thinking in American Culture*. Athens, Ga.: University of Georgia Press, 2001.

Shorris, Earl. *A Nation of Salesmen*. New York: Avon, 1994.

Shrady, Nicholas. *Sacred Roads*. San Francisco: Harper San Francisco, 1999.

Silverstein, Ken. "Trillion-Dollar Hideaway," *Mother Jones,* November-December 2000. http://www.motherjones.com/news/feature/2000/11/offshore.html.

Simon, Stephanie. "Scientists Inspect Humdrum American Lives," *Los Angeles Times,* October 28, 1999.

Slater, Philip. *The Pursuit of Loneliness*. Boston: Beacon Press, 1970.

Smith, J. W. *The World's Wasted Wealth. Part 2: The Causes and Cures of Poverty in Today's World*. Cambria, Calif.: Institute for Economic Democracy, 1994.

Sobel, David. *Beyond Ecophobia: Reclaiming the Heart in Nature Education*. Great Barrington, Mass.: Orion Society, 1996.

St. James, Elaine. *Simplify Your Life with Kids*. Kansas City: Andrews McMeel, 1997.

Stauber, John C., and Sheldon Rampton. *Toxic Sludge Is Good for You: Lies, Damn Lies and the Public Relations Industry*. Common Courage Press, Monroe, Me., 1995.

Steamer, James. *Wealth on Minimal Wage*. Chicago: Dearborn Financial, 1997.

Stein, Herbert, and Murray Foss. *The New Illustrated Guide to the American Economy*. Washington, D.C.: American Enterprise Institute, 1995.

Steingraber, Sandra. *Living Downstream: An Ecologist Looks at Cancer and the Environment*. Reading, Mass.: Addison-Wesley, 1997.

Strasburger, Victor C. *Adolescents and the Media*. Thousand Oaks, Calif.: Sage Publications, 1995.

Strasser, Susan. *Satisfaction Guaranteed*. New York: Pantheon, 1989.

Suzuki, David. *Earth Time*. Toronto: Stoddart Publishers, 1998.

Swenson, Richard. *Margin*. Colorado Springs, Colo.: Navpress, 1992.

———. *The Overload Syndrome*. Colorado Springs, Colo.: Navpress, 1998.

———. *A Minute of Margin*. Colorado Springs, Colo.: Navpress, 2003.

Theobald, Robert. *Reworking Success*. Gabriola Island, B.C.: New Society, 1997.

Thompson, William Irwin. *The American Replacement of Nature*. New York: Doubleday Currency, 1991.

Thurow, Lester. *The Future of Capitalism*. New York: Penguin, 1996.

Tischler, Linda. "What's the Buzz?" *Fast Company* 82 (May 2004), 76.

"Top 100," *Nation's Restaurant News*, June 24, 2002.

Twitchell, James. *Adcult USA*. New York: Columbia University Press, 1996.

———. "Two Cheers for Materialism." In *Utne Reader*, November/December 2000. Also in *The Consumer Society Reader*, edited by Juliet B. Schor and Douglas B. Holt, 167-172. New York: The New Press, 2000.

"2003 Market Measure," *Do-It-Yourself Retailing*, November 2002.

Urbanksa, Wanda, and Frank Levering. *Nothing's Too Small to Make a Difference*. Winston-Salem, N.C.: John F. Blair, 2004.

U.S. Census Bureau. *Statistical Abstract of the United States*. Washington, DC: U.S. Government Printing Office, 1999, 2004–5.

U.S. Environmental Protection Agency. Chemical Information Collection and Data Development (Testing) Web site. http://www.epa.gov/opptintr/chemtest/index.htm.

"Video Stores Seek Class Action in Suit against Blockbuster," *The Home Town Advantage Bulletin*, Institute for Local Self-Reliance, November 2000.

Wachtel, Paul. *The Poverty of Affluence*. New York: Free Press, 1983.

Walker, Bob. "Mall Mania," *Sacramento Bee*, October 19, 1998.

Walker, Rob. "The Hidden (in Plain Sight) Persuaders," *New York Times Magazine,* December 5, 2004. http://query.nytimes.com/gst/abstract.html?res= F20912FC3A5A0C768CDDAB0994DC404482&incamp=archive:search.

Wallis, Jim. *The Soul of Politics.* New York: New Press, 1994.

Walsh, David. *Designer Kids.* Minneapolis: Deaconess, 1990.

———. *Selling Out America's Children.* Minneapolis: Fairview Press, 1995.

Wann, David. *Biologic.* Boulder, Colo.: Johnson Books, 1994.

———. *Deep Design.* Washington, D.C.: Island Press, 1996.

Warren, Elizabeth. "Bankruptcy Borne of Misfortune, Not Excess," *The New York Times,* September 3, 2000.

Wattenberg, Ben. *Values Matter Most.* Washington, D.C.: Regnery, 1995.

Weil, Andrew. *Eating Well for Optimum Health.* New York: Alfred A. Knopf, 2000.

Weil, Michelle, and Larry Rosen. *Technostress.* New York: John Wiley, 1997.

Williams, Terry Tempest. *Refuge.* New York: Vintage, 1991.

———. *Leap.* New York: Pantheon, 2000.

Willimon, William, and Thomas Naylor. *The Abandoned Generation: Rethinking Higher Education.* Grand Rapids, Mich.: Eerdmans, 1995.

Wolf, Stewart. *The Power of Clan: The Influence of Human Relationships on Heart Disease.* Somerset, N.J.: Transaction Publishers, 1998.

Worldwatch Institute. *State of the World.* New York: W. W. Norton, published annually 1995–2000.

———. *Vital Signs 1995–2000.* New York: W.W. Norton, 2000.

———. *Vital Signs 2003.* New York: W.W. Norton, 2003.

Yalom, Irvin. *Existential Psychotherapy.* New York: Basic Books, 1980.

Yearning for Balance: Views of Americans on Consumption, Materialism, and the Environment. A report prepared by the Harwood Group for the Merck Family Fund: Bethesda, Md., 1995.

Yeoman, Barry. "Steel Town Lockdown," *Mother Jones,* May/June 2000. http://www.motherjones.com/news/feature/2000/05/steeltown.html.

Zablocki, Benjamin. *The Joyful Community.* Chicago: University of Chicago Press, 1980.

Zajonc, Donna. *The Politics of Hope.* Austin, Texas: Synergy Books, 2004.

INDEX

ABOUT THE CONTRIBUTORS

JOHN DE GRAAF has been a producer of public television documentaries for twenty-eight years. More than a dozen of his programs, including *For Earth's Sake: The Life and Times of David Brower, Running Out of Time, Affluenza,* and *Escape from Affluenza,* have been broadcast nationally in prime time on PBS. He is a frequent speaker at colleges and universities and has been a visiting scholar at The Evergreen State College and a lecturer on documentary production for the University of Washington Extension. He is also the national coordinator of the Take Back Your Time campaign (www.timeday.org) and the editor of the book *Take Back Your Time* (Berrett-Koehler, 2003). He was also coauthor of a children's book, *David Brower: Friend of the Earth.* He is a member of the steering committee of The Simplicity Forum (www.simplicityforum.org). He lives in Seattle.

DAVID WANN has written four books and more than a hundred articles and has produced many videos and television programs about sustainable lifestyles. His book *Biologic* (1994) discusses individual actions based on biological realities, while *Deep Design* (1996) looks at the prospect of an entire economy grounded in sustainable enterprise. He has taught at the college level, worked for more than a decade as a policy analyst for the U.S. Environmental Protection Agency, and helped design and build the co-housing village in which he now lives, in Golden, Colorado.

THOMAS NAYLOR is professor emeritus of economics at Duke University, where he taught for thirty years. He has also taught at Middlebury College. He is a writer and social critic and has consulted with governments and major corporations in more than thirty countries. In 1993 he moved to Charlotte, Vermont, where he writes about the search for meaning and community and for simplifying all aspects of our lives. His articles have been published in the *New York Times,* the *International Herald Tribune,* the *Los Angeles Times,* the *Boston Globe,* the *Christian Science Monitor,* the *Nation,* and *Business Week.* He has appeared on ABC, CBS, CNN, NPR, and the CBC. He is the author or coauthor of thirty books.

DAVID HORSEY is the *Seattle Post-Intelligencer*'s Pulitzer Prize–winning editorial cartoonist. His work is syndicated internationally by Tribune Media Services. The winner of numerous awards for his cartoons and written commentary, he has published five collections of his work. Currently, he is president of the Association of American Editorial Cartoonists. His career has taken him to Europe, Asia, Hollywood, and Washington, D.C., and through six presidential election campaigns. He lives in Seattle with his wife and two children.

SCOTT SIMON (foreword to the first edition) was the host of the TV program *Affluenza*. He is currently the host of *Weekend Edition Saturday* on National Public Radio and is a former host of the *Weekend Today Show* on NBC. The author of several books, he lives in Washington, D.C.

VICKI ROBIN (foreword to the second edition) is the coauthor of the best-selling book *Your Money or Your Life* and the founder and co-chair of the Simplicity Forum (www.simplicityforum.org). She also founded the "Conversation Cafes" and "Let's Talk America" campaigns. She lives on Whidbey Island, Washington.

ABOUT REDEFINING PROGRESS

REDEFINING PROGRESS (RP) is a nonprofit research and policy organization based in Oakland, California, that believes genuine progress entails providing a better life for all within the capacity of nature.

RP tools and policies emerge from three "Big Ideas":

SUSTAINABILITY is rooted in the realization that ever more of us live on a planet with shrinking regenerative capacity. RP uses the Ecological Footprint to document the overuse of resources and conducts workshops to explore fair and effective ways to live once more within the means of nature.

ACCURATE PRICES advances market mechanisms and incentives that provide accurate feedback about the full cost of our purchases and decisions to ourselves, others, and nature.

COMMON ASSETS recognizes the value of our natural and community-based resources in strengthening our communities. RP fosters policies to improve the health of these resources so that they can efficiently and equitably meet the basic needs of our communities and households.

RP also applies these Big Ideas to the problem of global warming through two campaigns to promote fair and low-cost policies to address **climate change.** For more information, visit the RP Web site at http://www.rprogress.org/.

ABOUT BERRETT-KOEHLER PUBLISHERS

BERRETT-KOEHLER is an independent publisher dedicated to an ambitious mission: Creating a World that Works for All.

We believe that to truly create a better world, action is needed at all levels—individual, organizational, and societal. At the individual level, our publications help people align their lives and work with their deepest values. At the organizational level, our publications promote progressive leadership and management practices, socially responsible approaches to business, and humane and effective organizations. At the societal level, our publications advance social and economic justice, shared prosperity, sustainable development, and new solutions to national and global issues.

We publish groundbreaking books focused on each of these levels. To further advance our commitment to positive change at the societal level, we have recently expanded our line of books in this area and are calling this expanded line "BK Currents."

A major theme of our publications is "Opening Up New Space." They challenge conventional thinking, introduce new points of view, and offer new alternatives for change. Their common quest is changing the underlying beliefs, mindsets, institutions, and structures that keep generating the same cycles of problems, no matter who our leaders are or what improvement programs we adopt.

We strive to practice what we preach—to operate our publishing company in line with the ideas in our books. At the core of our approach is *stewardship*, which we define as a deep sense of responsibility to administer the company for the benefit of all of our "stakeholder" groups: authors, customers, employees, investors, service providers, and the communities and environment around us. We seek to establish a partnering relationship with each stakeholder that is open, equitable, and collaborative.

We are gratified that thousands of readers, authors, and other friends of the company consider themselves to be part of the "BK Community." We hope that you, too, will join our community and connect with us through the ways described on our website at www.bkconnection.com.

This book is part of our BK Currents series. BK Currents titles advance social and economic justice by exploring the critical intersections between business and society. Offering a unique combination of thoughtful analysis and progressive alternatives, BK Currents titles promote positive change at the national and global levels. To find out more, visit www.bkcurrents.com.

BE CONNECTED

Visit Our Website

Go to **www.bkconnection.com** to read exclusive previews and excerpts of new books, find detailed information on all Berrett-Koehler titles and authors, browse subject-area libraries of books, and get special discounts.

Subscribe to Our Free E-Newsletter

Be the first to hear about new publications, special discount offers, exclusive articles, news about bestsellers, and more! Get on the list for our free e-newsletter by going to **www.bkconnection.com.**

Participate in the Discussion

To see what others are saying about our books and post your own thoughts, check out our blogs at **www.bkblogs.com.**

Get Quantity Discounts

Berrett-Koehler books are available at quantity discounts for orders of ten or more copies. Please call us toll-free at **(800) 929-2929** or email us at **bkp.orders@aidcvt.com.**

Host a Reading Group

For tips on how to form and carry on a book reading group in your workplace or community, see our website at **www.bkconnection.com.**

Join the BK Community

Thousands of readers of our books have become part of the "BK Community" by participating in events featuring our authors, reviewing draft manuscripts of forthcoming books, spreading the word about their favorite books, and supporting our publishing program in other ways. If you would like to join the BK Community, please contact us at **bkcommunity@bkpub.com.**